The Ethnographic Self

The Ethnographic Self

Fieldwork and the Representation of Identity

Amanda Coffey

SAGE Publications
London • Thousand Oaks • New Delhi

First published 1999

SAGE Publications Ltd
6 Bonhill Street
London EC2A 4PU

SAGE Publications Inc.
2455 Teller Road
Thousand Oaks, California 91320

SAGE Publications India Pvt Ltd
32, M-Block Market
Greater Kailash – I
New Delhi 110 048

British Library Cataloguing in Publication data

A catalogue record for this book is available from
the British Library

ISBN 0 7619 5266 7
ISBN 0 7619 5267 5 (pbk)

Library of Congress catalog card number 98–61542

Typeset by Photoprint, Torquay, Devon
Printed and bound in Great Britain by
Athenaeum Press, Gateshead

For Jules – with love

Contents

Acknowledgements

This book has benefited from a good deal of tender loving care – most of which has come from individuals other than myself. While I take full responsibility for the final text, and its inevitable flaws, there are a number of people who have helped the book along its way. I originally discussed my ideas for the book with Chris Rojek at Sage. I am grateful for both his initial encouragement and his support over the course of the writing process. I hope that, despite some deviation, the finished product retains the spirit of our earlier discussions.

Several people have been invaluable in the preparation of the manuscript. Laura Pugsley undertook several bibliographic searches on my behalf. The research committee of the School of Social and Administrative Studies, University of Wales, Cardiff supported the project with a grant from the SOCAS research fund. The staff of the Arts and Social Studies Library have been both helpful and efficient. Karen Chivers and Jan Stephens word-processed several early drafts. I am especially grateful to Jackie Swift for word-processing and editing the final text. Lesley Edwards and Mair Gaunt have supported me in my role as assistant dean, and have made the task of finding time to write much easier. Others have been kind enough to ask after the progress of the manuscript. I would particularly like to acknowledge and thank Ian Butler, Ian Welsh, Tom Hall, Jonathan Scourfield and Michelle Thomas. Paul Atkinson and Sara Delamont have both given me and my writing their unstinting support over the past eight years, including during the writing of this book. Their detailed attention to my drafts, constructive criticism and faith in me is always appreciated, although I am sure this is hard to believe at times.

I have left the most important acknowledgements until last. I am indebted to Julian Pitt, not least for his help on this book. Throughout the project he has provided intellectual support and practical help. More generally, his love, encouragement and sense of humour continue to enrich my life. Finally, thank you to Watney and Bramble.

1 Introduction

This book focuses on the relationships between the self and ethnographic fieldwork. It particularly addresses the personal, emotional and identity dimensions of undertaking prolonged fieldwork. The book is not, however, a textbook on how to 'do' qualitative research or ethnographic fieldwork. There are many excellent texts available which already fulfil that function. Nor is this volume a report of a singular research project. While I draw upon my own experiences of fieldwork, I do so in the context of a far wider body of literature and experiences. The idea behind the book is that ethnographers (and others involved in fieldwork research) should be aware of how fieldwork research and textual practice construct, reproduce and implicate selves, relationships and personal identities.

It has become increasingly fashionable for individual researchers to 'personalize' their accounts of fieldwork. But there has been little systematic attempt to reflect upon the experiences and emotions that are reported in any overarching collective or epistemological sense. All too often, research methods texts remain relatively silent on the ways in which fieldwork affects us, and we affect the field. It is perhaps more common than it once was for researchers to reflect upon their own fieldwork experiences. Indeed it is usual to find a personal dimension in the retelling of fieldwork and the analysis of data. However, such reflection remains at the margins of ethnographic scholarship. While there is increasing awareness of the personal nature of fieldwork, the self in the field is not something to which methods texts give substantial attention. Issues of identity, selfhood and emotionality are often referred to, and thereby understood, in tangential and semi-detached ways.

Encouraging more personalized writing of fieldwork is not the purpose of the book. Whether or not we choose to *write* about our self, and our emotional experiences, is not my primary concern (although I do explore the 'writing of the self' specifically in Chapters 7 and 8). What is central to the book is the recognition that fieldwork is personal, emotional and identity *work*. The construction and production of self and identity occurs both during and after fieldwork. In writing, remembering and representing our fieldwork experiences we are involved in processes of self presentation and identity construction. In considering and exploring the intimate relations between the field, significant others and the private self we are able to understand the processes of fieldwork as practical, intellectual and emotional accomplishments.

The purpose of this chapter is to set the scene for the book as a whole. It introduces the book in three main ways. I begin by reviewing some of the standard and current 'recommended' literature on the conduct of ethnographic research, as a way of exploring how the self and the emotional are conventionally understood and treated in methods texts. This is by no means an exhaustive review. Its purpose is illustration rather than generalization. Secondly, I introduce some of the contemporary debates and developments within ethnography, which place the topic areas of the book in a broader intellectual context. Thirdly, I provide a brief overview of the structure and organization of the book.

The Silent Space

The social research methods literature is now rich with 'advice' texts on the conduct and execution of qualitative methods, and more specifically ethnography. A widespread interest throughout the social sciences has encouraged a literature of general, introductory texts on the practical accomplishment of fieldwork. (Excellent introductions include Burgess, 1982, 1984; Delamont, 1992; Hammersley and Atkinson, 1995; LeCompte and Preissle, 1993; Lofland and Lofland, 1995). More specific texts on qualitative data analysis (for example Coffey and Atkinson, 1996; Dey, 1993; Miles and Huberman, 1994; Silverman, 1993, 1997; Strauss and Corbin, 1990) and ethnographic writing (Atkinson, 1990; Ellis and Bochner, 1996; Ely et al., 1997; Richardson, 1990; Wolcott, 1990) offer more detailed discussions of particular aspects of the research process. This literature has helped to establish qualitative methods and ethnographic fieldwork as cross/interdisciplinary and 'respectable' and, perhaps more importantly, teachable and learnable. The ethnographic self is not completely absent from this conventional literature. Indeed many texts make a virtue of the fact that fieldwork relies upon the social researcher as research instrument. Emphasis is placed on the stresses and rewards, and in that sense the emotions, of qualitative fieldwork. But relatively little systematic attention is paid to the emotional and identity work that frame the fieldwork experience.

To illustrate this in detail I will consider the contents of three widely known qualitative methods texts. A brief analysis of these reveals the simultaneous presence and marginality of the researcher self. The three texts I have chosen are all general introductions to qualitative research methods. Lofland and Lofland's (1995) *Analyzing Social Settings* is widely used in North America and the UK, and is in its third edition. Hammersley and Atkinson's (1995) *Ethnography* is currently a standard UK text for the teaching of qualitative fieldwork to both undergraduates and postgraduates. First published in 1983 it gives a thorough grounding in ethnographic principles and practice. LeCompte and Preissle's (1993) *Ethnography and*

Qualitative Design in Educational Research (2nd edition, with Tesch) I have chosen as an example which deals with general issues of ethnographic method from a particular disciplinary perspective. It is a widely used text in the USA and UK for graduate courses on educational research. These three texts are well used, reviewed and respected examples of one genre of 'how to do' methods texts. In different, complementary styles they do exemplary justice to the perspectives, procedures and processes of ethnographic fieldwork, analysis and writing. I use all three texts with my own students and would not hesitate in recommending them to colleagues. As 'cookbooks' they have been revised and updated to accommodate new ideas and new fieldwork. They engage in new debates and with new perspectives. As introductions to the theoretical principles and practical conduct of qualitative research they are broadly inclusive. Yet a rereading of them reveals gaps in the ways in which they address issues of the personal and the self in fieldwork. None of the books especially depersonalize the research process. A consistent theme is the need to engage personally with the processes of fieldwork. However, the texts confine the discussion of the personal and the emotional to particular aspects of the research process, rather than establishing them as pervasive to the whole enterprise. For example, LeCompte and Preissle (1993) have a chapter on the role and experience of the researcher. This chapter acknowledges the interactional qualities of fieldwork and the role of the researcher in that interaction. LeCompte and Preissle (1993: 91–2) advise the construction of a research identity as an instrument of the research:

> The personal characteristic . . . most affecting conduct of qualitative research is the investigator's identity as the 'essential research instrument' . . . The identity of data collector mediates all other identities and roles played by the investigator.

But their discussion does not engage in detail with the nuances of what this might involve, nor how the other identities and roles are constructed and mediated. Lofland and Lofland (1995) deal with the self more fully, but still work within a specific set of parameters. They have a brief discussion (five pages) on the relationship between fieldwork and biography, which mainly deals with choosing a fieldsite and warnings against autobiographic sociology. For example:

> A job; a physical mishap; the development, loss or maintenance of an intimate relationship; an illness; an enjoyed activity; a living arrangement – all these and many other possible circumstances may provide you with a topic you care enough about to study. (Lofland and Lofland, 1995: 11)

> Even when exceptionally well executed, reports analysing autobiographical data are often viewed by readers as borderline self-indulgence: when only competently executed, they are likely to be labelled 'narcissistic' or 'exhibitionist' and simply dismissed as uninteresting. (Lofland and Lofland, 1995: 14)

Lofland and Lofland return to the self in their chapter on 'getting along in the field'. Here they discusses issues of emotion, field roles and field relations. They highlight that fieldwork can be stressful and emotionally charged, and pay some attention to the fieldworker's identity:

> Obviously we do not refer here to donning a persona totally at odds with your natural demeanor. We are speaking, rather, of asking yourself questions such as an employer might ask herself about her behavior relative to her employees or a teacher might ask about his behavior relative to the children in his classroom. In many sectors of social life, goal achievement revolves in part around self strategies. (Lofland and Lofland, 1995: 55)

Like the Loflands, Hammersley and Atkinson deal with identity work in the context of impression management. They emphasize the necessity to activate strategies of impression management in order to secure access to a research site and fruitful field relations:

> As in other situations where identities have to be created or established, much thought must be given by the ethnographer to 'impression management'. Impressions that pose an obstacle to access must be avoided or countered as far as possible, while those that facilitate it must be encouraged, within the limits set by ethical considerations. (Hammersley and Atkinson, 1995: 83)

All three texts acknowledge that the researcher is part of the research process, and discuss, in some form, the nature of field relations and identity management. However, 'self' and identity are partitioned off (in both research terms and by the actual chapters of the text), rather than suffused through the process and the text. Identity work, the emotions of fieldwork, and the writing of the self are engaged with at a relatively superficial level. For example, while LeCompte and Preissle discuss the identity of the researcher in terms of discipline, research instrument and subjectivity, they give little space to an analytical discussion of how identities are constructed, reproduced, established, mediated, changed or challenged over the fieldwork process. Similarly Lofland and Lofland, and Hammersley and Atkinson place emphasis on the self-conscious production of a persona, only in order to facilitate good fieldwork relations.

> The researcher must judge what sort of impression he or she wishes to create, and manage appearances accordingly. Such impression management is unlikely to be a unitary affair however. There may be different categories of participants, and different social contexts, which demand the construction of different 'selves'. (Hammersley and Atkinson, 1995: 87)

Through concentrating on 'face sheet' characteristics (gender, age, race and ethnicity, religion) and impression management (clothes, the use of props, speech) Hammersley and Atkinson consider the consequences of managing identities in the field. They emphasize how the ethnographer manages the self in order to conduct fieldwork successfully. This also includes some discussion on the formation and maintenance of relationships in the field, and how the fieldworker manages this task. For the purpose of instructing researchers in the practical accomplishment of ethnographic fieldwork, all of these issues are entirely valid. But confining discussions to this self-conscious crafting fails to acknowledge the complexities of identities, roles and relationships that can characterize fieldwork. Identity and selfhood are primarily viewed relatively impersonally, and in terms of achieving successful access and research results. The researcher identity is to be 'managed', amended and constructed in order to facilitate the research process. Identity construction and fieldwork relationships are described in terms of getting the fieldwork 'done'. This sort of approach does not address, in any detail, how fieldwork shapes and constructs identities, intimate relations, an emotional self and a physical self.

The emotions of fieldwork are also discussed in relatively unemotional ways. LeCompte and Preissle do not really deal with the emotional tensions that fieldwork can pose, although they acknowledge that 'ethnographers share houses, raise their children, become ill, and have emotional crises among the people they study' (LeCompte and Preissle, 1993: 92). The Loflands, and Hammersley and Atkinson devote more attention to emotive qualities and dilemmas. Both books have a section which deals with the emotional stress of fieldwork. Lofland and Lofland suggest that although fieldwork can be emotional, even if we were able to catalogue that stress, doing so would not be epistemologically useful and might discourage potential field researchers. They give a typology of different sources of emotional stress caused by fieldwork – deception and fear of disclosure, loathing and the desire to withdraw, sympathy and the impulse to help, marginality and the temptation to convert. These cover a lot of ground, although on a rereading of their comments it appears that they tend to draw attention to these sources of stress without suggesting what fieldworkers should actually do with their feelings in the context of their lives or the fieldwork. Moreover the emotions they present are really all negative ones – i.e. as stress to be put up with or somehow dealt with. They do return to emotions later in the book, by suggesting that fieldwork is an adventure and should be engaging, and that writing can include discovery and surprise, though these feelings are not described and explored at length.

Hammersley and Atkinson (1995) take a similar approach, more concerned perhaps with alerting readers to the difficulties of fieldwork and to stressing that it is hard work, than with overly emphasizing the joys. They argue that fieldwork brings stresses and strains that can be both emotional and physical. They highlight marginality, like the Loflands, as one source of stress. While recognizing the potential alienation and isolation of remaining on the edge of a culture, they advise that ethnographers should avoid feeling too comfortable and at home, for fear of losing their critical perspective. More generally they remind their readers that 'field researchers do not always leave the field physically and emotionally unscathed, and they rarely leave unaffected by the experience of research' (Hammersley and Atkinson, 1995: 120).

These general methods texts do deal with some of the emotional issues of fieldwork – getting too close, or remaining marginal; coping with situations of dislike and like; entering and leaving the field. We are left in little doubt that fieldwork can be stressful. However, there is no acknowledgement that the whole research process can be emotional, only distinct portions of it. We are told a great deal more about the difficulties than the joys (perhaps this has much to do with the perceived necessity of qualitative research to justify itself as hard and difficult and therefore not a soft option). Moreover the emotional aspects of fieldwork are considered as issues to be acknowledged and if possible dealt with, rather than seen as epistemologically productive in the analysis of fieldwork and the fieldworker self.

Lastly in this illustrative overview I return to the reflective and writing practices of ethnography. This is, in part, a general issue of thinking about how the three texts deal with *both* the impact of the self on the research process and the impact of the research process on the self. Lofland and Lofland (1995) are cautious of what they term 'autobiographical sociology', whereby the self is used as the research site or source of data. They identify the need for balance between reflective fieldwork and self-indulgence. Despite this caveat the Loflands do recognize the importance of biography in qualitative research. From a sociological perspective, they argue,

> It is often said among sociologists that, as sociologists, we 'make problematic' in our research matters that are problematic in our lives. With the proviso that the connection between self and study may be a subtle and sophisticated one, not at all apparent to an outside observer, we would argue that there is considerable truth to that assertion. In fact, much of the best work in sociology and often social sciences – within the fieldwork tradition as well as within other research traditions – is probably grounded in the remote and/or current biographies of its creators. That such linkages are not always, perhaps not even usually, publicly acknowl-edged is understandable: the norms of scholarship do not require that researchers bare their souls, only their procedures. (Lofland and Lofland, 1995: 13)

The Loflands stress that emotional engagement is necessary for the comple-tion and quality of the project, and they imply that this involves some sense of connectedness between the self and the fieldwork. They believe that 'starting where you are' (from the biographical) provides meaningful linkages between the personal, the emotional and the intellectual rigours of fieldwork scholarship. However, while they describe writing in a personal way – having a secluded and indulging place to write, finding your own writing style – they do not offer advice or encouragement to write the self into the text. In their checklist of what should go into a report the self is confined to aspects of the methodological reporting rather than suffusing the whole text.

Hammersley and Atkinson (1995) have a useful chapter on ethnographic writing, in which they engage with different sorts of genres and writing skills. They also engage with contemporary debates over the relationship between writing, responsibility and authenticity. While discussing the craft skills of writing, and identifying ethnography as a textual enterprise, Hammersley and Atkinson neglect the self. They imply an active author crafting an ethnographic text, but they do not engage with, or explore, how ethnographic writing can or should incorporate, include, and represent the ethnographer self. Indeed they do not construct ethnographic writing in any sort of biographic or 'life' perspective.

Interestingly LeCompte and Preissle (1993) choose not to deal with writing specifically. In fact their text is notably silent on the textual production of ethnography. Further they do not address the place of the author and ethnographic self in the analysis and writing of data. They argue that

> most ethnographers present the conclusion to their studies in four stages: a summary presentation of data, interpretation of data, integration of findings within broader areas of interest, and applications or significance of the findings. (LeCompte and Preissle, 1993: 227)

They concur with this general approach, leaving out any references to the personal or emotional in the textual presentation of the fieldwork.

Hammersley and Atkinson (1995) as I indicated earlier, argue that ethnographers rarely leave fieldwork totally unaffected by their research experience. Yet they do not really go beyond that general statement to consider how fieldwork affects the self. Lofland and Lofland (1995) suggest that fieldwork can be both an adventure and a source of emotional stress. However, they do not suggest that fieldworkers are especially changed or challenged beyond the field. Similarly LeCompte and Preissle (1993) are silent on the impact of the research process on the self. All three texts do deal with the impact of the researcher on the research process. This is dealt with in terms of ethical considerations around choosing a fieldsite, gaining consent and minimizing harm or exploitation during fieldwork and publishing. There is, however, a lack of critical engagement with the ways in which ethnographers connect, relate, engage and have impacts on the field and the people, beyond these important but basic ethical principles. This is less about the contamination of the field by the researcher than about the ways in which fieldwork relies upon the interactions, relations and situatedness of the researcher and the researched. The ethnographic research process is fundamentally about the simultaneous connection and location of peopled and vocal lives. It is perhaps this that is most noticeably absent from the texts I have briefly analysed in this section.

To recapitulate, I chose the three texts to provide practical illustration and because they are well known, accessible and good. These texts, and others like them, have done much to widen the interest in and appreciation of qualitative methods. Qualitative methods are no longer the preserve of social and cultural anthropologists, and the odd sociologist. They are now actively learnt and pursued by educationalists, psychologists, geographers, nurses, pharmacists and researchers in media and cultural studies, business studies and social policy. Such texts have contributed to a general demystification of qualitative methods and more specifically ethnography. Qualitative methods are no longer simply 'done'. They are shared, taught, learnt, discussed, modified, criticized and practised, and that is good and positive. Despite this huge progress, some aspects of ethnographic research are still relatively neglected. There is widespread acknowledgement of the importance of self-management, and the emotional stresses of fieldwork. But such acknowledgement is to some extent premeditated and impersonal. Few sources offer the reader the positive opportunity to explore the multiple relationships between the researcher self, the field and the people of the field. In striving to legitimize fieldwork as 'real' research, which is difficult and personal but methodologically fruitful, we can lose sight of the fact that ethnographic research is peopled – by researcher and researched. Fieldwork is itself a 'social setting' inhabited by embodied, emotional, physical selves. Fieldwork helps to shape, challenge, reproduce, maintain, reconstruct and represent our selves and the selves of others. This text should not be seen as a replacement for the more orthodox texts. Certainly the books I have briefly reviewed here have served the ethnographic and qualitative cause extremely well. I now turn to a brief consideration of contemporary debates and developments, which will help to contextualize the book further.

An Intellectual Space

In this section I identify a number of key intellectual influences that have informed the ideas which I discuss in the book. These might be viewed as bases or catalysts, rather than prescriptive theoretical or methodological imperatives.

The Sixth Moment

In their recent, and in many ways authoritative, review of the development of qualitative research traditions, Denzin and Lincoln (1994: 7ff.) write of the 'five moments' of qualitative research. The first moment they identify as an objectivist and positivist programme, sustained by myth of the heroic lone fieldworker. Of researchers in this moment, spanning the years from 1900 to the Second World War, they write: 'They were concerned with offering valid, reliable, and objective interpretations in their writings' (Denzin and Lincoln, 1994: 7) The second moment is described as modernist and creative, characterized *inter alia* by attempts to formalize qualitative research methods. 'The modernist ethnographer and sociological participant observer attempted rigorous, qualitative studies of important social processes including deviance and social control in the classroom and society' (Denzin and Lincoln, 1994: 8). This modernist phase came to an end in the late 1960s, and was superseded by a third moment. This spanned 1970 to 1986, and is described by Denzin and Lincoln in terms of 'blurred genres'. There was, they claim, a new multiplicity of theoretical orientations and para-digms. Diverse ways of data collection and analysis also came to the fore during this moment. For instance:

> Diverse ways of collecting and analysing empirical materials were also available, including qualitative interviewing (open-ended and quasi-structured) and observa-tional, visual, personal experience, and documentary methods. Computers were entering the situation, to be fully developed in the next decade, along with narrative, content, and semiotic methods of reading interviews and cultural texts. (Denzin and Lincoln, 1994: 9)

The fourth moment coincides with a 'crisis of representation', in which canons of truth and method were challenged, not least through the critical examination of textual practices. As Denzin and Lincoln (1994: 10) suggest, 'the erosion of classic norms in anthropology (objectivism, complicity with colonialism, social life structured by fixed rituals and customs, ethnog-raphies as monuments to a culture) was complete'. The crises of this period or moment put in hazard not only the products of the ethnographer's work, but the moral and intellectual authority of ethnographers themselves. Finally, the fifth moment presented by Denzin and Lincoln is characterized by continuing diversity and a series of tensions. For instance, they write in their more developed account of this fifth moment:

> Qualitative research embraces two tensions at the same time. On the one hand, it is drawn to a broad, interpretative, postmodern, feminist, and critical sensibility. On the other hand, it can also be drawn to more narrowly defined positivist, post-positivist, humanistic and naturalistic conceptions of human experience and its analysis. (Lincoln and Denzin, 1994: 576)

Denzin and Lincoln also identify a possible sixth moment, towards which we are currently moving (see Denzin, 1997), characterized by reflexive, experiential texts that are 'messy, subjective, open ended, conflictual and feminist influenced (Denzin and Lincoln, 1994: 559). There is no doubt as to the general existence of the multiplicity of perspectives and practices which Lincoln and Denzin identify. Their discussion helps to identify and capture the cultural diversity of contemporary ethnography. However, the narrative development and periodization imposed by Denzin and Lincoln perhaps glosses over the tensions and differences that have always been present in ethnography. Each of their periods or moments – most especially the earlier ones – is too neatly packaged. The contrast between previous positivist, modernist and self-confident (but narrow) perspectives, and the contemporary carnivalesque diversity of standpoints, methods and representations, is too sharply drawn. It does something of a disservice to earlier generations of ethnographers, while suggesting that all contemporary research takes place in an intellectual field teeming with contested ideas.

There is perhaps greater continuity in the practical accomplishment and epistemological underpinnings of ethnography than Denzin and Lincoln allow. That continuity is not one of unbroken adherence to a single orthodoxy. Rather, there are tensions and differences that are themselves recurrent. It is as wrong to assume that all ethnography in past generations was conducted under the auspices of a positivistic and totalizing gaze as it is to imply that we are all postmodern now. There is a repeated dialectic between centrifugal forces – tending towards convergence on a dominant orthodoxy – and centripetal forces that promote difference and diversity. Rather than the temporal metaphor of 'moments', the more appropriate one might be that of 'vectors', implying the directionality of forces in an intellectual field. There is little need to appeal only to recent developments in ethnographic writing and commentary as evidence of 'blurred genres'. Relationships between the aesthetic and the scientific, or between the 'positivist' and 'interpretivist,' have been detectable for many years – indeed, throughout the development of ethnographic research this century. (Admittedly, they have not been equally remarked on, nor have they taken the same form at all time.) That said, Lincoln and Denzin's narrative account identifies ethnography and qualitative research as encapsulating a number of perspectives, debates and ongoing tensions.

It is clearly in the latter moments (perhaps moments four to six) of Denzin and Lincoln's model that the researcher self is most indicated and implied. This is not to say that past generations of fieldworkers have not experienced and lived the field in emotional, personal and subjective ways. But recent developments, as outlined by Lincoln and Denzin, provide a more recognized and acceptable environment in which to engage with such issues. For example the literary turn in ethnography has made it easier to utilize genres such as the auto/biographical and the personal narrative/confessional. And the significant contributions of feminism and postmodernism have made it both easier and more acceptable to think of the social world in terms of multiple perspectives and multiple selves.

Feminism and Ethnography

The debates which surround the relationship between feminism and ethnography provide a further framework for the book. These debates encapsulate, and to some extent mirror, the development of ethnography more generally. Before discussing the case for and practice of feminist ethnography, it is necessary to say something about feminism and social research more generally. Feminist critiques of social science and social research have, quite appropriately, argued that there are gendered questions in the choice of research programme, research strategy and modes of analysis. More specifically they have argued that the ideologies of gender have structured the social relations of research and the patterns of interaction during research. This can be seen as part of a complex set of arguments about how gender should be researched *and* which social research methods best serve a feminist agenda. Since the 1970s there has been philosophical debate within and beyond the social sciences about the nature of knowledge and 'scientific enquiry' (see Harding, 1987; Nielsen, 1990). In particular the basis of such knowledge has been questioned by calls for a re-examination of assumptions which have underpinned research and its social outcomes. These are the established assumptions about the dichotomies of masculinity/femininity, male/female, objectivity/subjectivity, mind/body, reason/emotionality and so on. The intellectual movement of the 1990s captured by postmodernism and post-structuralism has added fuel to this debate, based as it is in argument that there are no universal truths to be discovered, and that all knowledge is grounded in human society, situated, partial, local, temporal and historically specific.

> The essence of the post modern argument is that dualisms which can continue to dominate western thought are inadequate for understanding a world of multiple causes and effects, interacting in complex and non linear ways, all of which are noted in a limitless array of historical and cultural specifications. (Lather, 1991: 21)

These insights can be empowering to a feminist research agenda, throwing the objective foundations of knowledge into doubt and giving a forum in which feminists can legitimately abandon existing knowledges and create their own. The feminist critique of social research and the production of knowledge in turn places the researcher as positively present in empirical study. As Stanley and Wise (1990) argue, the researcher/researched relationship is a key to the research process and is about 'being there'. Emotion is a real research experience and our intellectual autobiography is constructed and reconstructed through social research. Stanley (1990) takes the position that social research can be recast as distinctly feminist – where (i) researchers account for the conditions of knowledge production; (ii) there is a focus on feminist research labour and a feminist labour process; (iii) power is positioned as central to research writing; (iv) where the relationship between epistemology and ontology is central. She argues that 'Feminism is not merely a perspective, a way of seeing; nor even this plus an epistemology, a way of knowing; it is also an ontology, or a way of being in the world' (Stanley, 1990: 14).

There is no consensus about the applicability of specific social research methods in feminist research praxis. Early commentators attempted to draw a distinction between research methods that are quantitative, 'hard' and 'masculine' and those that are qualitative, 'soft' and 'feminine'. However, this distinction artificially divided the strengths and weaknesses of different approaches, and did not engage with the process and praxis of research (Maynard, 1994, 1996). Stanley and Wise's (1990) position that no one set of methods or techniques, nor any broad category or type of method, should be seen as distinctly feminist is increasingly accepted. From this perspective feminist research praxis is not about particular methods or techniques, but rather about the methodological framing, outcomes and reflections of research and the research process.

> We emphasise that there is no need for feminists to assign ourselves to one 'end' or another of the dichotomies 'foundationalism v. relativism', 'idealism v. material-ism' and methodological individualism v. collectivism which have resurfaced in feminist discussions of methodology. We reject the disguised hegemonic claims of some forms of feminism and actively promote academic feminist pluralism. (Stanley and Wise, 1990: 47)

While the present book is not a textbook about feminist methods and research approaches, it is clearly grounded in a feminist discourse on the nature and process of social research. It draws upon the desire to locate the self as a gendered, embodied, sexualized and emotional being, in and of the research; discounting the myth that social research can ever be neutral or hygienic. It is concerned with demystifying the researcher and researched as unattached and objective instruments, arguing that research is personal, emotional, sensitive, should be reflective and is situated in existing cultural and structural contexts.

Thus far I have said very little about the specific relationship between feminism, qualitative methods and ethnographic fieldwork. As Olesen (1994: 118) argues, 'qualitative feminist research is not homogeneous but highly differentiated and complex' and feminists have utilized qualitative methods – life histories, ethnographic interviews *and* fieldwork. Several feminist ethnographers have reflected upon the practice of conducting fieldwork (Abu-Lughod, 1986; Skeggs, 1994; Tsing, 1993), and have assessed the usefulness of an ethnographical, interactional approach as a way of revealing women's standpoint (Farrell, 1992; Langellier and Hall, 1989; Stanley and Wise, 1990) as well as debating the representation of feminist ethnography in the production of texts (Behar and Gordon, 1995; Clough, 1992; Enslin, 1994; Stack, 1996; Wolf, 1992). Feminist anthropologists in particular have been engaged in an epistemological and methodological enterprise of establishing what a distinctive feminist ethnography is and how it is located within 'malestream' anthropological work (see, for example, Abu-Lughod, 1990; Jennaway, 1990; Strathern, 1987; Walter, 1995). In posing the question 'can there be a feminist ethnography?' Abu-Lughod

(1990) argues that it is time to explore the many things it might be. She considers the relationship between feminism and reflexivity in ethnography; the dichotomy of subjectivity and objectivity, the nature and locales of feminist ethnographical fieldwork; the exploration with form, and writing. She argues that 'what feminist ethnography can contribute to anthropology is an unsettling of the boundaries that have been central to its identity as a discipline of the self studying other' (Abu-Lughod, 1990: 26).

The impact of feminism on 'malestream' anthropology is a vexed point, and indeed some have argued that it has had a minimal impact (Strathern, 1987). The recent postmodern discourse within anthropology (and indeed sociology) has brought to the fore issues of feminist ethnography. Jennaway (1990) has argued for example that postmodern ethnography has resulted in the (dis)location of feminism discourse.

> The move towards egalitarian relations of textual production, dialogic and poly-phonic cultural scripts, collaborative authorship, the decentering of self and disalienation of the ethnographic other, the move away from systems of representation which objectify and silence the ethnographic other, i.e. the general reflexive stance, are things to [*sic*] which feminist theory (if not specifically feminist anthropology) has long been adverting. (Jennaway, 1990: 171)

The connections between postmodernism, ethnographic fieldwork and feminism have also been recognized by others. For example issues of how the self gets positioned and situated within social and cultural contexts; how the self gets defined and redefined through the mediation of culture and language; how voices and lives are captured and represented, are all connected links identified by Mascia-Lees, Sharpe and Cohen (1989). They suggest that what appear to be new and exciting insights have received attention in feminist theory since the early 1980s. That culture is composed of contested meanings, that language and politics are inseparable, and that the construction of the 'other' implies relations of domination are in this sense nothing new. They are a consistent part of feminist theorizing of life and culture.

It is not my intention to focus on any one perspective or current debate in ethnography. There is a variety of perspectives and debates in which ethnography, and therefore fieldwork, is positioned. The current 'movements' of (post) feminism, postmodernism and the literary turn form part of the intellectual backdrop against which this book performs. The content and context of *The Ethnographic Self* cannot be separated from past, contemporary and projected directions of ethnographic practice, theory and politics. Moreover in so far as this book is a contribution to ethnographic thinking it engages with the premise that 'We are our own subjects. How our subjectivity becomes entangled in the lives of others is and has always been our topic' (Denzin, 1997: 27).

Scope and Content

This book explores the relationship between the self and ethnographic fieldwork thematically. I have not separated out different sorts of ethnography, in terms of chronology, theoretical frameworks, disciplinary background or kinds of setting. Rather, each chapter refers to a range of empirical examples, monographs and accounts of ethnographic fieldwork. The materials used illustrate and illuminate different dimensions of identity, and the selves of fieldwork. The decision to draw cases from different field settings and disciplines is a purposeful one. I want to stress that the emotional and 'personal' aspects of fieldwork experience and positionality are relevant to more than simply a small cross-section of postmodern or feminist ethnographers. The complex relationships between field settings, significant social actors, the practical accomplishment of fieldwork and the self are present and salient for all of us who engage in qualitative research. They are not the realm of a few brave scholars who choose to write about them openly and critically.

Each of the chapters is reasonably self-contained and can be read independently. Where appropriate I have made cross-references between chapters. However, there is a thematic structure to the book as a whole which may guide the way(s) in which it is read. Chapters 2, 3, 4 and 5 explore the ethnographic presence in the field, and implications of this in and beyond the fieldwork. Chapter 2 considers some of the ways in which we create and establish the 'self' in the field. I argue here that fieldwork engages us in identity work, and that this can be both productive and problematic. Chapter 3 grounds ethnographic fieldwork in a social and interactional context, by looking at the ways in which the relational self implicates the research process. The nature and emotions of field relations are used to socialize and contextualize fieldwork. Chapter 4 turns our attention to the physical presence of the researcher in the field, by considering the body, and the embodiment, of fieldwork. Here I reanalyse the conditions of fieldwork from a perspective of the embodied self and the embodied field. In Chapter 5 I turn to an exploration of a specific kind of fieldwork presence and experience. Here I highlight and discuss sexualization of social settings and the self in the context of ethnographic fieldwork.

Chapters 6, 7 and 8 move from the experiences of fieldwork to their representation. The focus shifts to how we remember, retell and write ethnography and the self. Chapter 6 considers the ways in which we romanticize the memories and reminiscences of fieldwork, and draws parallels between our feelings towards the 'field' and other romantic attachments. Chapter 7 addresses the issue of self-representation in the writing of and about fieldwork. While all of the book is to some extent about the writing of the self, this chapter looks more closely at both conventional and contemporary strategies for autobiographical ethnography. Chapter 8 continues this theme, by placing the writing of ethnography in a broader context. Specifically, it addresses the relationships between qualitative analysis, ethnographic representation and the self. Chapter 9 forms the conclusion to the book. I have chosen not to provide detailed summaries of each chapter in conclusion, so the last chapter attempts to draw out some of the general issues of the book, which may inform the ways in which we think about, conduct and write about fieldwork and our experiences of it.

The last thing I wish to mention here is the presence of myself in the text. It would clearly have been hypocritical to embark on a project such as this and leave out my own voice and experiences. Equally, it was never my intention to produce a wholly autobiographical, self-referential text. I have written the text in the first person, and where appropriate included my own fieldwork experiences. While I hope to have captured some of my own emotions, relations and memories of fieldwork, I have deliberately not used the text to write an empirical monograph. I hope that my experiences and my 'readings' of others' experiences both confirms and challenges the ethnographic self and the emotional accomplishment of fieldwork.

2 Locating the Self

The anthropological novel *Return to Laughter* (Bowen, 1954) was ethnographic writing arguably ahead of its time, as it was one of the first accounts of fieldwork to explicitly adopt a fictional genre. The text is unashamedly and self-consciously a 'made-up' story, as it presents a fictionalized version of the author's fieldwork in West Africa. Yet the text draws on the *real* fieldwork and the *real* experiences of the author. The author's note to the American Museum of Natural History edition of the book (Bowen, 1964) makes this clear:

> All the characters in this book, except myself, are fictitious in the fullest meaning of that word. I knew people of the type I have described here; the incidents of the book are of a genre I myself experienced in Africa. Nevertheless, so much is fiction. I am an anthropologist. The tribe I have described here does exist. The book is the story of the way I did field work among them. The ethnographic background given here is accurate, but it is neither complete nor technical. Here I have written simply as a human being, and the truth I have tried to tell concerns the sea change in oneself that comes from immersion in another and savage culture.

This quotation also points to the way in which *Return to Laughter* represents an autobiographical account of fieldwork. The book gives a highly personalized and emotive view of the ethnographic endeavour. There is no escaping the mental and physical presence of the researcher – in the field and in the text. As the quotation from Margaret Mead on the back cover of the book (Bowen, 1964) notes, it was 'the first introspective account ever published of what it's like to be a field worker among a primitive people'. It presents a classic story of the anthropologist as outsider, personally involved and enmeshed in a different, even alien, culture.

The fictional genre of *Return to Laughter* maps on to contemporary concerns and debates about the writing and representation of ethnography (Atkinson, 1990; Geertz, 1988). In the same vein, the autobiographical style – the visibility of the self in the field and the text – has received much recent, critical attention. It has long been recognized that ethnography has a biographical dimension (the observing and telling of lives). Increasingly the autobiographical has also been identified as a key element of the task and writing of ethnography. This identification has established the personal narratives of fieldwork as legitimate ethnographic writing, of which *Return to Laughter* is one sort of example. As a fictional, though realist, account of a bush tribe in West Africa, it paints a vivid, dramatic portrait of personal engagement in the field. Despite the innovatory writing and autobiographical qualities of this classic anthropological novel, it did not go as far as it might have done, in terms of rethinking ethnography and the positioning of the self. The irreconcilability of the nature of the text with the original decision to publish under a pseudonym (Elenore Smith Bowen is the *nom de plume* of anthropologist Laura Bohannan) is taken up by Riesman:

> Because of the book's honesty in portraying the inner experience of field work, I was troubled at its initial appearance under a pseudonym, even though I was told by friends of the author that this was done to protect the tribe, which itself for further insurance is not named. The thought crossed my mind that the author herself may have feared that the book might hurt her reputation as a competent and objective ethnographer, perhaps particularly so among those literal-minded readers who could not separate the book's feeling-tone and subjectivity from its circumstantial chronicle. (Riesman, 1964: xvi)

This sort of debate continues to shadow the overt positioning of the researcher self, as an intrinsic part of fieldwork. There is by no means a taken-for-granted consensus over the appropriate amount of self-revelation and reflexivity that should appear in the ethnographic monograph proper. The legitimation of autobiographical ethnography continues to be fraught. Many of the personal narratives of fieldwork are published as appendices or as completely separate pieces. It is still relatively unusual, and often described as alternative (or experimental), for the ethnographic self to be central to the experiences, events and texts of the field. I return to the process of 'writing the self' into ethnographic texts in Chapter 7.

A later edition of *Return to Laughter* (Bowen, 1964) did put Bohannan's name to the text, with her consent, although she never herself gives an explanation for her 'divorce' from the self by the use of the pseudonym in the first instance. Perhaps more interestingly, a close examination of the text reveals a style of writing, albeit autobiographical, which confirms conventional wisdom about the ethnographic endeavour. Indeed, the author's note, quoted above, is highly indicative of this, referring as it does to the 'savage culture' in which she became immersed. This immediately gives an image of the civilized, Westernized even, ethnographer embarking on a journey among strange (and dangerous?) peoples. The introductory chapter of the book is a recognizable 'arrival' story (Atkinson, 1996).

> The truck alternately jounced and slithered over the dirt road; after last night's rain, the first of the season, it was a lake of mud with occasional reefs of laterite. To either side spread the grassland, dead gray grass patched with the green of yam fields and the brown of newly cleared land. Dotted about were their homesteads: circular clusters of round huts with thatched roofs like dinner bells, domed and golden in the sun. Men and women were out in the fields, hoeing and pulling grass. They straightened at the noise of our coming, shouted, and shook their fists

at me. Sackerto had thought to tell me that this was their form of greeting. I shook my fist in return. (Bowen, 1964: 1–2)

As the introduction continues it sets about constructing a 'field', that is a place 'elsewhere' and away. It constructs a picture of the ethnographer as stranger. It suggests a distant and remote site, which the ethnographer must learn about and endure.

The sun was high. The tall grass cut out any view and any breeze. Then the carriers began to sing, and my momentary depression vanished. Seeing them file down the path, boxes on their heads, made me feel like something out of an old explorer's book. True, I was not in traditional costume: neither Mary Kingsley's stays and petticoats, nor in the pith helmet, shorts and boots of the traveller's frontispiece. It's difficult to feel adventurous in tennis shoes, a cotton dress, dark glasses, a shoulder bag and a floppy hat, but I managed it. I even managed to feel competent, almost experienced. The water from the small streams we waded was running out of my tennis shoes just as I had been told it would. (Bowen, 1964: 4–5)

Throughout the text, Bowen (Bohannan) captures her sense of strangeness, alienation and quest of endurance.

I was constantly being given apparently arbitrary advice, until I almost gagged on it, yet I was always sorry when I ignored it. Nor was I always able to fool myself into a feeling of professional competence. Far from pursuing a schedule of research, I was hauled around from one homestead to another and scolded for lack of manners or for getting my shoes wet. Far from having docile informants whom I could train, I found myself the spare-time amusement of people who told me what they considered it good for me to know and what they were interested in at the moment. (Bowen, 1964: 38)

The self that Bowen presents is that of a stranger in an alien culture, attempting to make sense of that culture from an outsider's perspective. While she lived with the people and got to know some well, her account positions her as a distant or marginal native (Freilich, 1970). She remained poised on the interface between familiarity and strangeness.

Many of my moral dilemmas had sprung from the very nature of my work, which had made me a trickster: one who seems to be what he is not and professes faith in what he does not believe. But this realisation is of little help. It is not enough to be true to oneself. The self may be bad or need to be changed, or it may change unawares into something strange and new. I had changed. Whatever the merits of anthropology to the world or of my work to anthropology, this experience had wrought changes in me as a human being – and I had thought that what wasn't grist for my notebooks would be adventure. (Bowen, 1964: 290)

The imagery of the fieldworker as naive stranger or marginal native has long been propagated in texts on the conduct and epistemology of ethnographic research. The reality of fieldwork and the nature of estrangement is far more complex than many accounts suggest. Straightforward readings of standard methodological texts imply a position of ethnographer-as-stranger, progressing towards a familiarity and eventual enlightenment, while simultaneously achieving a professional and personal distance. Such conventional accounts are at best pedagogical simplifications and do not afford satisfactory accounts of research experiences. They certainly do not do justice to the complex dualities of the research settings and the fieldworker self. As Bowen's account demonstrates, the relationship between the field and the self is complicated by the personal embeddedness of the ethnographic research task. Involvement is to some extent inevitable and even desirable. Methodological and political critiques of social anthropology (and ethnography more generally) have, in recent years, called into question the image of ethnographer-as-stranger and marginal, challenging the dichotomies of strangeness and membership, experience and innocence, knowledge and ignorance, suggesting that they do not fully, or even partially, capture the complexities of the self in the context of meaningful and fruitful fieldwork.

The so-called conventional wisdom of ethnography has been premised on a duality of observed and observer. The observer-ethnographer is able, and encouraged, to adopt the position of ignorant outsider. Over-familiarity is considered a problem, rather than a strength, at least initially. The task of preventing over-familiarity has often been seen as part of a longer process of enlightenment. The ethnographer-as-stranger is a transitional and temporary state, an initial stage in a more lengthy process of status passage. In many conventional accounts of social anthropology, the ethnographer-as-hero surrenders love, family and familiarity in order to confront an unknown culture. The fieldworker initially and purposely divests him/herself of knowledge and personhood in order to achieve eventual understanding. The process of ethnographic discovery, and the simultaneous mortification of the self in order to achieve it, have set up a version of fieldwork premised on a self-evident distance between a self and an other. In this version, estrangement from home and self leads to an eventual enlightenment and a deeper understanding of the social world. The disorientation of strangeness and unfamiliarity is a preliminary to a more sustained period of mastery. The heroic displacement of the ethnographer to the margins of the culture in question, and to the social position of an ignoramus, is a preliminary to an even more heroic achievement of knowledge and understanding at the centre of the culture.

In accounts such as that of Bowen (1954) it is easy to see how the initial sense of strangeness was something which did not have to be strived for. The setting was unfamiliar and the people strangers. The anthropological journey of fieldwork, in other cultures and 'away' from home, immediately conjures up the image of a stranger entering a different, unfamiliar or alien environment. The dilemma of familiarity comes later, as the fieldworker begins to live, work and become part of that environment. Fighting familiarity (Delamont and Atkinson, 1995) is also an issue 'at home', as Geer (1964) noted in her paper 'First days in the field', where she reflected upon the difficulties of studying everyday, familiar settings. To an 'untrained', or over-familiar, observer 'nothing' may be going on and worth noting down in a hospital ward or school classroom. As Becker (1971: 10) comments:

> it takes a tremendous effort of will and imagination to stop seeing things that are conventionally 'there' to be seen. I have talked to a couple of teams of research people who have sat around in classrooms trying to observe and it is like pulling teeth to get them to see or write anything beyond what 'everyone' knows.

Accounts of fieldwork in familiar settings have also engaged with the ethnographic debates over distance, marginality and estrangement. Methods texts (see Delamont, 1992; Hammersley and Atkinson, 1995; Lofland and Lofland, 1995) emphasize the need to maintain, and if necessary re-create, a sense of strangeness during fieldwork. Estrangement is both harder to achieve, and possibly even more crucial, in studies of the familiar and the mundane. Delamont (1992: 42–9), in addressing educational researchers, devotes considerable space to the problem of over-familiarity. She stresses that a key task is to devise strategies to deal with this problem.

This view of ethnographic endeavour has been used as an important instrument for the practical accomplishment of fieldwork. There have been clear justifications of the analytic value of estrangement or alienation in the field (see Geer, 1964). Such justifications acknowledge the difficulties of achieving such a stance in some settings but argue that the cultivated naivety of the stranger-ethnographer provides an analytic cutting edge – allowing the researcher to pose original research questions and capture the complexities of social life. Paralleling this 'natural' progression from estrangement to enlightenment has been a process of personal learning and fulfilment. While conventional accounts of ethnographic discovery have played out and reinforced the distance between the fieldworker and the field, there have been implicit narratives of individual and personal self-development. The separatedness of the self and the field has sat alongside narratives of an explorer-self; an heroic-self; a self which is both mortified and better understood. The ethnographer embarks on a progression from ignorant stranger to wise scholar, treading a path through self-alienation to self-enlightenment. The denial of the self has been received as epistemological necessity. At the same time fieldwork has been taken as a setting and a context for personal growth. These contrastive aspects of the fieldwork experience have not, as might have been thought, disproven the distance between the self and the field. Instead the dichotomy has been reinforced and maintained. The two processes of ethnographic fieldwork and self-development have been seen as related though separate. The ethnographer can utilize the experiences of fieldwork to gain a better understanding of the self. Yet this self should remain distinct from and distant to the field setting.

The ethnographer cultivates strangeness and distance in order to gain insight and understanding of the cultural setting while experiencing personal growth, based upon a view of the self as a product of and subject to its own agency and will.

This position begins to make problematic the conventional view of estrangement and over-familiarity in fieldwork. It is easy to see how such a view is persuasive in pedagogical terms. It offers a methodological tool in the concept of 'strangeness', and an unambiguous and developmental position for the self. However, we should be cautious of accounts which uncritically render the ethnographer as stranger, or as marginal. These imply too stark a contrast between a culture (yet to be known or 'discovered') and an observer (yet to be enlightened). Such over-simplified images of ethnographer as ignorant outsider or stranger may be misleading and in fact may render mute the ethnographic presence. They may serve to deny the experiential in fieldwork. The ethnographic self actually engages in complex and delicate processes of investigation, exploration and negotiation. These are not merely professional tasks. They are also personal and social occupations, which may be lost if we revert to an over-simplified model of fieldworker as ethnographic stranger. As I have already noted, this model is particularly difficult to sustain if the fieldsite is a familiar one. The image of the heroic ethnographer confronting an alien culture is now untenable, and fails to reflect much of what ethnographers do, if indeed it ever did reflect the lived reality of fieldwork.

The conceptual machinery of familiarity and strangeness is also rendered problematic, although perhaps not without its uses. Ethnography is more often conducted by members of a culture or related cultures, than by complete strangers. Moreover cultures are not in themselves homogeneous, and never were. So who is a stranger or a member, an outsider or an insider, a knower or an ignoramus is all relative and much more blurred than conventional accounts might have us believe. The path between familiarity and strangeness; knowledge and ignorance; intimacy and distance is far from straightforward. Simply adopting the stance of 'stranger' or 'unknower' denies, rather than removes, the situatedness and connectedness of the fieldworker self, alongside other selves. It is not clear that, in practice, fieldworkers engaged in researching their 'own culture' actually manage to estrange themselves radically. Nor is it necessarily the case that forcing a distance from the mundane, lived, esoteric knowledge of a culture really enables relevant research questions to be posed, beyond the obvious and those devoid of cultural specificity.

There is always a balance to be struck between the healthy scepticism of the researcher and ingratiation into a culture. Yet, it is naive and epistemologically wrong to deny the situatedness of the self as part of the cultural setting. As a positioned and contexted individual the ethnographer is undeniably part of the complexities and relations of the field. The pursuit of cultural understanding and the process of personal development are intimately rather than tangentially related. Such an exposition embraces Bowen's (1954) use of the autobiographical in fieldwork, and problematizes the conception that the self can be at one and the same time involved and distant. This chapter takes this presumption as a starting point for exploring the lived experience of fieldwork. This does not deny the centrality nor importance of familiarity, strangeness, distance, intimacy, ignorance and knowledge in the conceptualization and enactment of fieldwork.

The Self as Conceptual Anomaly

The tension between strangeness and over-identification is a current theme for many social scientists engaged in research, not only for ethnographers. The general significance of this tension should not be dismissed. A researcher who is no longer able to stand back from the esoteric knowledge they have acquired, and whose perspective becomes indistinguishable from that of the host culture, may face analytic problems. Yet too often the tensions between strangeness and over-familiarity are drawn simplistically and crudely. Strangeness is often viewed as a form of epistemological virginity, to be cherished and never regained once lost. Such a dichotomous view of the ethnographic self relegates the relations and negotiations of fieldwork to a peripheral position. By concentrating on the dangers of too much rapport and identification, the much more messy and complex positioning of the fieldworker, in relation to others, is misplaced. Ethnographic fieldwork cannot be accomplished without attention to the roles of the researcher. And once we begin to document these it becomes increasingly difficult to justify a realistic stance of ethnographer-as-stranger. Fieldwork involves the enactment of social roles and relationships, which places the self at the heart of the enterprise. A field, a people and a self are crafted through personal engagements and interactions among and between researcher and researched. This negotiation or crafting of ethnographic selfhood in the process of fieldwork can be thought of as the establishment of a field identity or field role. Indeed many of the standard texts on conducting ethnographic fieldwork refer to the desire to establish appropriate field roles.

> Decisions about the sort of role to adopt in a setting will depend on the purposes of the research and the nature of the setting. In any case, anticipation of the likely consequences of adopting different roles can rarely be more than speculative. Fortunately, shifts in role can often be made over the course of fieldwork. (Hammersley and Atkinson, 1995: 109)

Such 'good sense' advice rarely captures the range of roles, nor the processes by which these are accomplished and challenged. The adoption and development of appropriate field roles are often described in relatively straightforward, and unproblematic ways. We go into the field and take on roles and identities as a way of *getting on* with the task in hand. These roles and identities are chosen or sometimes imposed; can adapt and change; can be singular or multiple. Occasionally we risk 'going native' and becoming over-familiar. This is to be guarded against. Such a perspective fails to address the amount of role juggling and negotiating that some people experience during fieldwork. Further it presents an uncontentious and unemotive conceptualization of the fieldworker-self.

Fieldwork can be recast as a process where the self is central. Undertaking ethnographic research can problematize and force a reconceptualization of the self, which goes beyond the narrow confines of the fieldwork itself. A well-documented example of this is Kondo (1990). Kondo presents a vivid account of everyday life on the shop floor of a Tokyo factory, based upon her ethnographic fieldwork. Aside from providing a portrayal of contemporary Japanese work, and family life, Kondo refers to the ways in which her fieldwork required the acquisition of a different selfhood. As a Japanese-American woman studying Japanese society, Kondo found herself to be something of a conceptual anomaly. While Japanese in appearance, Kondo lacked the cultural competencies of a Japanese self. These cultural competencies of how to act and behave; the nuances of interaction and engagement, were observed and consequently learnt by Kondo over the course of her fieldwork. Living with a Japanese 'host' family, she experienced what she describes as a recasting of her sense of self as Japanese. This process was the outcome of interactions between Kondo and her hosts. Kondo's *new* Japanese self was added to, rather than detached from, her other selves – for example as Japanese-American, female, academic researcher, anthropologist. However, her sense of being and becoming Japanese suppressed and challenged the way she had conceptualized her selfhood prior to her fieldwork. Her senses of self and identity were mediated by the experiences, relations and interactions of her fieldwork. Her hosts assigned to her culturally meaningful roles, which she embraced. These roles included those of honorary daughter, student, guest and prodigal Japanese. Kondo acknowledges that this recasting was a two-way process. The anthropological imperative to 'fit in' and become immersed in another culture intensified her desire to acquire the accoutrements of Japanese selfhood. At the same time her hosts also

> had every reason to make me over in their image, to guide me, gently but insistently, into properly Japanese behavior, so that the discrepancy between my appearance and my cultural competence would not be so painfully evident. I posed a challenge to their senses of identity. How could someone who *looked* so Japanese not *be* Japanese? In my cultural ineptitude, I represented for the people who met me the chaos of meaninglessness. Their response in the face of this dissonance was to *make* me as Japanese as possible. Thus, my first nine months of fieldwork were characterised by an attempt to reduce the distance between

expectation and inadequate reality, as my informants and I conspired to rewrite my identity as Japanese. (Kondo, 1990: 12)

Kondo's recasting of the self was her response to the management of cultural strangeness. Her account also points to the ways in which this was not an inert process, but one of interaction and negotiation. To an extent this was concerned with the assimilation and transmission of 'folk' knowledge about the setting. It was also contextualized by the giving and receiving of cultural knowledge and meaningful identities by others in the field. Kondo's 'decision' over appropriate field roles was not really a decision at all. Her sense of self was reformulated as a situated outcome of assimilated esoteric knowledge and the acquisition of meaningful identities.

This placing of the ethnographer, and subsequent recasting of the self, is a common experience. Fieldwork is not accomplished in isolation from the physical and social setting. The adoption of fictive kin and familial-type relationships can reformulate the etographer's sense of self. For example, Macintyre (1993) conducted anthropological fieldwork in Papua New Guinea, and became part of the family of her hosts. The intimate relationships and knowledge which originated from this process helped Macintyre to define her identity in the field. Moreover it redefined who she was away from the field. Her 'family ties' were not contrived, although they had been formed for the purpose of fieldwork:

> Set in a large lineage with two older sisters, a mother and three powerful men as my mother's brothers, as well as numerous younger siblings, I could be managed, instructed and guided in ways that did not threaten their dignity or mine. Although I was unaware of it at the time, there was a meeting of people who decided on my fate in these terms within days of my arrival. (Macintyre, 1993: 52)

Like Kondo, Macintyre was assigned culturally defined gender roles in the field. This helped in both the recasting and the reinforcement of self. For instance, separated from her own daughters by fieldwork, Macintyre was encouraged to adopt two young *Magisbu* daughters to live with her, and her maternal identity was confirmed in this way. It is clear from Macintyre's account that the relationship she formed with these young women was real, meaningful and familial. Yet it also reveals the tenacity of fieldwork relationships. The end of fieldwork meant separation from her 'daughters', just as the onset of fieldwork had separated her from *other* daughters. Macintyre's fieldwork identity as mother to these young women was both real and *temporary*. In seeking, being given and adopting appropriate field selves, the utilization of existing cultural roles for these women was crucial. The gendered identities of Macintyre and Kondo were also familial identities, significant in and beyond the field.

This process of identity construction, mediated by gender, race and family, has not only been reflected upon by women anthropologists. Wade (1993), for example, engaged in a recasting of his white, male, heterosexual self during fieldwork in Colombia. He particularly draws attention to the male friendships he struck up with two men *and* the two stable sexual relationships he had with women during fieldwork. Together these relationships engaged Wade in defining and to some extent confirming his identity and male selfhood.

> Fieldwork as a whole was a 'personal odyssey' for me . . . and certainly my close relationships with Eleon and Carlos, and with Marcela and Roberta were also personal odysseys within that overall journey. The interest of them for my analysis is the way they influenced how I as an anthropologist structured the encounter with my own concepts of close relationships and my own concepts of masculinity – always in interaction with local concepts of the same. (1993: 213)

The accomplishment of fieldwork is not a passive activity. We actively engage in identity construction and recasting. It is neither helpful nor accurate to treat these processes as cynical enactments of appropriate field roles in order to acquire rich ethnographic data. It is, on the one hand, easy to stress the need for the adoption of both plausible roles and professional distance in order to be ethnographically astute. On the other hand, the actual lived experience of conducting fieldwork confronts the self in ways that go beyond this enactment of a work process. Certainly many of those who have undertaken anthropological fieldwork 'abroad' have been met with the realization of a changing selfhood. The establishment of field roles has been personal and has had lasting impact on the conceptualization of selfhood, beyond the temporal and spatial boundaries of fieldwork. The analytical idea of the conceptual anomaly necessitates a position of realignment and redefinement. The result of this could be a fracturing or complicating of self-identity, rather than a process of clarification. Blackwood (1995) describes the ways in which she established and shifted between a number of equally valid identities during her fieldwork in Indonesia. She conducted prolonged fieldwork in a rural Muslim village in West Sumatra, with the intention of studying social change, gender and power. Interested in exploring the gender identity of lesbians, she met several and in the process fell in love with one of them. In preparing for fieldwork Blackwood decided to hide her lesbian identity. She identified herself as unmarried, and allowed the assumption to follow that she was heterosexual. She found that as an unmarried, supposedly heterosexual woman living with an Indonesian family she was expected to fulfil the ideals of this gender category.

> I resisted a field identity that conformed to their expectations for an unmarried woman. Although I cleaned my own room and sometimes swept the floors in the house, I never cooked or did my own laundry; instead, I paid other women to take care of these domestic duties for me. This failing did not surprise my host, who assumed that 'rich' privileged Americans would not be well trained in such matters. Where the dress code was at odds with my lesbian self, however, I developed the most resistance to reconstructing my identity. I could not force myself to wear skirts as any proper Indonesian woman does, except very

occasionally. My host sometimes remarked on this lapse because it raised deeper questions for her about my womanhood. (Blackwood, 1995: 57–8)

Blackwood's recasting of her sense of self in the course of fieldwork was both contrived and real. Clearly her (mis)identification as heterosexual, and her partial conformity to the gender ideals of Indonesian, Muslim culture were part of a self-conscious attempt at access and assimilation. Yet at the same time the relationships, both with her hosts and with her lover (Dayon) questioned and redefined her identity. To say that these were artificial or contrived would be to render them insignificant to Blackwood's biography and sense of self.

> My relationship with Dayon coalesced the identity conflicts that plagued me during my fieldwork. It helped to ease my sense of being ungrounded, restored to me my lost lesbian identity. I found a deeply rewarding and loving relationship that helped me survive the anomie and isolation of fieldwork, an isolation made more difficult by the need to keep my lesbian identity invisible. (Blackwood, 1995: 70)

Self-identity is concerned with both self-appearance and the social relations of the field. These simultaneously highlight the concepts of familiarity and strangeness, and complicate the differentiation between the two. The construction of self and identity in the field is also concerned with the acquisition and presentation of local and esoteric knowledges. In self-consciously seeking to acquire knowledge of social organizations and cultures the fieldworker may be involved in a more personal process of redefinition (Schutz, 1964). Commenting on his ethnographic fieldwork in the Edinburgh Medical School, Atkinson (1997) identifies how the acquisition of esoteric medical knowledge challenged his methodological stance of self-conscious novice:

> I found it necessary to manage the contrasting impressions of expertise and ignorance in the course of my fieldwork in the medical school. My general point here is to emphasise that the methodological stance of outsider, novice or stranger does not absolve the ethnographer from the requirement to make sense of the esoteric knowledge of a given community or occupation. One cannot make serious sociological sense of medical knowledge and medical culture if one remains stubbornly ignorant of what medical practitioners and their students actually do. (Atkinson, 1997: 65)

While Atkinson does not explicitly discuss this in terms of selfhood and identity it is clear that he was involved in managing his role as a kind of conceptual anomaly in the medical school. He found that during the teaching sessions he acquired a good deal of medical knowledge and information – which was crucial to his being able to 'understand' what was going on in the everyday world of the medical or surgical ward. At the same time he was conscious of the tenuous position this placed him in *vis-à-vis* the medical students.

> The students often found it hard to believe that I was genuinely capable of understanding what was going on – and on occasion would commiserate with me on my 'obvious' inability to follow what I was observing. They sometimes seemed unable or unwilling to believe that I was indeed able to keep up with at least the greater part of what was going on. Some students even appeared to resent my ability to gain some passing acquaintance with their subject, without the background training in the basic and medical sciences. (Atkinson, 1997: 61–2)

Here again, the emphasis is on the creation and maintenance of a fieldwork self in a relationship with others in the field. In the acquisition, assimilation and demonstration of knowledge the fieldwork self remains interactional, crafted out of the relationships with other selves. Methodological textbook approaches to the adoption and negotiation of field roles usually phrase such issues in terms of self-management strategies: of finding a role in order to do the job, collect the data, gain access to the understandings and knowledge of a particular cultural setting. Hence field roles are often cast in terms of the practical accomplishment of fieldwork. To this end the idea of managed strangeness is often what is actually being advocated. What such accounts miss, however, is the more complex reality of identities that are managed, crafted and shaped by the dialectic between researcher and researched. The crafting of selves in the context of fieldwork is not just about presenting an acceptable or plausible self, as a means to an end. It can actually be about becoming a different self over the course of and beyond the fieldwork. This process, moreover, is interactional and negotiated – the outcome of relationships or collusion with others. The roles, understandings and knowledges given, received and gained over the course of ethnographic fieldwork are shaped by who we are at the outset. They also go on to define who we become after fieldwork ends. Conventional views of the adoption of field roles, and the progression from naive stranger to informed 'knower', do not do justice to these contextual and interactional processes. The point I want to emphasize is that our fieldwork selves are fluid, negotiated and can be meaningful beyond the temporal and spatial specificities of the field.

Challenging Selves

In the summer of 1991 I began a period of ethnographic fieldwork in a large accountancy firm in a UK city. My interests lay in the occupational socialization and professional training processes of accountancy. I had arranged to 'shadow' a cohort of graduate trainees, as they began their professional careers. While I intended to conduct a series of ethnographic interviews over the course of my fieldwork, my main method of data collection was ethnographic observation, with varying degrees of participation. I took part in the initial training programme, undertook the preliminary bookkeeping classes, and participated in the extra-curricula and organizational social life alongside my 'fellow' new recruits to the accountancy firm.

There are well-established debates over how far the ethnographer should actively participate in the everyday life of the organizational or cultural setting (see Gold, 1958; Hammersley and Atkinson, 1995; Junker, 1960), and it is not my intention to rehearse them. The issue is of more general relevance in relation to the discussion here.

Prior to my fieldwork I had given very little thought to my field role(s), beyond a rather simplistic appreciation of the necessity to establish rapport. I did not anticipate that my fieldwork would challenge my sense of who I was. I was after all doing fieldwork 'at home'. I was not travelling overseas, or to a markedly different culture. While the actual organizational setting was strange to me, I expected that the kind of people there would be 'familiar' to me. I had a number of friends who were accountants in different firms. The graduates with whom I would be spending most time were of a similar age to me, had experience of university life in the same time frame as me, were individuals with whom I saw myself relating. Indeed I had even debated the possibilities of entering the accountancy profession a few years earlier. Although I had eventually decided against it, I felt my experiences of attending careers fairs and accountancy interviews gave me a common ground with my informants. In so far as I had any thoughts about my sense of self during fieldwork I assumed that I would have relatively little difficulty in combining my identities in and out of the field.

On the surface, my assumptions proved to be true. I was able to establish good working relations with the graduates and other members of the organization. While I had clearly differentiated relationships within the firm (for example my relationship with the senior partners was always more formal and structured than with the more junior members), I assumed that was a relatively normal part of the fieldwork experience. In any setting the ethnographer will establish a range of relationships with members, which mirrors the normal complexities of human interactions. Over the course of the fieldwork my experiences were relatively unremarkable, especially when compared with other, more challenging accounts of experiences during fieldwork. Yet I was unprepared for the ways in which the relationships I formed in the field would impact on my life and identity outside that particular 'work' context. I began to socialize more with the members of the setting than with friends and colleagues from outside the field. While I began by justifying this in terms of 'work', I became conscious that I wanted to be, and was increasingly accepted as, part of the 'scene'. I was hurt when I found out retrospectively about nights out planned and enjoyed by my 'fellow' accountants. Equally, I took my turn in organizing social activities. What began as working relationships became meaningful friendships to me. And as with all friendships, conflicts and tensions sometimes arose. I found myself increasingly dealing with those as personal rather than work situations. In addition to the ways in which I developed and came to rely upon these relationships, I also found myself drawn in to the everyday life of the organization. I cared passionately about doing my bookkeeping homework, and was able to empathize with the graduates over time spent grappling with technical problems. I was added to circulation lists for the distribution of routine documentation and information. The training tutor would discuss ideas and class material with me as a fellow teacher, rather than an observer.

On one level, the experiences which I have outlined may be judged as indicators of a successful ethnography. I was fully integrated into the firm, able to come and go as I pleased. I had developed good relationships and levels of rapport with my key informants. I had access to the formal and informal contexts of the organizational culture, as well as the documentary reality. I was in a position to collect solid and detailed data, with the full consent of the members. On a parallel level, I found that it became increasingly difficult to separate my life outside the firm from my life within it. I began to feel like a member of the organization, and especially part of the junior team. In fact I became concerned that I did not have a formal role within the firm, and began to offer to 'do' some of the teaching, and present at seminars. In retrospect, I realize that this was part of my attempt to justify and clarify who I was in the context of the organizational life. This is not to say that I underwent any form of identity crisis. On the contrary my commitments and relationships in the field were hugely rewarding, as well as intellectually challenging. But by actively participating in the everyday life of the setting, I found it impossible to divorce my fieldwork self from my other selves. My identities as teacher, friend, confidante, researcher, author, young professional woman, were mediated by a new identity of pseudo-accountant. These identities were all interwoven during the field-work, and continued to be so after the formal end of fieldwork. Who I am is different from who I was prior to my fieldwork in the accountancy firm. I return to aspects of my research later in this book, especially in the next chapter where I reflect upon my relationships over the course of the fieldwork. For my purposes here, I wished to draw attention to the ways in which the self and the field are interrelated. Moreover that issues of self and identity are not simply concerns for fieldwork in especially different, strange or difficult settings. The fieldwork self is always, to some extent, shaped by the cultural context and social relations of the field.

In many methodological accounts we find warnings and morality tales about the stereotype of 'going native' (I recognize here that contemporary sensibilities about linguistic practice have questioned the appropriateness of such terminology, while an increasing tendency to conduct fieldwork 'at home' also alters the exact meaning of the term). There continues to be a pedagogical assumption that the ethnographer should be advised against becoming totally absorbed in the cultural frameworks under study. We are not supposed to undergo total transformation in the course of fieldwork. Even with a growing sense of knowing and familiarity, a professional distance and 'strangeness' should be observed. One is not supposed to actually *become* a member of a host family, a model patient, a medic, an accountant, a storeman, a drug user or whatever. The argument for such cautiousness has already been rehearsed earlier in this chapter – if one's perspectives get too closely aligned with those of one's research 'subjects' or hosts, then the analytical cutting edge of cultural difference will be lost. Over-identification and rapport is held up as a source of doom and failure. Too close a rapport submerges the researcher in the new culture, to the detriment of the research endeavour and analytical astuteness.

> The comfortable sense of being 'at home' is a danger signal. From the perspective of the 'marginal' reflexive ethnographer, there can thus be no question of total commitment, 'surrender', or 'becoming'. There must always remain some part held back, some social and intellectual 'distance'. For it is in the space created by this distance that the analytical work of the ethnographer gets done. (Hammersley and Atkinson, 1995: 115)

This implies a view that analytical 'strangeness', once lost, can never be regained. Once crossed, the boundaries of culture, and therefore the opportunities for analysis, can never be redrawn. Equally it suggests that conversion is a possibility, and a dangerous one that should be avoided. Such a hard and fast approach can, in fact, be counterproductive. It tends to oversimplify the dynamics of crafting the self in the contexts of the field. Certainly not all ethnographers would subscribe to the usual strictures against 'going native'. Nor is the process of over-identification simple or linear, even if it has the potential to be pedagogically fruitful.

There are some well-documented examples of over-identification during fieldwork, and the consequent way this can lead to a skewed perspective of a cultural setting. Willis's monograph *Learning to Labour* (1977), based on an ethnographic study of working-class boys, is a case in point. Hammersley and Atkinson (1995) are particularly critical of the 'over-rapport' that Willis established with the 12 'lads' in his fieldwork. The monograph can be read as a celebration of these young men, based on an uncritical over-identification with them. Hammersley and Atkinson suggest that Willis became a spokesman for, rather than a researcher of, these boys and their social world. And because of this he gave a distorted description of schooling and an uncritical, partial perspective on working-class culture. The necessity to be intellectually poised between familiarity and strangeness (to use the terminology of Hammersley and Atkinson) is ignored by Willis, and his analysis is flawed because of this. Willis can be further criticized for his seeming lack of awareness of his sense of self in relation to the field and his key informants. He is remarkably unreflective on his own situated position. It is not so much his over-rapport as his failure to recognize and reflect, which is at fault. While acting as spokesman and biographer he himself remains invisible in the accounts and text. He is there yet is not there. We never get any real sense of his presence as a critical social actor in the field.

This lack of self-awareness and critical stance can certainly be an argument against immersion and over-identification within a cultural setting. Nobody could disagree with the general argument that becoming part of the cultural setting under investigation, and losing the intellectual capacity to recognize and reflect upon this, makes nonsense of fieldwork. Of course immersion must be accompanied by a critical, analytical, self-conscious awareness. However, some commentators have argued for full identification and total immersion in a culture, in order to facilitate analytical fieldwork. Here, the issue is one of recognizing the value of immersion to the intimate understanding of a culture. Jules-Rosette (1978) has argued from such a stance, documenting her religious conversion to an African church as part of her fieldwork experiences. This was not, in her case, merely the outward show of participation in a ritual. It was a personal conversion experience, which had personal and fieldwork significance. In a somewhat similar vein, Favret-Saada (1980) has written about her fieldwork engagement with witchcraft in rural France. Favret-Saada argued that there was absolutely *no* neutral standpoint to be adopted outside the discourses of witchcraft. She was, as she describes it, virtually compelled to become part of the system and its discourses. It was impossible to continue to study without doing so. Peshkin's (1985) experiences as a Jewish researcher of a fundamentalist Protestant school provide a further example, not necessarily of *conversion* but certainly of immersion. Being Jewish became an unavoidably salient aspect of his research subjectivity. While he set out to be a non-Christian scholar interested in a fundamentalist education in Bethany, Oklahoma, he soon found that his Jewishness was a personal fact that had a bearing on most of his research.

> Bethanyites let me define my research self, but could never rest easy with my unsaved self. I became forcibly aware that the threats to my identity as a Jew were not just a matter of history.
>
> For in the course of inculcating their students with doctrine and the meaning of the Christian identity, Bethany's educators taught us both that I was part of Satan's rejected, humanist world; I epitomised the darkness and unrighteousness that contrasts with their godly light and righteousness. They taught their children never to be close friends, marry, or go into business with someone like me. What they were expected to do with someone like me was proselytise. (Peshkin, 1985: 14–15)

Peshkin's account demonstrates that the ways in which we can become immersed are not always based on a sense of familiarity or belonging. Indeed immersion can capture the difficult position of the fieldworker, as both marginal to and fundamentally engaged in a cultural setting. As well as accounts of conversion and immersion, there are instances where researchers have reported extraordinary experiences that have occurred to them during fieldwork. These experiences are extraordinary in the sense that conventional fieldwork wisdom would dismiss or be unduly pessimistic about them.

For example, the collection edited by Young and Goulet (1994) includes a number of accounts by social anthropologists who have seen or experienced the unusual or unexpected during fieldwork. These include seeing a spirit (Turner, 1994); acquiring the powers associated with a shaman (Guedon, 1994); and witnessing the reappearance of the dead (Goulet, 1994). These accounts are based on the 'real' experiences of the researchers, and echo the experiences of other social actors (or members) in the field. They could be conceptualized (and indeed criticized) as 'going native' types of story. Yet they are presented in a somewhat different light: as evidence of knowledge gained that would otherwise have remained partial and opaque. Our concern is not so much with the 'truth' of such accounts, as with the ways in which they challenge the harsh rationality of the distinction between observer and observed in the conduct of fieldwork and reconstruction of culture.

Fieldwork is not always conducted by those who are social or intellectual strangers to the cultural setting. In the case of long-term ('lifetime') fieldwork, for example, the ethnographer becomes an insider or 'native' over time. Anthropologists describing their ethnographic careers of studying a distinct culture reflect upon the changing nature of their roles and relationships through time (see Fowler and Hardesty, 1994). There is, perhaps, also a contrast to be drawn between those who come to a setting from the position of relative stranger (where in theory the distinction between familiarity and strangeness is possible), and those who engage in fieldwork from an assumed position of 'knowing' – where the researcher already possesses some of the esoteric knowledge and an empathetic self. Key examples here would be ethnographies of occupational settings by members or ex-members, such as studies of nurses and midwives by practitioners in the field (Davies, 1988, 1994; Hunt, 1987) and Hockey's ethnography of British military life (Hockey, 1986, 1996) which was mediated by his past biography as an active soldier. His study of recruit basic training was emotional and meaningful, as it reminded him of his own experiences. After witnessing a demeaning incident for one of the recruits Hockey felt anger at the debasement he himself had experienced during training:

> The recall of one instance was quite vivid: me standing rigidly to attention next to my bed, with my equipment being laid out on the bed, being inspected by a Company Sergeant Major, who despite hours of labour on my part to make the items shining bright, proceeded to scream at me that there was filth in abundance and that I was a dirty horrible soldier and lazy! Then starting with my boots, he proceeded to throw items of equipment out of the window onto a muddy patch of grass. With this finished, he ordered me to ready the equipment for inspection again. (Hockey, 1996: 19)

School-based ethnography has been conducted by several former school-teachers (see Ball, 1981; Beynon, 1985; Burgess, 1983; Mac an Ghaill, 1988; Pollard, 1985; Riddell, 1992). Salisbury (1994) provides an example of this interplay between a past teaching self and a present educational ethnographer. Engaged in an ethnography of vocational teachers in training, she was able to bring to the research her experience as a classroom, school-based, teacher. This biographical feature helped her gain acceptance in the field, by both the 'teachers' (higher education lecturers) and 'students' (most of whom already had teaching posts in the further education sector). Her teacher identity also influenced the self that she presented and became over the course of fieldwork.

> Being a teacher of twelve years' experience, who had the fortune to 'tunnel out of the state school classroom for three years' I thought would give me some credibility with the trainees and provide me with a kind of retrospective access to the culture of teachers. (Salisbury, 1994: 44)

By emphasizing her teacher identity, Salisbury was accepted by the trainee teachers and the training staff. Yet Salisbury reflects that the role (and self) which she presented was not one with which she was completely comfortable. Having stressed her teaching experience and joined in with the teaching, planning and preparing of lessons she also found she became a confidante. She felt she became over-confided in; presented with 'guilty knowledge' she was unsure what to do with. Salisbury's biography as a teacher both enabled and disabled the sorts of fieldwork relationships and selves she made. Her teaching self interacted and reacted with her ethnographic self in the course of her fieldwork. Carter (1995) experienced similar 'mixed' emotions. As an ex-police-officer studying the occupational culture of prison officers Carter was given keys and open access to the prison setting. He was placed in a position of extreme trust, about which he was somewhat ambivalent. He welcomed the opportunities it afforded and the acceptance it implied, while being extremely wary of the level of familiarity and loyalty it assumed. His assumed 'insider' status was both opportune and something on which he had to continually and critically reflect.

The issues of over-familiarization and immersion (or 'conversion') are complicated by specific examples of total immersion, conversion, extraordinary experiences and 'insider' research. This is not to say that the debates and warnings about issues of over-identification are not valid discourses of ethnography. Indeed they provide us with a forum in which to explore the range of experiences and identities that occur in the process of fieldwork. While contemporary equivalents of 'going native' are difficult fieldwork positions to adopt, they do not necessarily deny the value of the fieldwork. Further these challenges or changes to our identity and sense of self in the field can be methodologically and personally significant in their own right. I have already discussed the crafting of the self that Kondo (1990) experienced during fieldwork in Japan. The redefinition of her identity was part of the processes of immersion and the formation of relationships. Kondo writes of the impact this had on her own perceptions of who she was and who she was becoming. She employs the concept of identity fragmentation to reanalyse the process. Kondo began to locate (and see) herself as

Japanese. She identified herself in terms of the culturally defined roles which were assigned to her in the field – Japanese daughter, housewife, female guest. On seeing a reflection of a 'typical' young, Japanese housewife in a shop window and upon realizing that what she was observing was her own image, Kondo's own sense of identity reached a point of crisis.

> This collapse of identity was a distancing moment. It led me to emphasise the differences between culture and among various aspects of identity: researcher, student, daughter, wife, Japanese, American, Japanese American. In order to reconstitute myself as an American researcher, I felt I had to extricate myself from the conspiracy to rewrite my identity as Japanese. (Kondo, 1990: 17)

This 'fragmentation of self', Kondo explains, was the result of a complex collaboration between ethnographer and hosts. Her identity was in the process of being rewritten and in part Kondo saw this as a threat to her own sense of selfhood. Recognizing that she was in danger of losing herself, Kondo moved out of the 'family' home where she had been staying. She moved into her own apartment as a means of re-engaging her former self. Her fear of losing her sense of self was genuine: 'Let me escape before I am completely transformed' (Kondo, 1990: 24). This sense of fear of initial immersion and loss of self has not been written about extensively. Indeed many of our initial fears may be about just the opposite. The fear of not fitting in or not being accepted may be a more common worry when beginning fieldwork. Yet the fragmentation of our lives that may come with prolonged fieldwork can throw our perspectives of who we are, and where we belong into chaos. With the momentum of fieldwork, and our desire to be part of the field, the self can be lost, found, altered and recast. Blackwood (1995), for example, describes a self that became lost, and refound over the course of fieldwork in Indonesia. The constraints and relations of fieldwork conspired to reduce her sexual self:

> And who am I, this amorphous creature with few reality markers to cling to, yet somehow conspiring to present a self acceptable to people here? Much of who I am, or considered myself to be, goes unrecognised . . . my gay identity is lost and crying out for recognition. (Blackwood, 1995: 59)

To an extent this complicates the interaction between the self and the field, by recognizing the tensions and fears in finding and keeping a fieldwork self. The balance between strangeness and familiarity, often stressed in pragmatic terms, is not an easily negotiated, emotional balance – between seeking an identity and losing an identity. Indeed what is emphasized here, and often not stressed in conventional discussions of field roles, is the way in which self and identity are not singular, fixed, bound entities (cf. Wengle, 1988). Selves and identities are fragmented and connected; open to shifts and negotiations. They are ambiguous, the outcome of culturally available and defined interactions, actions, meanings and values. The self is not so much complete and rounded, as partial and multiple. This has consequences for the self in the field and the ways in which the self interconnects with others in the field. Haraway (1991: 193) argues that one needs to reformulate the self as 'partial in all its guises, never finished, whole, simply there and original; it is always constructed and stitched together imperfectly and therefore able to join with another, to see together without claiming to be another'. This is, in many ways, faithful to social interactionist perspectives on self and identity (Denzin, 1989) and the idea that everyday life is multilayered, with multiple perspectives and voices. However, such perspectives are often discussed as part of the more general framework of ethnographic practice, than as specific points from which to explore the ethnographer. This conceptualization of the self as partial and fluid is useful in locating the multidimensional and complex aspects of selfhood, which many field researchers experience. In particular it helps to make sense of the fragmentation, negotiation and reconstruction of the self during fieldwork.

Conclusion

In this chapter I began by setting out the relative positions of familiarity and strangeness in the conduct of fieldwork. In doing so I suggested that at the very least the concepts of ethnographer-as-stranger and over-identification are pedagogical simplifications and do not do justice to the full range of research experiences. Simplified and unqualified versions of strangeness, immersion and familiarity fail to engage adequately or completely with the positionality of the self in the context of fieldwork. Conversion and over-immersion in the field have conventionally been perceived as negative, analytically weak and, in research terms, deviant in the extreme. Such accounts are usually located in the genre of the morality tale; tending to serve as a warning of getting too involved. These accounts can actually be both unhelpful and paralysing. The choices between involvement and immersion, rapport and over-rapport, familiarity and loss of self are often too starkly drawn to accurately reflect the full range of chosen and imposed identities, assumed during and beyond the field. The issue is not necessarily one of conversion, immersion or not, but a recognition that the ethnographic self is the outcome of complex negotiations. Moreover the definition and location of the self is implicitly a part of, rather than tangential to, the ethnographic research endeavour. One of the strengths of ethnographic enquiry is the real involvement of the fieldworker in the setting under study. A weakness is not the possibility of total immersion, but a failure to acknowledge and critically (though not necessarily negatively) engage with the range of possibilities of position, place and identity.

I would like to add a caveat to what has gone before. It would be easy to assume, on the basis of my discussion, that full immersion and identification is always (a) possible, (b) desirable, and that fieldwork is only truly meaningful when we are fully engaged, and indeed challenged. Both of these conclusions take my general argument too far. It is totally necessary and desirable to recognize that we are part of what we study, affected by the cultural context and shaped by our fieldwork experience. It is epistemologically productive to do so, and at best naive to deny the self an active, and situated place in the field. However, it is not necessary to make the self the key focus of the fieldwork, and to do so would render much ethnographic work meaningless. We should not lose sight of the ethnographic imperative that we are seeking to understand and make sense of the social worlds of others, albeit using ourselves as key research instruments. Lastly it would be wrong to suggest that most of us ever really become part of the cultural setting we study, and that our identities have a lasting impact on those cultural settings. That implies a far greater level of self-importance than most of us enjoy, and quite rightly so. Most of us intrude in a setting for a relatively short period of time. Even where the relationship between field-worker and setting is lengthy, the fieldworker comes and goes and is rarely a constant element. It is extremely self-centred of us to think that we can ever be a 'fully paid up member' of an accountancy firm, a hospital, an opera company, a village community in Papua New Guinea or whatever. On occasions we may feel as though we belong, and rarely we may actually undergo a sort of conversion experience. Far more likely, however, we remain an honorary member or 'friend' of the setting, despite or because of our self-conscious relationship with the field. In attempting to make sense of the relationship between the self and the field we should not lose sight of this, nor see our objective as changing this. The reality that the impact of fieldwork is usually greatest for us and not for our hosts should remain the firm reason why we should be open about our attachments to and emotions about fieldwork and our hosts.

3   The Interpersonal Field

Fieldwork takes place in a variety of social and cultural settings. We use the term 'the field' to refer to a heterogeneous group of locations and contexts. Everyday life as an area of social enquiry makes the boundaries of observation and analysis almost limitless. While generalizations about the field are difficult, and often unhelpful, all fieldwork sites will have at least one common factor. The field is a site peopled by social actors and, implicitly, by the social researcher. The primary task of the fieldworker is to analyse and understand a peopled field. This task is achieved through social interaction and shared experiences. It follows, therefore, that fieldwork is dependent upon and guided by the relationships that are built and established over time.

As a social process, fieldwork necessitates relational work of a unique and intense kind. From initial access to developing field roles; from collecting the data to analysing and publishing. In all stages of the ethnographic enterprise social relationships remain key. Furthermore, how we experience and remember fieldwork is through the interactions and relations we share with others. The people of the field and our relationships with them provide not only the bulk of our data. They also provide us with the building blocks of our identity in and beyond the field. It is inevitable and desirable that we seek to develop positive relationships with those we are engaged in studying (with). The interactional quality of fieldwork relies upon the formation of such relationships. In comparison, poor or difficult fieldwork relations can affect the collection of data, as well as our experiences and memories of fieldwork.

It is difficult to conceive of effective fieldwork without paying attention to the relationships and interactions that help to characterize it. We cannot escape the necessity of developing rapport and a level of intimacy during the pursuit of prolonged fieldwork. Yet such relations, on the surface at least, are different from other relationships we engage in. Fieldwork relationships are at once professional and personal, yet not necessarily readily characterized as either. Many professional, or even research, contexts rely upon social relationships that are courteous and polite, though distant. While we might hope to establish an ease of rapport, polite acquaintance is usually an entirely appropriate response. Yet in fieldwork the professional, research relationship also has a far more personal quality. It is not enough to simply go through the motions of politeness and professional courtesy. Fieldwork simply will not generate good data and interesting analyses without personal investment in the relations of the field. However artificially, and perhaps cynically construed in the first place, fieldwork relationships are real in their consequences, both in terms of the quality of the data and the lived experience of the research. Fieldwork is easier, more enjoyable, and possibly more productive where good social relationships are forged. Equally, extremely poor relations can make effective fieldwork difficult, though they can none the less be illuminating in themselves. Adopting a middle stance, field relations must be such that the researcher is engaged and included (actively and/or passively) in the life and everyday activities of the social world being studied.

Establishing field relations is not an even or straightforward process. Certain limits and boundaries exist, at least initially. The onus is firmly on us to initiate a working rapport and level of trust. We are locating ourselves within a particular setting. We are the ones for whom the relationships matter, in the context of our research agenda. That is not to deny the meaningfulness of fieldwork relationships for other social actors in the field. Indeed one of the qualities and potential problems of ethnographic fieldwork is the shared and significant relationships that are often forged. But at least at the commencement of fieldwork it is up to the researcher to actively pursue these social relations. Given the possible variety of fieldwork locations, this is bound on occasion to result in attempts to establish relationships and common ground with social groups with whom we have explicitly very little in common. It is also possible to envisage situations where at first there are genuine shared views and personal engagement. In both instances managing the resultant relationships, both personally and professionally, can be challenging.

The distinctive dependence on social interaction and relations establishes fieldwork as a form of personal identity work. As I discussed in Chapter 2, our relationships with others in the field can provide a source of self-identification. Moreover the shared nature of the relationships suggests that others, too, might derive meaning and identity from them. Although they arise out of a particular situated context – a researcher engaging in ethnographic fieldwork – field relations come to depend upon a level of rapport and sharing. Clearly the level of reciprocity is a crucial issue. At a base level the fieldworker is gaining field data, and usually personal satisfaction. The gains and benefits to the other social actors in the field (the 'subjects') are less easily assessed. How reciprocity and trust are developed, established, tested and lost in the pursuit of fieldwork is key to understanding the relations of fieldwork.

So far I have talked generally about the centrality of social relationships in the pursuit of field data. These social relations are, however, fundamentally interactions between individuals. While we can think collectively about the researcher's 'relationship' with a field site or a people, what we are really concerned with are individual social actors getting along (or not). Over the course of ethnographic fieldwork we develop relationships with key individuals. Sometimes these are sought out early on in the research process. The selection is personal and highly reliant upon shared understandings and a desire for friendship. At other times we may have no choice as to whom we rely upon as key individuals; the nature of the research site or the framework of our access may link us automatically to one or a small number of people.

In most cases fieldwork becomes reliant upon one-to-one interactions and relations. How these develop over time is not prescribed. Some field relationships are short term, lasting for no longer than the fieldwork, or a particular part of it. In these cases the relationships are bounded by the formal research strategy and situated context of the field. This does not absolve them from being mutual and meaningful, nor their ending from resulting in a sense of loss. This pattern does not capture all field relationships. For example, some relationships forged in the field last well beyond the fieldwork. Long-term friendships can be made, which draw on the usual conventions of friendship: trust, rapport, respect, personal commitment, sharing, mutual interests, emotional feelings and so on. Equally, though less frequently documented in practice, individual fieldwork relationships can be testing. Certainly during fieldwork itself, difficult assignations are hard to walk away from. We are so dependent upon the quality of our field relations that we may quite easily find ourselves engaging in conversation with people whose views we particularly despise, or participating in social activities which leave us feeling awkward or uneasy. In such cases it is difficult to call it a day, say we are tired or indeed to go home. There is also a case to be made that we should not pursue arguments, clashes or difficulties – in a way that we might with personal friends or work colleagues. Not only is it sometimes necessary to form relationships with individuals whom we would rather not interact with ordinarily. We are also restricted in how we can deal with particular interactional difficulties. While we are responsible for forming the relations of fieldwork, the social dynamics that result are often guided by others rather than ourselves. If anything we sometimes have to discipline ourselves and our interactions in order to maintain fruitful fieldwork relationships.

Genuineness and reciprocity are vexed issues for the ethnographer. Imbalances in the degree of trust, commitment and personal investment can lead to potentially exploitative or unbearable situations. These can occur on both sides. Postcolonial commentators (see Said, 1978) and feminist writers have been particularly critical of the privileging of the ethnographer, and the potential exploitation of the researched (see Chapter 8 for a discussion of how these critiques have been used to rethink ethnography and issues of representation). In contrast, the reliance of fieldwork on our personal relationships also places us at risk of vulnerability, exploitation and hurt. Like reciprocity, issues of power also have the potential to cut both ways.

Who controls field relations, and how that control is manifested, may set the parameters for the fruitfulness and the longevity of the relationship.

This introduction has set out one of the central characteristics of field-work. The relations of fieldwork, and the social interactions inherent in those relations, provide the building blocks of this sort of research approach. It is impossible to separate the field from the social actors that people the setting. Not only do the relations of fieldwork facilitate the research and generate the data, they also help to define our experiences and understandings of fieldwork itself. They provide the interactional context in which we shape our field roles, and ultimately our identity, certainly during fieldwork (and often beyond). In the rest of this chapter I explore some aspects of the relations of fieldwork. I have specifically concentrated on the relationships between individual social actors. In particular I look at the notion of ethnographic friendship and the means by which we craft field relationships. Towards the end of the chapter I highlight some of the problematics of field relations. There are different sorts of relationship that we can have in and with the field and its people. Some of these are addressed in other chapters. For example, sexual relations are dealt with in Chapter 5, and emotional commitments in Chapter 6.

Key Informants and Best Friends

It would be wrong to suggest that fieldwork relationships cannot be based on genuine commitment. But they are clearly situated within social, cultural and organizational contexts. More often than not the reason for the initiation of the relationship is tied up with the actual pursuit of fieldwork. While that does not necessarily detract from the value of the relationship it may serve as a limiting framework for any long-term commitment, since participation has been constructed within the boundaries of recognizable fieldwork relations. Yet there are many examples of mutual friendships that develop over the course of prolonged fieldwork, and several instances of these surviving beyond the research. The issue of friendship in ethnography is not uncontentious. While there are many accounts of friendships being forged during fieldwork it has long been recognized that there are problems associated with combining the role of friend and informant. Crick (1992), for example, argues that the context of fieldwork is somewhat at odds with the formation of genuine friendship. In particular Crick considers the motivations for the pursuit of friendship:

> The relations between ethnographer and informant are more accurately seen, perhaps, as mutual exploitation. Both parties risk and exchange information; and one of the risks is necessarily the relationship itself between them. While the

ethnographer clearly has the accomplishment of professional work as a central motivation, in the case of informants a range of motivations is possible. (1992: 176–7)

Crick contends that field relations are inevitably ironic. Ethnographer and informant conspire to create a working fiction of a shared world of meaning. Crick suggests that in reality this is often a falsehood. Over time field agreements can fall apart, ethnographer and informant reverting to separate and perhaps mutually incomprehensible social worlds. Crick's account indicates that establishing fieldwork friendships can be problematic – with potentially contrastive motivations, shared social worlds and long-term commitments. His own friendship with Ali, a key informant during fieldwork in Sri Lanka, encapsulated some of these difficulties.

> I always referred to him [Ali] by his first name, and in fact, he only once told me his full name. He, on the other hand, always called me 'Doctor'. This difference in mode of address no doubt well expresses the asymmetrical character of our situation. If I call Ali a 'friend' or 'informant', both labels would say too much and also leave something important out. (1992: 176–7)

The ambivalent experience of combining fieldwork and friendship is a common one. El-Or (1997) conducted fieldwork in Tel Aviv. Her account of her friendship with Hanna serves to highlight the differences in the lives of these two women. El-Or found the boundaries of mutual understanding and sharing difficult to traverse. As a non-religious Jewish woman attempting to become close to an ultra-orthodox Jewish woman (who was also a member of an ultra-religious sect), El-Or found bridging the distance between their cultures problematic. It was especially difficult to narrow the gap between them without violating the other's belief systems and boundaries of intimacy. In many ways El-Or and Hanna did become close friends. Their relationship developed over a two-year period and could be characterized as a conventional friendship. They met two or three times each week. They shared stories and visited each other's houses. They developed mutual respect, trust and understanding. Yet El-Or notes that the friendship was always mediated by the boundaries of fieldwork. Theirs was always a working relationship. There were shared expectations of conversation and activity. Both adopted and maintained the field roles of researcher and researched. These working relations demanded different parameters of intimacy and closeness than those of other personal friendships. In turn these arrested the long-term development of the relationship. El-Or concluded that she could never be true friends with Hanna, precisely because Hanna was the object of the research, and both of them knew that.

Despite these potential difficulties and limits placed on the nature of ethnographic friendship, there are instances of long-term and meaningful relationships forged during fieldwork. Inevitably we only tend to have the researcher's account of these friendships, and their significance. Romantic narratives of personal friendship and reciprocal rapport are arguably useful to fieldwork. It is desirable to present good field relations, as a way of validating the research. However, the sometimes emotional and evocative accounts (and memories) of field friendships stress their personal significance. Hendry (1992), for example, describes her relationship with Sachiko, whom she met before she began any formal fieldwork in Japan. They met while Hendry was teaching English in Japan, and Sachiko invited Hendry to stay with her family. Later Sachiko worked as an *au pair* in England. Their friendship spanned two decades and was temporally, spatially and research bound. Sachiko was a fellow student who became a friend, and later a key informant.

She acted as an informal gatekeeper for Hendry's Japanese fieldwork and was a neighbour to her during that fieldwork. Later Sachiko and Hendry worked together as research collaborators. They shared anthropological, familial and personal experiences. Their relationship was bound by the ethnographic research process (and their relative positions within that process) as well as by the stresses and strains of friendship. From Hendry's account it is clear that the fieldwork exacerbated and tested the boundaries of conventional friendship. The personal relationship she formed with Sachiko was paradoxical and potentially difficult. Vulnerability, inequality and conflict of interests were experienced by both Sachiko and Hendry over the course of their friendship. Having an informant as a friend was problematic for Hendry. Having an anthropologist as a friend was problematic for Sachiko. The boundaries and roles of fieldwork and friendship did not always coincide. Hendry is philosophical in discussing how this realization was epistemologically productive, though personally challenging at times.

> In general, during fieldwork, it might be thought better to avoid expressing negative opinions about matters close to the hearts of informants. In other words, one can really only pretend to be a friend. Nevertheless . . . I sometimes grew tired of the role I was playing, and made the mistake of revealing this to my host, as friend, rather than as informant . . . however, my mistake actually led to a deeper understanding of the people I was investigating. (Hendry, 1992: 172)

For Hendry, exploring and understanding the boundaries of friendship was epistemologically meaningful, though (as her relationship with Sachiko turned sour) personally difficult. During my own fieldwork in an accountancy firm I became friends with Rachel, a key informant and the graduate accountancy tutor. My experience of friendship did not mirror exactly that of Hendry, although I came away with similarly ambivalent feelings of ethnographic friendship. Rachel and I were the same age and at equivalent stages in our professional careers. We had graduated in the same year (although from different universities). We lived in similar houses, in the same city. We both originated from the English midlands, and had both chosen to settle in Wales. We had interests in common and even mutual friends. I was a lecturer in a university department, and had trained as a teacher. Rachel was involved in the training of graduate trainees, as a professional tutor. We had teaching experiences in common.

Over the course of fieldwork, a mutual respect and friendship developed. Rachel was an invaluable source of introductions and she allowed me to sit in on her classes. Later she gave me access to the trainees' progress, organized meetings for me and generally became a partner in the research process. She would suggest ways of 'getting at' issues, of interviewing the trainees and approaching people. Our interests overlapped – we were comfortable meeting after work and occasionally went out together on a social basis. I think our friendship was genuine, although mediated by my role as researcher, and hers as informant. This did place some expectations on the balance of our relationship. On the occasions that Rachel suggested a night out or an after-work drink I usually felt compelled to say yes, even when I was tired and did not feel like socializing. I felt it was expected that I would always ask about Rachel's day at work, and the progress of her class. We shared a working understanding that I was interested in what she did and what she said. I was in fact uneasy about talking about myself. Not because of some huge fear of self-disclosure, but simply because the overt reason for our relationship was my interest in Rachel and her workplace. Even within these boundaries I came to see Rachel as a personal and close friend. In her capacity as informant and friend she shared stories and conversations with me. She read some of my fieldnotes and empathized with the everyday complications of the research. Over time, I became more willing and able to talk about myself, outside of the context of the fieldwork. I came to think of the friendship as something that transcended our research roles and the field context. We shared gossip, our plans for the future, and the odd emotional crisis.

What I have presented here is a highly personalized account of my friendship with Rachel. It would be impossible for me to presume that this was also the way in which Rachel understood, and indeed remembers, the friendship. My friendship with Rachel benefited my fieldwork enormously, of that I have no doubt. It eased my continued access to the field and the people in the field. On a practical level Rachel could always help me to arrange meetings, attend classes and visit work sites. Analytically the relationship enabled me to share and test ideas, gain another perspective and analyse beyond my own interpretation. The friendship also established a location for my personal self within the context of the field. I was able to be myself and interact as such, knowing that I had a key informant who was also a friend. My sense of self and belonging was enhanced by the relationship.

Hendry's account of her friendship with Sachiko (Hendry, 1992) high-lights the paradoxes of combining friendship with fieldwork. In particular she notes the potential role conflicts that may emerge. Sachiko expressed a feeling of vulnerability in being an object of study, and Hendry examined how this sense of inequality was incompatible with the Japanese under-standing of friendship. Likewise Rachel and I did not have an equal relationship. As well as 'a friend', she remained my key informant during the course of fieldwork. And that distinction became more rather than less important. Rachel was a critical social actor in the field. She knew she was a key informant. At times we did conflict, though usually not irreconcilably. I recall thinking that if only for the sake of completing the ethnography I could not afford to lose her friendship – which perhaps says more about the friendship then than I dared to admit at the time.

At the end of the fieldwork, when I had left the field it became clear that Rachel and I did not share the same interpretations of the events and interactions that had occurred in the field. Our respective professional positions meant it was difficult to 'agree' on what had happened, or more importantly what I chose to write about. The inequitability of our relation-ship became increasingly clear. I was writing about Rachel's activities, interactions and career. But I was writing for an academic audience and not for her. She evidently felt hurt and betrayed by me. My writing and analysis were of her experiences. She had few, if any, opportunities to analyse and write of my experiences. Equally I felt hurt that she did not understand enough about my work or career. I actually began to resent the fact that she did not want to know about me and my life – or so it seemed. Yet the nature of our relationship, bounded by fieldwork, meant it was almost impossible for me to articulate this. She was still part of the field, where it was necessary for me not only to be polite but to be grateful and interested. The trust we had built up became violated on both sides. I felt unable to challenge the situation and was uneasy about it becoming emotionally charged. Yet I wanted the friendship to continue. I had made the mistake of assuming that our friendship transcended the boundaries of the field. In retrospect this did not seem to have been Rachel's understanding. The context of fieldwork created, encouraged and eventually limited our friend-ship. If our relationship had not been bound up with the formalities of fieldwork, perhaps I would have been less reluctant to challenge Rachel, and better able to fight for the friendship on personal terms. Our relationship was situated within the domain of fieldwork. The trust was both real and contrived. The reciprocity of our relationship was based on our relative positions in the field. The difficulties of sustaining the relationship beyond the field were precisely because we could not reconcile our fieldwork and other selves.

The conflicts in reconciling the roles of informant, researcher and friend span other types of fieldwork interaction. For example, fictive kin are a common feature of social anthropological fieldwork. The relationships here encompass friendship and familial ties. Macintyre (1993) had to manage friendship and 'adoptive motherhood' during fieldwork in Papua New

Guinea, while Briggs (1986) and Kondo (1990) had to reconcile the roles of ethnographer and 'daughter'. Fowler (1994) emphasizes the problems of writing about 'family' and 'friends' made during fieldwork. Of her fieldwork in North America and the relationships with two key informants she refers to as Grandma and Grandpa, she comments that

> maybe what I was doing could hurt Grandma and Grandpa. Perhaps the community would get angry with them for having sold out, telling me things I had no business knowing. How could I be sure? The safest bet was not to say or publish anything. Also, what I was learning was not doing them any particular good, in the practical sense. (Fowler, 1994: 157)

As I indicated in Chapter 2 there is a long-standing debate in ethnography about the analytical tightrope between familiarity and strangeness. Clearly the issue of personal and fulfilling friendship in the field demands that some attention be paid to notion of over-familiarity and over-rapport. However, it is simplistic, and in many cases unhelpful, to argue that we should avoid friendship in order to remain marginal and able to provide a critical perspective. The essence of the ethnographic enterprise is predicated on shared understandings and reciprocal arrangements. Good ethnographic practice, data collection and analyses rely upon genuine empathy, trust and participation. It is inevitable that prolonged fieldwork will promote emotional ties and personal attachments that go beyond the parameters of the field. Just as important are the parameters that the field will impose on the long-term nature of those attachments. Ethnographic friendships can simultaneously be strong (based on shared understandings and fieldwork objectives) and fragile (non-meaningful outside the field and the fieldwork). The narratives of ethnographic friendship are indicative of social actors sharing lives and biographies in the field. They serve to remind us that we are part of what we study. In researching, constructing and writing the lives of others we are engaged in negotiating and writing ourselves. Significant ethnographic friendships can also exaggerate the contradictions of fieldwork (Crick, 1992). The relationships we create in the field raise our awareness of the ethnographic dichotomies of, for example, involvement versus detachment, stranger versus friend, distance versus intimacy. The friendships we experience are part of the contradictions and ambiguities that denote the essence of fieldwork. Friendships can help to clarify the inherent tensions of the fieldwork experience and sharpen our abilities for critical reflection. The emotions, commitments, and indeed betrayals of field relations are not necessarily insurmountable or negative. They do affect the ethnographer's gaze and it is important that that should be so. Moreover they firmly establish fieldwork as relational, emotional, and a process of personal negotiation. In the next section I discuss this in more detail, by considering the craft work of creating relations in the field.

Crafting Relations

Fieldwork relationships do not just happen. They are the outcome of negotiation between the social researcher and the social actors in the field. We are not always consciously and self-critically aware of this staging of our relationships: it is often incredibly difficult to reconstruct how some field relations were created and developed, or how some became difficult. In suggesting that field relations are negotiated and crafted I am not implying an exclusively self-conscious or critical approach. Of course, the early stages of field research are often characterized by a necessity to explicitly pursue working and reciprocal relations. More generally though, the relations of the field are the outcome of a series of interactions, transactions and implied contexts. Throughout the research process we are actively engaged in creating working and personal relationships. These relationships may well be bound by ethnographic tensions – for example between familiarity and distance, engagement and strangeness. They will also be bound by social and cultural norms and expectations. Different sets of normative values and expectations will be brought to bear by the participating members. These will contribute to the development, establishment and form of the emergent field relations.

Such values and expectations span a variety of socio-cultural aspects of individual and group situatedness and identity, and may include aspects such as biographical experiences, gender, age and race. What I am suggesting is that field relations are the outcome of particular sorts of relational craft work. Consider, for example, the specific sorts of male friendships that have formed a mainstay of much classic and contemporary ethnographic work. The infamous relations between Liebow and Tally (Liebow, 1967) or Whyte and Doc (Whyte, 1981) are well-rehearsed examples of fieldwork friendships which proved key to the execution of the research project and subsequent writing. Both Liebow and Whyte were able to draw on culturally driven, masculine values to forge close working relationships with their two key informants. It is difficult to imagine how *Tally's Corner* or *Street Corner Society* could have happened without the creation of these relationships. Equally it is difficult to imagine such close relationships occurring without the shared male understandings which the various social actors brought to the field. These are classic examples of how fieldwork friendship establishes the sharing of experiences, settings and the shaping of identity.

Contemporary studies also illustrate this general point. Take, for example, D.R. Wolf's (1991) anthropological study of a brotherhood of outlaw bikers in North America. In attempting to study the 'Rebels' Wolf had to be both initiated into a particular masculine culture *and* accepted as a biker with a distinctive masculine identity. Wolf became a fully fledged member of the Rebels, and counted himself as a friend of a number of the members of the brotherhood. The friendships which Wolf embarked upon, and came to value, were predicated on a particular sort of male identification. The brotherhood operated within the bounds of a specific form of machismo that provided its male members with a distinctive sense of personal male identity. Such identification was ensured by, and relied upon, a set of symbols, rituals and behaviours which emphasized a certain sort of maleness. As an anthropologist, Wolf was involved in establishing relationships by acting upon these symbolic rituals. These served to reinforce his commitment to the group and their particular enactment of male identification. Wolf recalls an early encounter at a brotherhood party to which he was invited (Wolf's name in the brotherhood was Coyote).

> Jim discovered that the rear tyre of his motorcycle had gone flat. Jim, along with everyone else, was too 'wasted' to even consider detaching the back wheel, breaking the bead on the tyre, removing the tube, isolating the tear, scrounging around for patches, and so on. As wee Albert had commented: 'It sure is drunk out tonight!' Luckily I happened to be 'packing' a can of Flat Proof in my saddlebags. I was able to seal the leak from inside by removing the valve stem, squeezing the Flat Proof into the tube, then reinflating the tyre using an air pump that I carried. The whole process was completed in a matter of minutes. Jim had an ear-to-ear grin when he saw the repair. 'Hey look at this! Coyote's a fucking mechanic! Haw! Haw! Haw!' Jim filled a quart container with draft beer from one of the kegs and brought it over to me: 'Tell you what, Coyote. Why don't you and Sandy (my lady) come over Sunday afternoon and my ol' lady (Gail) will cook us this goose that I shot last week!' I accepted the invitation. (Wolf, 1991: 67)

This demonstrates the developing acceptance of Wolf as a friend of the brotherhood. Wolf was able to show his commitment by repairing the tyre. Yet even this is not as simple as it might first appear. Wolf had to make implicit decisions about whether to undertake this task. He had to have an awareness of how appropriate it would be for a relative newcomer to repair a fellow brother's tyre. Implicit in this is an understanding of the brotherhood code of conduct. Wolf had to judge and assess the risk of unacceptability. His account demonstrates the craft knowledge of the brotherhood, more generally the biker. He was in a position where he clearly knew what was involved in repairing a tyre the conventional (and permanent) way. He could also demonstrate his craft skills of doing an instant repair at the roadside. This ritualization of biker knowledge gained Wolf the respect and acceptance of the brotherhood as a 'knower'. We could argue that this is simply a case of a male anthropologist joining a very macho/masculine subculture. But the dynamics of gender are more complex than that. Wolf had to recognize and make judgements about how biker masculinity was expressed and reproduced, and how in turn this reinforced his commitment to the brotherhood. The relationships being negotiated drew upon shared and expressed understandings. They extended from the field to the personal. While women could not be members of the brotherhood, relationships with women were a distinctive element of the biker persona. Male biker interaction with, and about, women helped to define particular forms of masculine identity and status. The distinctive form of masculinity identification which the Rebels, and in turn Wolf, endorsed and reproduced depended in part on the heterosexual relations of production. The 'ol' ladies' – long-standing partners of individual club members – were a distinctive part of the gendered framework within which the men operated. The biker's lady had to display congruence with the male subculture:

> for an ol' lady to be able to adapt to a potentially wide range of social circumstances, it is necessary for her to develop both flexibility and control in a manner comparable to that of her ol' man. There must be sufficient overlap between her value system and cognitive model of the external world and that of her ol' man to allow her to both interpret and generate behaviour in a manner that is congruent with that of her ol' man and the club. As one Rebels member stated: if she doesn't know the rules, then she shouldn't be around. (Wolf, 1991: 161–2)

Wolf's partner (Sandra) became part of this gender culture – learning and adapting to the rituals of the women of the brotherhood. Wolf's own status and acceptability to the male biker subculture was enhanced by the demonstration of an appropriate and understood heterosexual relationship with Sandra. Wolf was able to utilize his personal relationship to enact some of the craft knowledge and interactional modes of the bikers. Wolf (and Sandra) learnt and were able to demonstrate ritualized expressions of masculinity and heterosexuality. Wolf's relationships with the brotherhood rested on enacted understandings of biker masculinity and gender positionality. The level of negotiation depended upon explicit acceptance and enactment of gendered cultural norms. It also rested upon his personal relationship with Sandra, as an acceptable biker companion. Wolf's own expression of gender, and his within- and between-gender relations, contributed to a particular approach to the biker subculture, contextualized by a particular masculine construction.

Other male ethnographers have also contextualized their field role and experiences within situated masculine frameworks. Moffatt (1989), for instance, undertook fieldwork in an American college. From the beginning of his fieldwork he faced dilemmas about his understandings and expressions of acceptable masculinity and sexuality. The first days in the field were spent covertly as a mature first year college student. Later he came out as a college professor and pursued his fieldwork with that explicit identity. During his first days in the field he found himself engaging in 'light banter and friendly talk'.

> It was not all that hard to keep up with them – to think, at thirty-three years old, of a line or two that might be amusing to eighteen year olds. Just as I had to watch my high or academic talk among the freshmen, however, I discovered that I had to watch my low talk as well. Maybe intimate sex-talk was more explicit among people my own age; maybe I was making the wrong assumptions about 'college men'. In any case, I found myself being smuttier than they were if I wasn't careful. (Moffatt, 1989: 7)

Moffatt found that his own masculine identity was reformulated and checked as he attempted to gain the friendship of a group of male college students. Indeed his own memory of college life and his perceived understandings of male friendliness were to some extent out of step with the fieldwork reality. His thirty-something male identity and language were not the same as that of his 'room-mates'. As a room-mate, Moffatt was a fellow student, with roles and expectations to enact. This meant joining in and relating to his fellow room-mates' masculine identities in the context of college culture. Likewise the expression and discussion of sexuality was also a process of learning.

> In my first couple of days in the dorm, I was finding the generally suppressed sexuality of the co-ed dorms, which I had never experienced in my own college years, a steamy business, more than a little stressful for my thirty-three year old libido. Sexuality was something students alluded to a great deal in dorm chit chat and in other forms of expression – in musical lyrics, for instance, or in the human icons that decorated the walls of the rooms. But the students only discussed sexuality honestly with close friends, if they discussed it honestly at all. (Moffatt, 1989: 9)

While most of Moffatt's fieldwork was carried out overtly, as a college professor, these early fieldwork experiences can be seen as essential orientation exercises, not only to the culture of the male college students but to the construction of their gendered masculinized identities. Moffatt had to check his own behaviour and adapt his own experiences and gender identity to be compatible with, if not to mirror that of his college peers (and later informant friends). At the outset Moffatt was conscious of his breadth of experience, his relative age and appearance. But he had not problematized his gendered identity and sexual cultural norms. The first days in the field established the framework for the field relations that later developed. His position as a gendered, sexual self was mediated by the gendered identities and sexual cultural norms of the subculture to which he was attempting to connect. Age and sexuality had to be negotiated, alongside acceptable gender norms.

Moffatt's experiences of researching adults younger than himself raises issues not only of identity and experience but also of age. His ideas about appropriate vocabulary and behaviour had to be modified to accommodate the gendered identities of the younger college men. These experiences are pertinent in other settings where the age differential is marked, for example in researching children. There are some excellent accounts of the challenges and dilemmas of conducting social research with children (for example Butler and Shaw, 1996; Corsaro and Streeck, 1986; Fine, 1987) and it is not my task to rehearse them here. But in connection with the crafting of field relations, these fieldwork contexts illustrate the pertinence of age and generational issues as situated contexts. Take for example Fine's (1987) ethnography of little league baseball. The relationships which he developed with the boy baseball players was crafted in terms of friendship, though this was potentially problematical between adult researcher and child participants.

> Because friendship is not a typical relationship between adults and children (although there often are friendly authority relations), time is necessary to develop it. I vividly recall that in my first weeks in Beanville I was surprised at how 'nice' the boys seemed and how few obscenities they used. Only after several weeks had I become sufficiently accepted for the children to drop their reserve. (Fine, 1987: 224)

In a methodological appendix to his monograph Fine reflects how his personal biography reacted with the biographies of the boys. The negotiation of field relations was predicated on shared understandings of adult–child interactions. His age and male gender were both significant variables in his crafting of relationships. Fine was able to engage with the game of baseball as a knower. He was asked to umpire and to help with coaching. His self-admitted lack of sporting prowess meant he did not threaten the experts – boys and officials. He knew enough to talk about baseball and to be a participating researcher. He recalls one such occasion:

> An intra squad game was organised by the coach of the Angels. Since they did not have the necessary number of players, I was asked to play center field. In the field only one ball was hit toward me and fortunately was sufficiently far from where I was standing that I didn't need to be embarrassed about not catching it, and actually made a fairly decent throw to hold the batter to a double. At bat I struck out my first time up, grounded out in my second time up, becoming known as an 'early out'. Finally, in my third bat, I singled. (Fine, 1987: 226)

Fine was able to engage with the boy baseball players; be privy to a male, pre-adolescent subculture through his negotiation of acceptable field relations. In crafting a self in the field, Fine was also crafting relationships with individual social actors. As well as relating to the field and the people in a general sense he developed specific relationships which gave him access to the social world he was seeking to understand. He was able to see and hear about the everyday world of the baseball boys. (Although Fine recognized that a fine line existed between what he was permitted to see and hear, and what he felt was censored by the boys.) The nature of his friendships was bound by expectations of usual adult/young people relationships in the context of the baseball setting. The relations of fieldwork were bounded by both the context of fieldwork and the boundaries of the field setting. The fieldwork established the need to develop active and fruitful relationships while maintaining a sense of professional distance. The field setting had cultural norms and expectations of relationships that guided how, in practice, Fine's relations with the boys were established, developed and checked.

Field relations are contextualized by cultural expectations, as well as being temporally and spatially located. This craft work occurs in particular temporal frames and places. In my own fieldwork in an accountancy firm my field relations were guided by a physical locale and a temporal framework. My fieldwork mainly took place during the office hours of the firm. During the working day and the working week I sought to develop relationships with various social actors in the field, including Rachel and graduate trainees. During those 'on duty' fieldwork times it was legitimate for me to ask questions; observe and take notes; talk to and actively engage in the development of rapport with these social actors. The offices of the accountancy firm offered a number of specific spatial contexts for the pursuit of these relationships. The classroom, the coffee machine area, the entrance hall, the open plan office suites, the boardroom, and the meeting rooms all afforded settings appropriate to relationships I was trying to foster and develop.

Away from these spatial and temporal contexts, the relations of fieldwork took on different agendas. For example, outside office hours and the locale of the office it was unclear what my legitimate relations with the graduate accountants could or should be. It was difficult, in this context, to arrange times to interact. The familiarity and commonality of the office relations became problematized. This was particularly noticeable if I happened to come across one of the graduates at a weekend in a setting which was 'strange' to our relationship. For example on a number of occasions I saw individuals in the city centre or in the supermarket. I became incredibly conscious of how I looked, who I was with, how I acted and what I said. Sometimes I would go out of my way to avoid interactions (self-consciously ensuring I did not bump into them in the supermarket by switching aisles). When we did physically meet I would be both embarrassed and anxious, unable to say more than hello or to generally enquire after their well-being. I suspect I often appeared rude or uninterested. Yet on Monday morning at 8.30 a.m. I would be back in the office being interested, engaged and talkative – and being actively talked to. It was legitimate again for me to be crafting the relationship, and expected that I should be doing so.

One of the difficulties of the nature of ethnographic work is how field relations are (and should be) bounded by the time and the place of fieldwork. The entry into the setting and the self-conscious pursuit of field relations are both legitimized and (at least implicitly) agreed by researcher and researched. It is acceptable and expected that both parties will work at some sort of productive relationship. The fieldworker is expected to talk to, and develop relations with, members of the field. The people in the field expect to be talked to by, and to engage in the negotiation of a relationship with, the fieldworker. What is less certain is what happens outside of the field setting and the field time. For those of us who engaged in fieldwork with clear on-duty and off-duty times these problems are both exaggerated and managed by physical and temporal distance from the field. For those who 'live' in the field these issues are less easily discernible but equally valid. The times and places for the legitimate and agreed negotiation and development of field relations are much harder to discern if the fieldworker is living as well as working in the field. Without space and time out the negotiated agreement of appropriate situations for field relations may be confused. All times and all places may be open for the active pursuit of the relations of fieldwork. The rules and boundaries will be less sharply defined, while being more readily violated.

The acknowledgement that the relations of the field are negotiated and crafted through time and place helps to identify fieldwork as a craft skill. The essence of fieldwork – its relational and interactional quality – is precisely the aspect of the field which is often talked about in rather abstract or clinical ways. In self-consciously attempting to develop field relations we should go beyond a simplistic understanding that this 'happens' – albeit sometimes more easily than others. Rather the data collection, data analyses and experience of the field are intimately related to both our ability to craft relations and our understanding of how those relations are culturally, temporally and spatially framed. The constraints and situated contexts of these crafted relations are addressed in the following section.

Difficult Relations: between Reality and Falsehood

The relational necessity of fieldwork serves as both a strength and a weakness. The quality of our data (and our analyses) relies upon the establishment, development and critical reflection of ultimately personal relationships. But these relationships are subjected to the same rigours and tests of all human relations. They are fragile, complex and multidimensional. Meaningful personal relations usually rely upon a level of trust and reciprocity, as well as a common focus. Relations break down in circum-stances where trust and the values of reciprocity are violated. The relations of the field are characterized by these same expectations and values. Where these aspects are deficient, violated or absent the whole fieldwork enterprise is, at best, challenged, and at worst threatened beyond repair.

In general we can characterize the relations of fieldwork as a balance between reality and falsehood. Field relations usually begin as 'false' in that they are artificially contrived by the researcher for the purposes of data collection. This does not diminish the strength of the relationship nor the quality of consequent data. The purposefulness with which field relations are sought emphasizes the interest and commitment the researcher usually has in understanding social worlds and the accounts of social actors. A commit-ment to cultural relativism, and the importance of folk knowledge, means that the forging of relations in the field is both sensible and desirable. We aim to explore and understand, through the participant's lived reality, a social or cultural world. The initial impetus for relationships in the field is usually that of the researcher, but this does not mean that this initiation, nor the resultant relationship, is not genuine. The researcher is genuinely interested in forging ties. The participant social actors may seek and gain genuine understanding, respect and ultimately friendship. But the situated context of these relations may in itself be artificial. It will almost certainly be in the interests of the fieldworker to maintain relations during fieldwork, even if those relations become strained or difficult.

Unlike personal relationships outside of the boundaries of fieldwork, they may feel that their choice over how or whether to continue the relationship is constrained. At root, the researcher is reliant upon maintaining the relations of data collection and analysis. This may involve appearing more amenable, sociable and interested in other lives than might otherwise occur. The constraints of field relations may also be felt by others in the field. In the interests of the research and the telling of their story individuals or groups of social actors may remain more willing to engage and interact than might otherwise be the case. Like you, they may see the fieldwork and the relations of the field as *work*. That is, field relations are part of the research project in which they too have a stake. The telling and understanding of their lives and their social world relies upon not only their co-operation, but their active participation in the realities and relationships of the field. The crafting and then maintaining of field relations may be actively managed by both parties.

The contrived context of initial, and sometimes long-term, relations must be set alongside the reality of feelings, emotions, lasting friendship and occasionally painful memories that they can bring. Both parties in field relationships can find these 'work' relations meaningful, reciprocal and based on a shared commitment. Feelings of trust and of betrayal are equally revealing of a relationship which had real emotional and personal consequence. Many field researchers have written autobiographical accounts of the friendship, commitment and love that they found in the field; and where that has diminished, of feelings of hurt, betrayal and guilt. For any of us who have developed friendships in the field, or experienced the consequent demise of such a friendship, the idea that somehow that relationship was false and only 'good' for the collection of data is clearly abhorrent. Whether or not field relations last beyond the formal fieldwork phase is to some extent irrelevant in this context. For relations to last, and where there is commitment from one or both parties, is testimony to the real quality of those relations. While for some the ending of fieldwork is a welcome respite, for others the leaving of the place, and more often the people, can cause sadness, anguish and pain. The difficulties of maintaining relations, or in some cases the necessity not to, is evidence that those relationships mattered. Of course the reality of the relationship is not a neccessarily positive one. The reality of particular relationships may have been precisely their difficulty and stress. In the field we can have negative feelings; relations of antagonism or dislike that are real and emotionally significant.

The balance between reality and falsehood will be unique to each social relationship in the field. The path between the two is not a simple one, nor easily discernible. In any one field site, and indeed in any one field relationship, we may simultaneously experience the real and the false. The nature of how field relations start in the context of field*work* and the consequent development of those relations – as social interactions between social actors – means that they may contain both falsehood and reality. The actual balance will depend on a number of situated and local factors. These include the personalities and positions of the participating social actors (researcher and researched); the disposition of the social actors to forge relationships; the differential and contested meanings attached to the field-work; the expectations each has of the fieldwork; the commonalties and differences of the social actors; and the perceived and real outcomes of the research. The nature of the relations of the field is contained not only in their initiation and establishment, but also in the consequent expectations and outcomes of the research.

Significantly, a strength and a weakness of field research – the quality of the social relations that are forged – needs to be considered in reflexive and self-conscious ways. We cannot conceive of field relations purely as unemotive and purposive work. Nor can we take a position that the relations of fieldwork will always be emotional and positive for ourselves and the people of the field. While working towards the establishment of the contexts of fieldwork relations and interactions, we need to be aware that field relations born out of a falsehood can have real emotions and consequences.

Conclusion

Qualitative research generally and ethnographic endeavour in particular is, by its very nature, interpersonal and intimate. Fieldwork relies upon the establishing and building of relationships with significant others in the field. It is these relationships which give ethnographic research its intensity, its quality and insight into the everyday social world. This does not imply that meaningful social relationships are not formed during other types of research. Nor does it imply that fieldwork relationships are all equally valuable or uniform in nature. Indeed, recognizing the complexity and variety of the interpersonal is a crucial part of one's apprenticeship and subsequent practice of qualitative research. The interpersonality of fieldwork enables us to connect with a place and a people in a personal and subjective way. It is not necessary to enter into philosophical debates about the dualities of subjective/objective, science/art, rational/emotional to acknowl-edge that fieldwork pivots on personal relationships and experience. The interconnectedness of researcher, researched, social actors and significant others is the very essence of fieldwork. To a large extent the quality of the research experience (for all involved) and the quality of the research data is dependent upon the formation of relationships and the development of an emotional connection to the field.

Research which is reliant upon sustained periods of fieldwork is a shared (and more often than not an emotional) experience. Fieldwork spawns data, texts *and* personal relationships. Friends, acquaintances, antagonists, loves, enemies can all be made, maintained and lost during the course of fieldwork. Time, space and emotions are all invested in ethnographic fieldwork – connecting the personal, the political and the professional. It is impossible to differentiate the subjective, embodied self from the socio-political and the researcher-professional. Our own sense of personhood – which will include age, race, gender, class, history, sexuality – engages with the personalities, histories and subjectivities of others present in the field. Our own subjective personality is part of the research and is negotiated within the field. Ethnographers are not outsiders looking in. They have to be reflective insiders, negotiating roles and subjectivities, looking out. Like all human relationships, the relations of the field can be immensely fulfilling, long lasting and intimate. They can also be fragile and potentially exploitative. What I have been concerned with stressing in this chapter, however, is not so much the different sorts of relationship that can ensue. My emphasis has been on recognizing the interpersonal and emotional craft work that forms an integral part of the philosophy and practice of ethnographic work. Most crucially, fieldwork involves emotional labour (Hochschild, 1983), of a particularly managed kind. We are often simultaneously engaging in public and private relations of meaning. In bridging these, the private use of emotions is tempered by a reality of fieldwork as *work*.

> In private life, we are free to question the going rate of exchange and free to negotiate a new one. If we are not satisfied, we can leave; many friendships and marriages die of inequality. But in the public world of work, it is often part of an individual's job to accept uneven exchanges, to be treated with disrespect or anger by a client, all the while closeting into fantasy the anger one would like to respond with. (Hochschild, 1983: 85–6)

I am not arguing that the relations of fieldwork are those of service provider and client (though it would be an interesting debate as to how the different social actors of the field would be characterized according to such a schema). Nevertheless, I am stressing the necessity of viewing the relations of fieldwork as both private and public. As such they are bounded by different rules and values from solely private relationships. It is not enough simply to characterize the relations of the field as purely personal. Nor is it adequate to view the crafting of these relations as impersonal 'work' tasks. Rather in recognizing the interpersonal and relational aspects of fieldwork we should critically engage with both their practical and their emotional production.

The next chapter considers a different aspect of the relationship between the self and the field. Thus far I have explored how the concept of self is crafted and challenged by fieldwork, and the specific relational contexts in which this is achieved. Chapter 4 engages with the contemporary articulations of the embodiment of social actors and everyday social life. In doing so it explores the relationship between the body and fieldwork.

4 The Embodiment of Fieldwork

Fieldwork is necessarily an embodied activity. Our body and the bodies of others are central to the practical accomplishment of fieldwork. We locate our physical being alongside those of others, as we negotiate the spatial context of the field. We concern ourselves with the positioning, visibility and performance of our own embodied self as we undertake participant observation. Moreover, our observations and fieldnotes are often scattered with implicit and explicit references to the body. We note and analyse how social settings provide physical and cultural space for the performance and management of the body. The body is negotiated in everyday life, serving as an agent of cultural reproduction and as a site of cultural representation. Bodies are adorned, used, abused, touched and forbidden. They work, play, interact, gesture and fail. In the same way as fieldwork is dependent on the relational, it is also reliant upon the analyses of bodies and body work. Such a claim positions ethnographic fieldwork alongside contemporary scholarly interest on the body and the nature of embodiment.

There has been an outpouring of research and literature on the centrality of the body and embodiment that has spanned a number of disciplines (Featherstone and Turner, 1995). These include linguistics, psychology, psychoanalysis and social philosophy, as well as anthropology and sociology. The body has been reframed as a legitimate area of social enquiry and social theorizing. Its role and symbolic significance have become key to our understandings of the social world and social interaction. The body has been recast as a site of discourse and action; as a form of representation; as intimately linked to biography and the crafting of the self. In turn these are all key aspects of the theory and practice of fieldwork. Ethnographic observation and participation incorporates discourse, action, representation and auto/biography.

In calling for a more embodied sociology Scott and Morgan (1993) argue that attention should be paid to the physical, social and sexual body in our reasoning and theorizing about the social world. This draws on the earlier work of Frank (1990, 1991), who argued that sociology was failing to accord centrality to the body. Frank's analysis provides four substantive categories for the centrality of the body in social life. These are (1) talking bodies – recognizing the interactional qualities and language of the body; (2) disciplined bodies – how the body is framed by contexts of control, regimentation, rules and desire; (3) sexualized bodies – recognizing the gendered and sexualized contexts of the body; and (4) medicalized bodies – the body as a site of health, medical and cultural appropriation and representation. The emergent discourses of the body have elaborated upon this sort of analytical framework to centralize our everyday experiences as inevitably *embodied*. It is possible to adopt similar frameworks for characterizing the practice and experiences of fieldwork. The interaction, language and discipline of the body form the very essence of fieldwork. The sexualized and gendered body affects both our own experiences of fieldwork and the nature of the data we collect. The body as medicalized, healthy, failing or appropriated has significance beyond instances of fieldwork in explicitly medical settings. It has become usual to recognize that the body bears upon the experience of fieldwork, although arguably this recognition has to date been at a rather superficial level. For example, the body has been readily discussed in terms of the self-presentational skills of the researcher (see, for example, Delamont, 1984; Patrick, 1973; Shaffir, 1991; Van Maanen, 1991). Warren (1988: 24–5) captures this kind of body work:

> What is presented to the host culture is a body: a size and shape, hair and skin, clothing and movement, sexual invitation or untouchability. The embodied characteristics of the male or female fieldworker affect not only the place in the social order to which he or she is assigned, but also the fieldworker's and informant's feelings about attractiveness and sexuality, body functions and display.

While such skills of self-presentation are important to the successful negotiation of fieldwork, taken alone they do not capture the full consequences, nor explore the full potential of an embodied fieldwork. The relationship between fieldwork, the body and the contexts of embodiment can be construed more comprehensively. The aim of this chapter is to explore this relationship by concentrating on the body work of ethnographic research. The chapter is in three main parts. First I consider how the body can inform the content and analyses of fieldwork. Secondly I conceptualize fieldwork as a site for the management and production of the body. Thirdly I broaden the discussion, by recasting the characteristics of fieldwork in terms of their embodied properties.

Body Work

The body can be a distinctive site for social research and observation in its own right. There are some settings which lend themselves especially well to the study of the body in everyday social life. In such contexts the embodiment of fieldwork is an explicit aspect of the research process – bodies are most obviously watched, analysed and noted. Nobody could deny that the nude beach (Douglas et al., 1977), the naturist club (Parry, 1987), professional boxing (Wacquant, 1995), or the dance club (Lewis and Ross, 1995) have the body as central to their everyday activities. Studies and accounts of such settings which did not explicitly focus on and analyse the present, performed, active and managed body would be instantly deemed deficient. It is hard to envisage these settings not being, at least in part, sites for an ethnography of the body and body work. For example, Wacquant (1995) explores the social world of the professional boxer and examines how the human body is invested in, shaped and displayed through the articulation of the sport. He explores how practitioners of the 'bodily craft' of boxing conceive of their bodies as a form of capital. Based on ethnographic fieldwork at a boxing gym, Wacquant (1995) provides detailed description and analysis of the physical and mental body work of boxers:

> a highly intensive and finely regulated manipulation of the organism whose aim is to imprint into the bodily schema of the fighter postural sets, patterns of movement, and subjective emotional-cognitive states that makes him into a conversant practitioner of the sweet science of bruising . . . it practically reorganises the entire corporeal field of the fighter, bringing to prominence certain organs and abilities and making others recede, transforming not only the physique of the boxer but also his 'body-sense', the consciousness he has of his organism and, through his changed body, of the world around him. (Wacquant, 1995: 73)

In documenting how boxers learn to know and monitor their own bodies, Wacquant highlights the body as a site for sacrifice, risk, management, discipline and satisfaction. It is evident here that the embodiment of fieldwork is contained in the subject matter of the field. The body becomes an obvious site for description and analysis. It would be difficult to consider an ethnography of the everyday life of the boxer without paying considerable attention to the detail of the body work.

Other settings are more implicitly concerned with the body. For example a number of commentators have analysed social and work organizations in terms of the body and sexuality (Hearn and Parkin, 1987; Witz et al., 1996). Witz et al. (1996) explore the embodied nature of different sorts of contemporary organizations – the hospital ward, the public sector office and the financial institution. Their analysis focuses upon the relationships between embodied social actors, the organization of the body and gender relations. More generally they propose a three-dimensional politics of the body in organizations. First there is a spatial dimension: bodies are organized and physically present; there are rules about proximity and touch; bodies are physically, personally and symbolically spaced. Secondly Witz and her colleagues identify a verbal dimension: bodies are talked of and talked about; the body forms part of the everyday talk of the organization. Thirdly they note the physical dimension of the body: here they are concerned with the ways in which bodies are presented, adorned and managed.

Witz et al. suggest that these dimensions are interrelated rather than discrete, and collectively enable an analysis of the embodied nature of contemporary organizational life. Such an analysis lends itself to a discussion of the embodiment of fieldwork on more than one level. It helps to establish the potential for embodiment and body work in a far greater variety of settings, if not all of social life itself. Moreover the practice of ethnography in organizations is recast as necessarily embodied – concerned with spatial, verbal and presentational dimensions of both our own body and the bodies of others.

A focus on the embodied nature of social settings opens up new avenues of analysis and potentially contributes to a rethinking of many conventional sites of ethnographic fieldwork. For example Schilling (1993) has argued that the school is a place where bodies are regulated, managed and disciplined, and that social research of the school should make its embodied aspects more explicit. The school as a cultural site of 'body work' is a rather different way of constituting the school ethnography. In a recent paper, Delamont (1998) reanalyses fieldnotes taken during observation at a secondary school in England in the late 1970s. She does so in the light of the literary turn and recent attention to the textual production of ethnography (Atkinson, 1990; Clifford and Marcus, 1986; Denzin, 1997). Yet the fact that she chooses to reanalyse a physical education lesson and draws on an embodied perspective (Frank, 1990, 1991; Hughes and Witz, 1997) establishes the school as a site for body work. This is something that was largely absent from her earlier analysis (Delamont and Galton, 1986). Delamont argues that the methodological exercise had substantive significance, drawing attention to the pervasiveness of the body in educational encounters. She concludes that

> For many years, however, the social body has remained largely implicit in most educational ethnographies. The embodied nature of educational work, the expressive body of teachers, and taught, the disciplined body in the school or classroom regime, the embodied enactment of pedagogic performances – these have all remained part of the taken-for-granted background of educational research until recent years. Retrospective and secondary analysis of ethnographic data can help to rescue and render visible such embodied phenomena. (Delamont, 1998: 16)

A focus on the body can be epistemologically productive for a reanalysis of settings and data. This focus establishes social life as necessarily embodied and physical. In addition it recasts the act of fieldwork as embodied. As ethnographers we also engage in body work. This includes the conscious self-presentation of the body in terms of appearance (discussed at greater length in the next section of this chapter). It also includes the spatial positioning and negotiation of our body in the field. We experience fieldwork as embodied social actors. While this is arguably the case in most, if not all social settings, it is most easily illustrated by settings where the body is readily identified. Take, for example, a Tokyo hostess club (Allison, 1994). Through working as a hostess, Allison collected data on the everyday activities of the hostess club. She was especially interested in the way this particular form of Japanese corporate entertainment was spoken about, contextualized and accounted for. Allison describes such clubs as a setting in which male 'work and play' are accomplished in the company of female hostesses. The club which Allison studied was not a brothel. Indeed actual physical (sexual) activity was explicitly forbidden. Yet a lot of the talk and activity that took place on the club premises was embodied and sexualized. The general conversation focused on the body, as subject and object. The work of the hostess was located within this body talk. Allison described the rules and boundaries of 'talk' at the hostess club:

> The task should be unstructured chatter about things so insignificant that they need not be recalled later. Such unforgettable conversations build a commonality among men . . . Although the hostess participates in the conversation, she often becomes its subject. Four customers . . . were in the club and for about an hour I served as their sole hostess. The atmosphere was jovial and light-hearted, and the talk consisted of playful put-downs, directed primarily at Hamano, the highest ranked among them, sexual banter about me, sometimes addressed to me, and rambling, seemingly insignificant chatter . . .
>
> References to sex were constant. Hamano suggested that I should try him out as a boyfriend, gesturing toward his penis and saying in English, 'cock'. Agata protested, arguing that Hamano would tire me out because he had 'too much energy'. Yamanoto had just returned from a year in Amsterdam, and they joked about how tired he was because he hadn't seen his wife for a year and had climaxed 'eight, nine times' the previous night.
>
> Hamano said to me, 'oppai okii' (your breasts are big), and then started talking to Agata about the kind of woman he liked. Agata told me that Hamano liked big-breasted women even if they were not pretty; Hamano denied this, saying that he liked pretty women even with small breasts like mine (though earlier he had said mine were big). He declared that some women have bodies of three dimensions, sketching out three increasingly large curves in the air, starting at the chest, moving to the stomach and ending at the hips. (Allison, 1994: 46–7)

In Allison's descriptions of the hostess club talk, women's bodies are particularly in evidence. There was a recognized vocabulary for body talk within the context of the club. Allison drew upon this vocabulary to describe her own experiences of working and talking at the club. She participated in the talk – either as a subject of discussion or in interactional situations. The physical appearance of the body was part of such description and talk. Indeed 'breast' talk was characterized as a key transitional moment for men attending the club. Talking about the breasts of hostesses signalled 'the expression of men at long last released from formality . . . as often as I heard a comment about a breast made, it never failed to get the same reaction: surprise, glee and release' (Allison, 1994: 48). Talking about breasts of the hostesses created an informality and a relaxed atmosphere. The talk established the women as a safe object of the male gaze and signalled leisure time. This talk was accompanied by club rules of touch. For example, female breasts could be touched for only short periods of time, and in ritualised and understood ways.

Allison's own body was central to her fieldwork experience. As a hostess her physical presentation and body were open (in principle at least) to attention, talk, description and touching. In establishing herself as a part of the field, she positioned her body as central to the fieldwork experience. As a novice hostess she was spared actual physical touching (men were only permitted to touch the bodies of veteran hostesses). However, she did have to accept constant references and vocal attention to her body. In that context Allison's fieldwork was body work in a very real sense. Allison is remarkably unreflective about the ways in which her body was an implicit and explicit part of the experience of fieldwork and the collection of data. Yet it is clear from her account that the concept of the embodied researcher was very real. A significant element of her monograph is actually about the positionality of her physical, sexualized, gendered body in a setting where the body is central.

Where the body is an explicit focus of the research it is relatively easy to see how an embodied ethnography might exist and be epistemologically productive. Indeed the body and embodiment are, in these cases, key analytical frameworks, pivotal to the wider research endeavour. However, by focusing on such an explicit example as that of Allison (1994) it is also possible to argue for an embodied ethnographer regardless of the explicit focus of the project in hand. As embodied social actors we engage in fieldwork. Much of the 'work' of fieldwork is about locating ourselves as embodied individuals. The rules and rituals of a social setting often demarcate the body. The interactional qualities of fieldwork are embodied as well as language based. The vocabulary of the field is performative as well as semantic. The body work of fieldwork encapsulates both the body as focus of enquiry (either as an explicit or implicit aspect of the social setting/ institution/organization/everyday life) *and* the fieldworker as an embodied social actor. The embodiment of the fieldwork experience also locates the body as part of the identity work of the ethnographer. That is, as well as engaging, actively or passively, in body work, many field researchers are also concerned with the active production of a physical body image, acceptable to the research setting.

The Production of the Body

The 'self conscious' presentation of self (Goffman, 1959) has been well documented as a salient consideration of fieldwork. In particular, dress and personal appearance have been referred to as part of the impression management that is carried out during access negotiations and the establishment of acceptable field role(s).

Where an explicit research role must be constructed, forms of dress can 'give off' the message that the ethnographer seeks to maintain the position of an acceptable marginal member, perhaps in relation to several different audiences. They may declare affinity between researcher and hosts, and/or they may distance the ethnographer from constraining identities. (Hammersley and Atkinson, 1995: 87)

The impression management of the ethnographer's body goes beyond dress and adornment. Demeanour, speech and the use of props are aspects of the construction of identity and role during fieldwork. All are concerned with the production of a fieldwork body which is both acceptable and plausible. Clothing can establish a particular sort of embodied image. Speech vocalizes the physical body. Demeanour is concerned with the positioning and performing of the body. Props (such as jewellery, instruments, artefacts) are used to decorate, and may be used to legitimize the fieldwork body. Thought of in this context, the practical accomplishment of fieldwork is synonymous with the practical accomplishment of body management, production and image.

During my own fieldwork (Coffey, 1993) I was extremely conscious of the need to manage and produce an acceptable body to the fieldsite. I was concerned with presenting a personal front which mirrored that of the social actors in the field. I attempted to dress 'like an accountant'. This in itself was based on my assessment of the acceptable body in accountancy – as smart, self-assured, confident and well managed. I dressed in a black interview business suit with straight skirt and fitted jacket, rather than denim jeans or Lycra leggings. I wore pale blouses rather than T-shirts in loud colours. I wore heeled shoes rather than training shoes or loafers. This sort of self-conscious attention to appearance is well documented by other fieldworkers (Warren, 1988), and applies to men as well as women. For example Patrick (1973) recalled the attention he had to give to appropriate dress in order to fit in with a Glasgow, male gang. Van Maanen (1991) had to try and dress 'like a policeman' without actually wearing a uniform, during observation of working policemen in the USA. Many of the general texts on the conduct of fieldwork deal with the issue of dress and physical appearance as part of the necessary impression management, often giving advice on how an appropriate image is to be achieved and maintained. Yet these rarely go beyond a relatively superficial discussion of appropriate clothing and general appearance. In many instances the production of the fieldworker body extends beyond these straightforward aspects.

The social setting of the accountancy firm is not in or of itself especially bodily. Nor is accountancy an activity generally associated with the body. The work of accountancy is, from the outside looking in, financial and organizational. Yet this organizational setting is imbued with issues of bodily conduct and bodily presentation, which in turn encompass aspects of gender and sexuality (for an exploration of the sexuality of organizational settings see Acker, 1990; Hearn and Parkin, 1987; Savage and Witz, 1992;

Witz et al., 1996). Both formal codes and informal rules deal with aspects of the body, some intimately so. The physical appearance of accountants is of course important. Certainly to an outsider the accountant is perceived as fulfilling certain expectations about dress and demeanour. In Western Ridge, the firm in which I conducted fieldwork, new recruits (in this case graduate accountants) were given implicit and explicit guidance on their personal appearance. This included not only dress but also advice on skin care, make-up, hair-style, body hair, and the use of props such as jewellery and briefcases. For these junior accountants the body was implicated in their daily work lives. By association it was also implicated in my personal and practical experiences of fieldwork.

The production of my body, alongside the production of accountancy bodies, became central to how I understood and made sense of daily life in the office. I was conscious of the need to produce myself (Baudrillard, 1975) as part of the fieldwork. The physical appearance of my body was negotiated and understood in relation to the normative codes of the field setting. In that sense my experience of fieldwork was embodied. The public world of the work organization and the private world of the body intersected in the conduct of fieldwork. Yet the public work of the organization and the professional vocabulary of the setting did not lend themselves to an explicit implication of the body. Apart from introductory talks to the new recruits on the expected standards of dress and general personal appearance the body was rarely discussed or problematized. The self-presentation of the body quickly became a taken-for-granted element of the production of the self as accountant *and* fieldworker.

During my fieldwork I was not particularly self-conscious or reflexive about the production of my own body: certainly not beyond the realities of needing to look the part in order to achieve access and an acceptable fieldwork persona. In retrospect I have come to realize that I was engaged in negotiating and producing a fieldwork body. In doing so I was responding to norms and rules of the organization. I crafted my body as part of the crafting of the field, and this was not something that was confined to the actual fieldwork setting. The ways I 'chose' to dress, wear make-up, style my hair, even shave my legs were part of a bodily performance which I subconsciously thought necessary for the successful accomplishment of the fieldwork. My body is part of the way in which I experienced fieldwork and an important aspect of my fieldwork memories. I will always remember the ways in which the graduate accountants sought to craft the image of accountant. As too I will remember the way in which my feet ached after a working day in high-heeled shoes!

Thus far I have confined my discussion here to the production of the body in terms of the ways in which it is presented – through dress, adornment, props and so on. The production of the body image is not confined to, but is mediated by, the needs of fieldwork. There are instances where issues of nudity and privacy are at stake. The production and management of the body can be concerned with the norms, rules and rituals concerning nakedness. (Rarely are fieldworkers faced with conducting fieldwork in the nude – see Parry 1982, 1987 on conducting ethnographic fieldwork in a naturist club). Moffatt (1989) undertook fieldwork in an American college, at first covertly then overtly. There was a number of ways in which the physical appearance of his body was implicated in his fieldwork relationships with the college freshers he was studying. While he was sharing a dormitory with other male students, the issue of nudity was something which he had to confront. Posing as a 'freshman' considerably older and more experienced than the other students, Moffatt (1989: 9) noticed that bodily privacy was more significant for his student peers.

> Other freshmen stopped by our door regularly and peered in looking away in embarrassment if they happened to catch one of us in our underwear. Total nudity, I noticed, was generally masked even between male room mates.

When the freshers 'discovered' that Moffatt was really a college professor, the body remained an important part of his fieldwork relations

> [John] told me his fantasy about me. I was a 'returned Vietnam vet infiltrating the system to take knowledge back to the Vietcong'. My long hair and wire rimmed glasses had looked 'radical' to him. I had slept a lot (I had really been listening in on them with my eyes closed). I had been quiet and apparently relaxed when everyone else had been zinging with nervous tension. 'Vets can sleep under fire in foxholes,' John explained. (Moffatt, 1989: 11)

Moffatt goes on to say that the students performed a number of practical jokes on him which included stealing his clothes while he was sleeping, forcing him to run naked on to a balcony in order to recover them. Moffat's physical appearance and the concept of the private, naked body were part of his experience of fieldwork. Moreover they were part of his fieldwork self. Privacy and nudity were both problematized and used by the students over the course of his fieldwork. His exposed body was actually part of the relationship he had with his fellow students. Furthermore the reactions to the body were significant in locating the values of the students and the position of Moffatt in relation to them. The establishment of his identity in the field was mediated and bounded by his physical, and in this case naked, body. The production of the body here went beyond issues of dress to concerns with viewing the body, exposing the body, and privacy. Again the setting (a North American college campus) was not particularly embodied in any explicit sense. Yet Moffatt's experience of fieldwork was embodied. Moreover by discovering and exploring the rules and expectations of the body, he was able to gain insight into the social world of college freshers.

Not all fieldsites centralize the body. Nor is it always necessary for the researcher to engage in overt body impression management. However, the concept of research that is embodied and bodily can still prove important in understanding the personal and the practical in fieldwork. In the next section I broaden the discussion in order to consider how embodiment can be used to characterize key conditions of ethnographic fieldwork.

Bodies in the Field

The main aim of this chapter is to explore the ways in which fieldwork is embodied. There are particular sites that readily implicate the body and fieldwork activities that are particularly physical. Yet all fieldwork can be conceptualized in terms of the body. Not only is fieldwork concerned with the spatial location of bodies (the fieldworker and other social actors). It is also concerned with the interaction, regulation, management and use of the body in everyday social life. Fieldwork includes the observance and analysis of the body as an embodiment of culture. At the same time our engagement with the field is both intellectual and physical. We cannot divorce our scholarly endeavours from the bodily reality of being in the field. To elucidate and expand on the embodied perspective of fieldwork, what follows is a revision of the conditions of fieldwork, as discussed by Le Compte and Preissle (1993). LeCompte and Preissle present six conditions which affect the practical and intellectual accomplishment of fieldwork. These are (1) personal issues; (2) participatory issues; (3) advocacy issues; (4) roles and relationships; (5) boundary issues; and (6) ethical issues. Le Compte and Preissle provide a very general comment on the ways in which the mental and physical condition of the fieldworker may affect the conduct of the research, but they do not consider how the conditions of fieldwork relate to an understanding that fieldwork is embodied. Yet all of the conditions they outline can be used to further explore the relationship between fieldwork, the body and the nature of embodiment.

Personal Issues

The relationship between fieldwork, biography and identity is a recognizable one. It is difficult to separate fieldwork from our own sense of self. In the course of fieldwork we are often engaged in the (re)construction of our own biography and the biographies of others (I deal with this in considerable detail in Chapter 7). Fieldwork is necessarily subjective and personal. The impact of personal characteristics and looks on the conduct of fieldwork is reasonably well documented. Fieldwork is personally experienced through and by our body. What our body looks like, how it is perceived and used can impact upon access, field roles and field relationships. Weidman (1986), for example, provides an account of how her own looks affected her ethnographic study of Burmese women. She had certain physical characteristics which were considered to be desirable in Burmese women, especially lightly coloured skin and naturally arched eyebrows. Yet other characteristics, notably her slim and angular appearance and short hair, were less desirable, and were problematic, as they made it potentially difficult for the Burmese to determine her gender. Others have noted similar impact of their skin and hair colouring on the establishment of field relations. Golde (1986) has written about how her 'whiteness' and curly hair contributed to her research access. Fordham (1996) racially identifies herself as African-American and describes how this and her status as an involuntary diasporic – a wanderer – was a key aspect of who she was and who she became in the cause of fieldwork in an African-American school in the United States. She was acutely aware of her dual status as black self and anthropological self. Her skin colour and racial self-identification was central to her experience of the field. These are personal aspects which give an embodied dimension to the experience of fieldwork. Like dress, they help to locate the ethnographer as part of, or as distinct from, the social world they are seeking to study and understand.

The personal body also enables us to view fieldwork in other ways. For example fieldworkers have often commented on the physical, bodily exhaustion of fieldwork, and the effect this has had on their ability to function in the field. Fieldwork involves physical as well as intellectual involvement. It can be physically stressful, time consuming and trying. Kenna describes her memories of her first fieldwork experiences in Greece in an explicitly bodily way:

> painful sunburn from May to September, shivering in the clammy chill of the winter months when my landlord was in Athens, flea-bites, bruises on thighs from cafe chairs and wooden donkey saddles, prickly rash from sitting on horse-hair sofas, hay fever at threshing time, period pains during long church services, split and bleeding feet, eye strain from reading and typing by paraffin lamplight, and blisters from pulling up buckets of water every day. (Kenna, 1992: 155)

Kenna comments that compared to the dangers experienced by fieldworkers in Africa, South America and New Guinea, whose texts she was brought up on as an undergraduate, her own physical miseries were minor. Equally, many of us will have engaged in fieldwork not nearly so physically arduous as that of Kenna. Yet some of my own enduring memories of sustained fieldwork are aching feet, tiredness, the physical uncomfortableness of stuffy rooms on wet days, headaches from sitting under artificial light for much of the day, a wrist that hurts from writing up fieldnotes late into the night. Yet I was not faced with physical dangers or particularly arduous activities. I was conducting fieldwork in a modern office, in a metropolitan city close to home. The physicality of fieldwork was not premised on difficult activities, nor on overtly uncomfortable and unfamiliar surroundings. The personal issues of fieldwork are, of course, about biography, selfhood, subjectivity and first-hand experience. They are also about the ways in which fieldwork imposes upon, and manages the body.

Participatory Issues

Our body in the field is often a participating body. Present and active, our body may well be taking part in the everyday life of the social world we are observing. There is a long-standing debate in ethnography over the degree to which the participant observer should in fact take part. In attempts to map out the rules that fieldworkers may adopt (see Gold, 1958; Junker, 1960) the issue of immersion or complete participation is a central one. A number of commentators have dealt, in some detail, with the pros and cons of participation and it is not my intention to add to this debate here (see Hammersley and Atkinson, 1995 for a useful summary). However, it is important to note that the issue of participation is physical and bodily, as well as intellectual and methodological. Bolton (1995) and Styles (1979), for example, both describe their physical and 'body' participation during fieldwork which focused on gay male sexuality. Bolton engaged in sexual activity during the course of fieldwork, while Styles became a bodily participant during fieldwork in gay bath houses. Styles describes his first visit to a bath house, where his bodily participation was a key aspect of his experience:

> My first project – scouting out the layout of the bath itself – consisted of twenty or thirty minutes of pushing my way between naked and almost-naked men jamming the hallways . . . I could see few details of behaviour and gave up on the orgy room when, after squeezing through a mass of bodies, I stumbled around in the dark, bumped into a clutch of men engaged in group sexual activity, and had my towel torn off me while one of them grabbed for my genitals. (Styles, 1979: 138)

Most of us are not necessarily engaged in such overtly 'bodily' settings as the bath house or, as Parry (1982) studied – the naturist club. Yet that does not exclude us from being bodily participants in the field setting. For example Atkinson (1997: 42) describes 'gowning up' his body during fieldwork in a hospital theatre:

> If we were in an open theatre, rather than behind a glass screen, we all had to put on gowns, caps and masks. With only our eyes showing it became difficult to recognise who was who.

Atkinson's body was hidden and gowned, alongside the bodies of medical students and surgeons. His body was a 'prop' and aid to his negotiation of field roles. Similarly Fine's active participation on the baseball field (Fine, 1987) as player and umpire was a form of bodily participation. His physical presence was a key part of his field role. Oboler (1986) provides a further example of the relationship between the body and fieldwork participation. In this case the body of her husband was a crucial aspect of fieldwork. The fact that he had been circumcised (a factor crucial to the male life cycle of the Nandi, the Kenyan people Oboler and her husband were living with) made her acceptance and entry into the field much easier. Oboler notes that an uncircumcised husband would have made fieldwork in Nandi extremely difficult. More centrally for our discussion here, the experience of Oboler and her partner illuminates the ways in which participation can also include the exposure and disclosure of the ethnographic body.

Advocacy Issues

The relationship between advocacy, voice, affiliation and fieldwork is a long-standing issue for those engaged in ethnography. This is, in part, a concern with commitment to the participants of the research. Advocacy also highlights the politics of fieldwork, for there is ongoing debate about the extent to which we can, and should, speak for, or intervene in, the lives of our participants. Such questions relate to some of the more general issues of the validity or reliability of ethnography (Hammersley, 1991; Lather, 1986) and the impacts of our research on policy, understanding and emancipation. On the surface it is not easy to relate the body to these sorts of concern. However, there are aspects of advocacy which do attend to the embodiment of fieldwork. For example we might wish to argue that there are advocacy issues of, say, white researchers studying black culture that are bodily as well as cultural (for example Gillborn, 1990; Mac an Ghaill, 1988). Race and ethnic identification is physical as well as cultural. Or that the physical experience of pregnancy has implications of advocacy and empathy for those studying mothers and motherhood (Bolak, 1997; Schrijvers, 1993). The ability to serve as advocate or representative or participant is mediated by our physical looks (looking 'right', looking the part) and the status of our body. Issues and considerations such as age, gender, race and class are social characteristics but they also have physical manifestations that may actually be more explicitly significant.

The ability to 'look' as we are expected to (or not!) is a key factor in our ability to conduct the research; to promote trust and reciprocity; and to establish the roles of participant or advocate. The potential for asymmetrical field relations and power differentiation in fieldwork is concerned with status on a number of levels, including that of the body. This includes what is perceived as acceptable/desirable/normal in terms of physical appearance, as well as what is seen as threatening or intimidating. Being particularly beautiful or ugly; large or small; short or tall will be important in certain social or cultural settings. How we relate to others in the context of fieldwork can be dependent upon physical (bodily) markers of status or class, of both the fieldsite and indeed one's own culture. The potential relations between participant and fieldworker may be based on physical impressions and interpretations, even before the establishment of emotional or intellectual commitment. This relates to the more general link between the body and the roles and relationships of fieldwork.

Roles and Relationships

There is no doubt that the body is a key characteristic of our field roles and relationships. Some researchers explicitly use their body to aid the development of a role in the field. For instance, Parry (1982) established herself as a fellow naturist. This included the decision to expose her body within the parameters of the club. Allison (1994) had a role as a hostess in a Japanese club. This role was a physical one. The appearance and adornment of her body was key to her fieldwork relations with the male members of the club, as was her tolerance of explicit conversation about her body. Humphreys (1975) established his role as 'watchqueen' during research on male sexual activity in tea-rooms (public conveniences) in North America. His role involved him positioning his *body* at the entrance to the tea-rooms, providing a physical presence as a means of reciprocal access to his key informants. All of these established a field role which had a distinctively bodily aspect.

There are a number of examples of women who have developed particular sorts of fieldwork roles during the physical state of pregnancy. Schrijvers (1983, 1993) describes how her experiences of pregnancy and her status as mother were central to the ways in which she experienced the field. Her relationships with her female informants were predicated on this shared physical state. Similarly Salisbury (1994) describes her experience of pregnancy as she undertook fieldwork in the education department of a university. Some of her informants were trained midwives, engaged on a teacher training course. They helped to mould her field role and her pregnancy. Salisbury's immediate experience of pregnancy and her memories of her pregnant self were shaped by the advice, interest, roles and biographies of her informants. Her changing body state (and status) were a significant aspect of her field role and relationships.

Aside from examples like those above, many of us who engage in fieldwork are learning embodied skills which are used in the course of developing and negotiating field roles and relationships. As part of understanding the everyday social life in particular fieldwork contexts we learn how to perform and regulate our body according to perceived or understood norms and expectations. Some fieldwork relationships are clearly predicated on body performance, actively participating in the physical activities, work or leisure activities of the field. In certain places taking part in the physicality of the setting may well be part of gaining insight or understanding into that setting (for instance in factory work, sporting activities or dance clubs, physical participation may be deemed desirable). Equally, establishing and managing intimacy and distance is a bodily skill. We 'learn' the craft skills of body work during fieldwork participation. We get to know when it is appropriate or acceptable to touch bodies – whether that be affectionate slaps on the back, hugs, shaking hands, physical proximity or kissing. Moreover we learn when it is unacceptable to engage in body contact – where the body is distinct and bounded. Violating body rules can jeopardize the role of the researcher and the quality of field relations. The body is implicated in the roles and relationships of fieldwork both in terms of how our body becomes part of our experience of the field *and* in the necessity (albeit often implicit) for the ethnographer to learn the skills and rules of embodiment in the particular social setting.

Boundaries

> Because ethnographers almost always study groups whose cultures are not identical with their own, boundary-spanning skills are critical to the success of a research project. Boundary spanning in some senses is similar to cultural brokering in so far as ethnographers often act as intermediaries or go-betweens. (LeCompte and Preissle, 1993: 103)

Ethnographers also span *body* boundaries during the course of fieldwork. As a visitor to a cultural setting, the fieldworker has to carve out a space for the physicality of their body. As cultural boundaries are negotiated, so too are boundaries of the body. At a very simple level, the ethnographer has to sit or stand or lie or be *somewhere*. Whether that place is at the back of a class-room, to the side of an operating theatre, in the middle of a gathering or on the street corner, is no matter. A space has to be made, or found, or negotiated for the body-thereness of the ethnographer. Fieldwork often invokes the physical awkwardness of the body. There may be no proper, ready-made or appropriate place for the ethnographer to co-locate. Actions and physical articulations may be awkward responses to awkward situations. Facial expressions of interest and engagement are all too important. The 'fixed' smile which demarcates interest and empathy, and the accompanying stereotypical actions and positions, are something to which many field-workers may relate. It is often difficult to know what to physically *do* in the field in order to look natural, comfortable, engaged and welcoming, while not appearing bored, threatening or judgmental. Immersion and integration are physical aspects of fieldwork, as well as academic and personal ones. The fieldworker is a visible as well as a watching body.

The physicality of the fieldwork and the spanning of body boundaries is particularly visible in ethnographies of children and childhood. Corsaro (1981, 1985) is an example of an adult male studying the everyday activities of a nursery school. Corsaro discusses his fieldwork experiences in terms of asymmetry of age between researcher and researched, and the ethics of studying children (see I. Shaw, 1996). Yet one of the most startling aspects of the adult researcher in this context was his physical size. Bill (Corsaro) was *big* and therefore the children at the nursery school were reluctant to include him in their games. It wasn't so much that he was an adult. Corsaro had to negotiate his physical size with the nursery school children, in order to be allowed to play with them. 'Big Bill', as he became known by the children, did get to play eventually! Yet Corsaro experienced fieldwork in terms of his bodily size. Part of his explicit negotiation in the field was distinctively embodied. King (1978) also studied the everyday world of small children. Conducting a study of infant school classrooms King sometimes observed 'from inside the Wendy house' (King, 1978: 340). The impact that this male, adult body would have had on the play potential of the Wendy house is not discussed by King at all. King's body was also present (and absent) in other areas of the research. He notes that he spent whole days in close (one supposes physical) proximity to the class, and at times had children request to sit on his lap. King's lack of critical discussion of his body presence and body boundaries does not absolve them from being a key aspect of his research experience. It is clear that where he placed himself, and how he negotiated his physical, body space (alongside that of the children) was important to the conduct of the research, his field role and field relations. The acquisition of and potential negotiation of personal space also involved the establishing, blurring or violating of body space.

Ethics

The politics and ethics of fieldwork are increasingly recognized and explored. Discussions and debates around the ethical dimensions of ethnography span a number of key issues including informed consent; distinctions between public and private; the status of privacy; harm and exploitation; and risk. These are concerns for social research generally, not only for ethnographic fieldwork (see Homans, 1991; Punch, 1986 for useful discussions on the ethics of social research). There are ethical dimensions to the relationships we have with the people studied, observed and interviewed. Questions of ethics are particularly salient to the consequences, dissemination and publishing of our research. All of these are not so much arguments against ethnographic fieldwork as a case for ensuring that we remain reflexive and critical. Clearly, many of the ethical dimensions of fieldwork are implicated in an ethics of the body. For example the body can be considered to be private or even sacred. Yet fieldwork and observation often makes public the private body. We watch and note the body. Moreover our own body can be exposed and observed during fieldwork. The boundary between the private body and the public body is a fieldwork dilemma and an ethical dilemma. Negotiating and managing privacy is an issue for both researcher and researched. Similarly, informed consent is not just an intellectual or academic concept. It also has real, physical implications. In many contexts consent to watch bodies is requested, given or denied – as they work, play, perform and interact. Fieldwork may also mean watching bodies at risk of harm or exploitation. Equally some fieldwork contexts may place our own body at risk of harm or exploitation. While these may be rare occurrences, their possibility highlights the body-ethics of fieldwork. The fact that fieldwork involves physical co-location of bodies means that ethical aspects surrounding the body are also ethical aspects of fieldwork. It is difficult to divorce the ethical boundaries of privacy and touch from the fieldwork experience. As boundaries can be recognized and enforced they can also be spanned and broken. If a consideration of ethics (regardless of the particular ethical stance you choose to advocate or adopt) is part of the condition of fieldwork then account should also be taken of the ethics of the body as an experience of fieldwork.

Conclusion

The embodied field and the embodied fieldworker are concepts which capture a physicality of ethnography. Turner (1984) noted that the social sciences had often neglected the fact that human beings have bodies and are embodied. And while there has been substantial scholarly interest over the last two decades or so (for example in the development of a sociology of the body), this has not really extended to a methodological interest in the body and the nature of embodiment. More specifically, while the literature on ethnographic research is now significant (and growing) little has been made of the embodied nature of the fieldwork task. This is not to say that all ethnographical accounts have silenced the body. As I have noted, issues of bodily presentation have always been part of narratives of access and the development of field roles. We also know, from recollections of fieldwork, that it can be physically demanding and tiring. What this chapter has done, however, is to take these obvious aspects of embodiment as starting points. While the concept of self-presentation and the physical demands of fieldwork are important, widely acknowledged and experienced, they touch only the surface of an embodied fieldwork perspective. Both the physical body and the symbolic, cultural significance it has are central, rather than peripheral, aspects of ethnographic fieldwork. Clearly an embodied perspective does not imply a privileging of the body. But we should recognize that a lot of what we are undertaking in the field is body work of one sort or another. We are observing, interpreting and analysing the bodies and body perspectives of others. At the same time we should analyse and use the physical ways in which we experience fieldwork, rather than denying them or simply taking them for granted. This general case is subjected to scrutiny in the next chapter, where I consider sexual aspects of field research.

5   The Sex(ual) Field

Associating sexual activity and ethnographic fieldwork is nothing new. Indeed the sex lives and sexual relations of *others* have long been a concern of social anthropology. For example, both Malinowski (1987) [1929] and Mead (1949) [1928] focused on the sexual lives of 'primitive' societies. Yet despite this fascination and documentation of the 'sexual', anthropologists (and other fieldworkers) have been relatively silent about their own sexuality and sexual experiences. This chapter focuses on aspects of sexual activity, experiences and desires in ethnographic fieldwork. My aim is to explore how 'sex in the field' can aid the quest for a better understanding of the emotional and personal dimensions of fieldwork, by examining some of the different dimensions of the sexual in fieldwork. This includes the sexual status of the researcher; physical sexual activity which occurs during fieldwork; *and* fieldwork which is conducted in sexual and/or explicitly erotic settings. As Kulick (1995) notes, sexual relations during fieldwork are not unproblematic, though they can be epistemologically fruitful:

> every fieldwork situation will include numerous circumstances in which sexual relations between anthropologists and individuals in the field would be unethical and exploitive [but] perhaps more than any other type of interaction, sex can urge an exploration of the basis of, nature of, and the consequences of relationships entered into in the field. (Kulick, 1995: 22)

It is not necessarily my intention to advocate or encourage those engaged in fieldwork to seek sexual liaisons with informants or fellow researchers. On the contrary, there are issues of ethics, safety and power that may well work to encourage quite the opposite. Nor is it my aim to criticize, moralize or pass judgement on those fieldworkers who do report sexual encounters during fieldwork. Indeed from a perspective of fieldwork peopled by physical, embodied and emotional social actors, it would be hypocritical to cast the researcher as asexual, or devoid of desire. My concern is with the ways in which sexual activity, desire and expectation impact upon the lived reality of fieldwork. I contend that the questions and issues raised by focusing on the 'sexual perspective' both illustrate and exaggerate a number of features of fieldwork research. For example, the characteristics of the fieldworker (age, gender, race, sexuality); the relational nature of the research process (establishing and negotiating field roles, relationships, boundaries); and the possible emotions of fieldwork (love, hate, excitement, risk, power, belonging, alienation) can all be analysed through such a focus.

The very fact that sexual status and sexual encounters *are* issues for discussion tells us something of the personal and physical intensity which fieldwork involves. That sexual intercourse is a *possibility* and a *reality* (see Kulick and Willson, 1995) demonstrates how intellectual curiosity, physical desire and emotional investment can be construed and experienced in combination. This takes us beyond a consideration of the actual physical, sexual act toward a much broader set of experiences, constructions and emotions.

Fieldwork, especially but not exclusively in social anthropology, has often been charged with the exotic, and often by implication the erotic. In studying and positioning 'the other', ethnographers have often associated the people they have been studying with excessive, perverse or, at the very least, *different* sexualities. There is a long tradition of describing the sexual availability, erotic pleasures and sexual lives of other people. The field has often been portrayed as erotically charged. By contrast it is far more unusual to represent fieldwork (and the ethnographer) as sexual, erotic, pleasured or desiring. And yet the fieldworker, as emotional and embodied, cannot help but have a sexual positionality. This does not necessitate physical enactment, but the reconceptualization of the researcher as sexual and desiring does impact upon the ways in which the experience of fieldwork is constructed. Our sexuality, emotional and physical desires do not disappear on entering the field. The question is, how does an explicit focus on them add to (or change) our understanding of fieldwork as lived experience? By focusing on the sexuality and erotic subjectivity of the researcher we can examine the diversity of biographies and identities that shape (and are shaped by) ethnographic fieldwork. Kulick argues that:

> at a time when anthropologists are finally beginning to examine and even celebrate various dimensions of their subjectivity in their fieldwork and in their writing, it seems propitious and crucial to place the erotic subjectivity of the anthropologist firmly on the anthropological agenda. (Kulick, 1995: 6)

This chapter attempts to establish how a consideration of the sexual and the erotic is epistemologically productive. Drawing on accounts and 'confessions' I explore the ways in which a sexual perspective may be fruitful. I have been necessarily selective in my review and discussion. I have certainly not attempted to undertake a comprehensive review of all available references to sexual encounters that have occurred during fieldwork. Nor have I set out with the aim of analysing all the possible 'sexual settings' in which fieldwork either has occurred or could occur. By drawing on a range of settings and experiences, however, I hope to be able to demonstrate how fieldwork can be shaped, negotiated, understood *and* problematized by erotic subjectivity and sexual identity. To facilitate this, the discussion that follows is divided into three sections, each of which takes a slightly different focus. The first section identifies how sexual status is defined, confronted and tested during fieldwork encounters. The second examines how boundaries are identified and maintained in field settings that are themselves eroticized or sexual. Thirdly I consider the meanings and consequences of sexual encounters that have occurred during fieldwork. This draws on accounts of physical and emotional intimacy and intimidation.

Virginity, Marriage and the Ethnographer

Sexual status has been a recurrent theme in accounts of fieldwork. Women researchers, in particular, have reflected on their sexual status and its impact on fieldwork and relationships. In this context sexual status has often been associated with marital status (see, for example, Abu-Lughod, 1988). It has been less common for men to address the issues of marriage and associated sexuality in their accounts of fieldwork (see Abramson, 1993, who does discuss his sexual status and the ways in which it impacted on his fieldwork experience). The focus on marriage is indicative of a more general set of fieldwork issues. Virginity, sexual activity and celibacy are all aspects of the fieldworker-self that have been the subject of curiosity and concern. Day-to-day interactions have often included, by inference at least, the perceived and real sexual status of the researcher.

Social anthropology has conventionally given some prominence to the issue of virginity, particularly female virginity. So it should not be so surprising that, in turn, the sexual status of the researcher has also been the subject of some scrutiny. Virginity has been central to analyses of honour and shame. It is a concept that has been used to examine and critique the rhetoric of hegemonic masculinity in some societies. As Lindisfarne (1994: 90) notes, 'the celebrations which follow the bloodied proof of a bride's virginity are extensively documented in the ethnographic literature'. Female virginity has often been seen as a status to be simultaneously prized and solved. On the one hand it is portrayed as a desired state, especially in young women who are single. On the other hand virginity implies being unattached, unmarried, potentially vulnerable and in some cases abnormal. Hence it is indicative of a problem for which the solution is attachment, usually to a man and usually through marriage. The same attention to the unmarried status has been afforded to women undertaking fieldwork. For example, Hutheesing's (1993) single status was an issue for her informants during fieldwork in the Lisu mountains of northern Thailand:

> my status as a single person was somewhat odd in their judgement, a situation which they attempted to rectify by trying to marry me off to various types of Lisu men. From time to time I appeared in the village with western male friends who were immediately identified as my husbands. (Hutheesing, 1993: 97)

This is a relatively common experience recounted by women anthropologists. Dua (1979) and Golde (1986) were both advised by informants to go home and get married. Karim (1993) was encouraged to 'choose a spouse' for the duration of her Malaysian fieldwork. Similar attention was also paid to Abramson (1993) during *his* fieldwork in Fiji. He was unmarried and this was a subject of advice. He says he was encouraged to 'plant a few shoots in my "father's" plantation, just as I was often encouraged to marry, throw down roots ("weka") metaphorically, and stop "fucking about" in the world' (Abramson, 1993: 71).

The issue of marital status is not confined to anthropologists, as Lees (1986) discovered. Conducting fieldwork in an educational setting with teenage girls, Lees found that the girls had initially assumed she was a lesbian (partially because she wore dungarees!). This only came to light when she happened to mention she had a husband and child. This not only highlights how our sexuality gets constructed by our informants. It is also indicative of the heterosexual parameters within which fieldwork is often conceived. The perceived importance of marriage, and conversely the 'dangers' of being single, especially for a woman, have led some ethnographers to adopt strategies to conceal their 'true' status. Abu-Lughod's (1988) experience of living in a Bedouin culture is a particularly good example of this. She conducted fieldwork in a society where for young, single women to live on their own was considered problematic. Abu-Lughod tried to counter this by ensuring she always conformed to appropriate codes of dress (ensuring modesty and so forth). She was also careful in the way in which she described her home life, in Harvard, to her Bedouin informants. The Bedouin could not imagine that unmarried women would live on their own. It was considered to be both dangerous and odd. Abu-Lughod responded to this by letting her hosts believe that she lived near to her father (although in actual fact Harvard is in Massachusetts and not Chicago, where her father lived). She did not attempt to correct the mistaken assumption that her hosts had made. While Abu-Lughod did not conceal her single status she attempted to make it seem less problematic.

Others have made more conscious decisions to either actively or passively let it be thought that they were married (when in fact they were not). M. Wolf (1996) is quite open in admitting that she lied about her marital status, while Katz (1996) let the inhabitants of the Sudanese village where she did fieldwork *think* that she was married to her partner as she assumed that cohabitation would be viewed as sinful. In these cases the ethnographers thought that marriage was a more acceptable status to adopt. But the assumption of marriage can also be part of a process of making fieldwork 'safe' for women. The lack of marriage, and therefore a stable heterosexual relationship can be perceived as an indication of character. For example, Dua (1979) notes that, as an unmarried, female anthropologist in India, she was the recipient of several unwanted marriage proposals and sexual advances. These left her feeling unsafe at times. Warren (Warren and Rasmussen, 1977) wore a ring on her 'wedding' finger and used the title 'Doctor' to keep her marital status ambiguous, in order to lessen the potential for sexual harassment during her fieldwork. Gurney (1985) notes that sexual hustling is more likely to occur when a female researcher is perceived to be single or unattached to a male. Being perceived as 'attached' may reduce, though not eliminate, sexual attention during fieldwork.

Marriage has also served as a source of identity for some engaged in fieldwork. Again it is noticeable that this has usually been reported on by women. Their marital status has impacted on the quality of field relationships, especially with other women. Macintyre (1993) found that marriage was a state and set of experiences she had in common with the women of Papua New Guinea, although her husband was not actually accompanying her during her fieldwork. Her consequent admittance of temporary celibacy was a cause of mirth, empathy and discussion among the women. Even where the status of marriage was secure, the issue of sexual activity was still extremely relevant. In contrast Berik (1996) was accompanied during her fieldwork in rural Turkey by both her husband and her father. Berik found that her day-to-day interactions and treatment were highly dependent upon their presence. The kinship relations and idioms of the rural Turkish community were a key aspect of conformity to which she acquiesced. Yet here again, despite her confirmed marital status, questions were still raised, this time related to the status of the marriage in terms of procreation. As a married but childless woman, Berik was the recipient of a great deal of public concern.

> In rural Turkey, being childless is probably the worst predicament that could befall a woman (or a couple), and there is intense social pressure on couples to have a child right after marriage. After finding out how many years we had been married (two years at the time), men and women would offer their sympathy and consolation. It was difficult for them to comprehend and believe that this was by choice. At my age of twenty-nine the choice was clearly anomalous. Whether by choice or not, however, childlessness was an attribute that disempowered one, relative to married women with children. (Berik, 1996: 61–2)

While not explicitly dealing with the sexual activity between Berik and her husband, the concerns over her childlessness were multiply focused on her 'odd' choice and on the underlying issue of ability to conceive. Her status as childless was to some extent set against the 'success' of her marriage. Kenna (1992) had similar experiences. When she first undertook fieldwork in Greece she was unmarried. This concerned the women friends she made. When Kenna returned to Greece some time later she was married but childless.

> Just as my women friends had been worried . . . about my finding a husband, they were now worried I was still childless; I had lost a great deal of weight which meant, in Greek terms, that married life, particularly its physical side, was not satisfying. (Kenna, 1992: 158)

Measor (1985) also recalls how her childlessness was an issue for her 12-year-old female informants during fieldwork in schools. Once it had been established that she was married but child-free she was attacked as being selfish and only caring about herself. (In contrast, the presence of one's children in the field can also affect field relations, as Fleuhr-Lobban and Lobban (1986) document.) Clearly the role and experience of marriage extends beyond procreation. Several researchers have discussed how their marital arrangements were challenged by fieldwork. For example Friedl (1986) and Freedman (1986) both consider the problematics of fitting their marital relationships in with the gender and cultural norms of the societies they were studying. Vera-Sanso (1993) provides an account of how her husband, accompanying her during fieldwork in southern India, contradicted local gender norms in terms of the domestic division of labour. His behaviour and their marriage were the subject of scrutiny by the local people. Pettigrew (1981) conducted fieldwork in the Punjab and was also married to a Jat Sikh (from the Punjab). Her marital status was both facilitating and problematic. She was able to gain access because of her marriage but was subjected to cultural assumptions and attitudes based on her status as a Sikh wife.

This interest in the marital and sexual status of the fieldworker demonstrates a key way in which identities are established and maintained. The perception and reality of sexual experience and attachment often, though not always, located within marriage are used by informants and the researcher to construct and shape the relations of fieldwork. In just the same way that other aspects of our character or personal life can be exposed during fieldwork, these accounts show that the sexual self is not absolved from scrutiny. Our virginity, celibacy, sexual relations, reproductive choices and capabilities are all possible sites for passing judgement, asking questions, interference and curiosity. This makes fieldwork a deeply personal event for some. But the value of these experiences takes us beyond the personal. There is ethnographic value in addressing these issues. Marital status and sexual status are located within cultural norms and frameworks. They are bounded by rules and understandings of the acceptable and unacceptable, the desirable and the unwanted. They relate to issues of gender conformity and sexual norms. The gendered structures of particular societies, institutions and social settings can take on more transparent meaning when one is experiencing them first-hand. How marriage and sexual status are enacted on a day-to-day basis can serve as an important aspect of the analysis of a cultural setting. This can be the analysis of the rituals of the marriage ceremony, courtship or the loss of virginity. Equally it can refer to the everyday discourses and actions which are used to establish cultural norms and frameworks by which individuals (and groups) negotiate, establish, maintain and alter their sexual identities. Hence the issues of sexual and marital status link the personal to the ethnographic in vivid ways. The experiences of researchers, negotiating these statuses in the context of fieldwork, can be used as data. That is they provide first-hand, 'stranger' accounts of how sexual mores, status, attachments and marriage are accomplished in the cultural setting. The ethnographic is thus linked to the personal. In turn the personal informs and becomes part of the fieldwork.

Sex(y) Settings

The relationship between the personal and the ethnographic is exaggerated in those settings where sex forms part of the explicit research agenda or context. Thus far I have chosen to concentrate on the sexual status of the fieldworker, not necessarily in explicitly sexual settings. This helps to establish the idea that sexuality is a condition of fieldwork in a general sense. There are some sites of fieldwork where sexuality and sexual status are part of the everyday talk and activity. The sexual dimension of the social setting can have implications for the conduct of fieldwork and the sexual engagement of the researcher. Of course there are sex settings and there are sex settings. It is not necessary for sexual activity to be explicit in the setting for it to be conceived as sexual. There are a number of social settings where sex and sexual activity are explicitly present. Sex workers (Barnard and McKeganey, 1995), brothel madams (Heyl, 1979), and the sex scene of Times Square (Karp, 1980) are all undeniably concerned with sexual activity of one sort or another. As sex settings they structure the context of fieldwork. Everyday activities and conversations will include sex. Sex will be part of the vocabularies and routines of the setting and the fieldwork. There are other settings where this might well be the case, even though the setting is not explicitly a sexual one. For example in some contexts sexual activity is explicitly limited, restricted and forbidden, as in the case of the naturist club (Parry, 1982, 1987). Or the sexual aspect of the setting is implicit though not formally recognized, as Douglas et al. (1977) found in the case of the nude beach. In such settings the sexual dimension may still inform and contextualize the data and the personal fieldwork experience.

There are practical, ethical and personal aspects to fieldwork in sex settings. As Bolton (1995) notes, actual sexual behaviour is not easily observed. How the research is conducted and how data are collected are questions which are particularly relevant. Sexual settings can crystallize the issue of personal involvement or non-involvement for the researcher. Involvement and observation may also have ethical as well as methodological problems attached. Bolton's study of the Belgian gay community (Bolton, 1995) confronts these issues. He participated as a sexually active social actor during his fieldwork. For him it was a natural and inevitable part of both his research and his personal experience.

> As a gay man studying the erotic culture of gay men, I was drawn to them for both personal and professional reasons, and my interactions simultaneously affected my work and my private life. (Bolton, 1995: 148)

Bolton argues that his active, sexual participation was a valuable means of gaining information and insight into the Belgian gay community. Indeed the sorts of data he was able to collect were only available because of such participation. Without his physical and sexual engagement with the field, his data might well have been different.

> Information obtained post-coitally (except in quick sex encounters in public places), when people tend to relax and open up about their lives, was always richer, more from the heart and more revealing than the data gathered in a more detached manner. Once one has shared physical and emotional intimacy, sharing other knowledge about oneself seems easier. (Bolton, 1995: 148–9)

Bolton was an *active* member of the gay community. Indeed he argues that it would be extremely difficult for a gay man to investigate in a highly charged erotic environment such as gay sauna baths (where he conducted fieldwork) and not be tempted to participate. He had sexual, intimate and emotional desires which could not easily be divorced from his researcher role. Nor did Bolton advocate that they should be. 'Hanging about' gay venues, bars, baths and steam rooms was part of his fieldwork and became part of his private life. Engaging in sexual activity was by choice – personally and professionally. Bolton is careful to report that he never engaged in sex purely for the purpose of collecting data; that he never participated in unprotected sex *and* that he was always interested in sexual partners as people *not* simply as convenient informants. The sexual life and activities he participated in were not that different from what he would have done 'back home'. Not to have engaged in them would have been to have denied his own sexuality. Although Bolton emphasizes his choice and his ethical standpoint he freely admits that in a culture where sexuality and shared sexual experiences are paramount, it would have been difficult to have fully engaged with the everyday experiences without participating sexually.

> By experiencing them, I came to learn of blow jobs from bartenders, when the door was locked at closing time, of jacking off in cruising spots in a park near the Grand Place in particularly public view, of sexual encounters in alleyways between someone headed home from the bars and someone on his way to work at dawn, of sexual action in the dunes along the coast and on the piers in Ostende and in the backrooms of discos and in the bathrooms of ordinary bars. (Bolton, 1995: 148)

It is not necessary to participate sexually in such settings in order to undertake fieldwork, as Humphreys (1970) demonstrated. Humphreys did not engage in sexual activity, although his research setting was explicitly sexual – he was studying gay male sexual encounters in public lavatories ('tea-rooms'). His participation was limited to that of a lookout or 'watchqueen':

a man who is situated at the door or windows from which he may observe the means of access to the restroom. When someone approaches, he coughs. He nods when the coast is clear or if he recognises an entering party as a regular . . . by serving as a voyeur-lookout, I was able to move around the room at will, from window to window, and to observe all that went on without alarming my respondents or otherwise disturbing the action. (Humphreys, 1970: 27–8)

Humphreys was able to observe homosexual acts that took place in the tea-rooms, something he would have found much more difficult without some form of active participation. It also meant he was in a much better position to engage the participants in meaningful discussion about their activities. He adopted a sexual role in the field in order to facilitate his data collection. He was a sexual player, even though he was not a participant in the sexual activity *per se*.

Tearoom Trade has been the subject of some criticism. This has mainly focused on the ways in which Humphreys chose to follow up male customers who frequented the tea-rooms (see Humphreys, 1975 for a methodological and ethical discussion of this). More generally the social setting and Humphreys's participation highlight the practical and ethical dilemmas of conducting fieldwork in explicitly sexual environments. These are complicated further if we consider gender. For women to participate in 'sexual' fieldwork is perhaps less easy – not least because of the complex juxtaposition of safety and reputation. This should not be taken to imply that physical and sexual safety are not concerns for both men and women, but it is more usual to associate these concerns with women fieldworkers. Sexual reputation is a gendered concept, with gender-specific routes (sexual prow-ess versus sexual purity). Bearing this in mind, some women have found a level of participation to be possible and fruitful. For example, Allison (1994) participated in the everyday life of the Tokyo hostess club. She worked as a hostess in an environment where sex talk was a norm. Sexual activity was also part of the implicit context of the club. Allison did not conduct covert research but she did participate in the everyday interactions and activities of the club. She was part of the sex talk and the sexualizing practices of the club – as both a subject of male desire and as an interactional player. She did not, however, engage in any sex acts, nor did she observe sexual activity. Her level of participation and the social setting were sexualized but not explicitly sexual.

There is little doubt that participation (more or less) in 'sex' scenes during fieldwork can result is fruitful data. More doors are open, more conversa-tions possible and meaningful; more everyday practices and routines explicit. The personal dimensions of the experience can also be self-illuminating, in just the same way that any sexual encounter (positive or negative, scheduled or not) can be. The collection of 'sexy' data, and the possibility of personal sexual experience are two outcomes of fieldwork in sexual settings. Such fieldwork also illustrates and exaggerates the issues of boundary and positionality in research. The cultural importance and central-ity of sex may make it more difficult to establish and recognize the boundaries between the personal and the professional, the fieldworker and the self. Even where participation is limited, the sexualizing of the self becomes a crucial part of the fieldwork experience. For Bolton (1995) sex was a necessary part of fieldwork experience. For Allison (1994) the sexualizing of her body and her feminine sexuality was a key aspect of her fieldwork interactions. In these, as in other instances, sexuality, privacy and data collection were interwoven. The cultural importance of sex in these settings made the positionality of the sexual self more transparent and real, yet more difficult to separate from the fieldworker self. Explicitly sexual settings make it possible to acknowledge the ways in which fieldwork can be sexual and embodied. They can provide a sexual vocabulary and a context within which to test and explore the rules of behaviour and action.

Settings do not need to be conceived as sexual to be sexually charged – for researcher and researched. For example, the nude beach is not neces-sarily a sexual scene – yet the association between nudity, sex and beach life makes it so. Douglas et al. (1977) observed very little in the way of public sexual acts, but there were stories and accounts of sexual intercourse, sexual activities and sexual violence happening on the beach. Indeed while sexual activity was not part of the nude beach in any explicit sense, sex was part of the everyday world the researchers observed and heard. As partici-pant observers, Douglas and his colleagues contributed to this social world:

> An important part of this 'going natural' was learning the body code and the situated body language of the nude beach. The situated language, the subcultural dialect of a universal body-code, is being created slowly to deal with the scene as people come increasingly to grasp and understand it. Much of the communication on the beach, especially the most important kinds about sex, is done entirely in terms of the body-code – facial expressions, the way one walks, autonomic responses (from erections to quavering voices). (Douglas et al., 1977: 15)

From the exposure of the body to the interpretation of language, behaviour and action, Douglas and his colleagues immersed themselves in the 'sex' scene of the nude beach. Aside from its reputation (which is not necessarily reality) as a sexual intercourse zone, the nude beach was sexually important. The beach was 'told' as a place for sexual display, finding partners, dealing with hang-ups and frigidity, voyeurism and gay cruising. All of these were ongoing and contributed to the nude beach as a site of sexual narrative and sexual activity. Sex was part of the vocabulary, rituals, interactions and everyday activities of the beach. Hence it was a central part of the ethnographic analysis of understanding the social world of the nude beach. Sex was analytically significant.

Parry's (1982) research in a British naturist club is less explicit about the ways in which sex is implicated in an everyday context. Unlike the nude beach, the naturist club was mainly a social location for married couples (indeed there were restrictions on membership by single, unattached males and females). Parry notes issues around sexuality and sexual display. The naturist club had strict rules about certain aspects of sex-related behaviour. Naturism (nudity in a particular social context) was explicitly presented as non-sexual. Physical and overtly sexual contact was, in fact, less acceptable in the club than in many other social settings. The demonstrative actions of fondling, hugging and kissing were usually viewed as inappropriate and certainly not encouraged. While nudity was explicit, physical displays such as penile erection were denied as sexual. Men developed strategies, such as turning on to their fronts, to manage this denial. Parry participated in the social activities of the club. She was an unusual member, being a single woman who joined on her own (she did not conduct covert research, but access to undertake the study depended upon her becoming a member). While the club was aware of her researcher status, a condition of her attendance was adherence to the club rules – including nudity and attention to the 'sexual' rules. Her observations suggest a conscious attempt by the club to desexualize a potentially sexually charged environment.

In just the same way as explicitly sexual settings, examples like the nude beach and the naturist club present the fieldworker with rules, boundaries and vocabulary about sexual behaviour, display and appropriateness. Sometimes these rules and boundaries are implicit – the nude beach did not have explicit rules about sex, yet what was appropriate, acceptable, desirable or lewd was discernible. Very public, very overt sexual activity was 'not permitted'. The naturist club had much more explicit rules, understood by its members. Many of Parry's informants were reluctant to discuss matters of a sexual nature. They were seemingly unwilling to sexualize their club participation and activities, and certainly did not wish to give Parry any reason to do so. Yet in divorcing nudity from sex, the club and its participants were engaging in a sexual dialogue with each other and with the researcher, albeit unspoken and muted. This desexualizing of the naturist club reflects a particular aspect of fieldwork and ethnographic writing. Ethnography, to some extent, trades on ironic contrasts with regard to sex and sexuality. Both intrinsically and contemporarily the fieldworker has often been keen to 'look beyond' the sexual in explicitly sexual settings. The sexual has often been desexualized – sex has been taken to be indicative of more general social interactions and cultural events. Rituals around sexuality have been analysed in terms of the everyday activities of the fieldsite. In this way, sex has almost been accidental or incidental to the analysis of the social setting. Sex(ual) settings have been reanalysed in terms of their interactional process and personal-structural context, shifting the focus away from the sexual and the erotic. By contrast, settings and organizations not explicitly sexual have been sexualized; that is the *hidden* sexuality of the site has been brought to the fore and used as a tool of analysis. For example contemporary studies of organizational settings have focused on sexuality as an analytical framework. (There is a whole literature on sexuality and organization: see for example Hearn et al., 1989, Witz et al., 1996).

The idea of sexualizing the social (cf. Adkins and Merchant, 1996) is a useful one in exploring the relationship between sex and fieldwork. This chapter concentrates on the ways in which sexuality and sexual activity is implicated, experienced and challenged in fieldwork. While it is relatively easy to accommodate this perspective in sexually charged settings, the points are more general ones. This section has concentrated on fieldwork where the relationship to physical sexuality is obvious. By focusing on such settings issues of participation and embodiment are discernible, in relation to both fieldworker and informants. As I have noted, such settings allow for a much clearer understanding of the rules, boundaries and vocabularies of sexual activity. Yet the very nature of the settings makes the issues of selfhood and engagement more, rather than less problematic. In the section that follows I turn my attention to *actual* sexual experiences of fieldworkers engaged in prolonged fieldwork.

Intimacy and Intimidation

The actual or perceived sexual status of the researcher has a number of implications – for incorporation into the field, fieldwork relations and relationships, the maintenance of fieldwork boundaries, the reproduction of gender and so on. While the physical act of sexual intercourse is perhaps implicit here, it is contextualized in terms of marriage, love, children, *and* for women especially, personal safety and cultural expectations of appropriate behaviour. Such aspects are all, of course, bound up with the expectations and assumptions of a sexual relationship, although the physical act of sex is still a relatively taboo subject for the ethnographic account. However, there is a small corpus of authors who have chosen to write about the sex act in fieldwork from a personal, experiential perspective, most notably the contributors to the Kulick and Willson (1995) collection of anthropological fieldwork experiences. The particular nature of anthropological fieldwork may make some anthropologists especially susceptible to the formation of personal (and sexual) relationships in the field. It is documented (and more generally assumed by the anthropological community) that, for social anthropologists, fieldwork is a deeply bounded, prolonged, personal experience. Doctoral students, for example, are expected to 'go' to the field for extended periods of time, often in a foreign country, with little or no contact with 'home', their university department, colleagues or supervisor. Even where doctoral fieldwork does not involve travel to foreign parts there is still the expectation that students will 'go it alone', and not necessarily have regular contact with their academic department during the main fieldwork stage (Coffey and Atkinson, 1996). The tradition and expectation of (partial) immersion in the field is still strong. So it is both understandable, and perhaps unsurprising, that deeply personal relationships are formed. The anthropologist in this context, 'lives' the field and is most intimately a part of the place and people that are being studied. While not all social anthropologists 'go away' and there is an increasing amount of anthropological fieldwork being conducted 'at home' (often referred to as indigenous ethnography), the bounded, insular and private conception of the fieldwork experience still holds. 'In the field' and then 'coming back from the field' are still real categories and temporal boundaries.

For others engaged in fieldwork, full immersion and engagement are less often the norm. For example some sociologists and educationalists have immersed themselves in the field and lived there for an extended period of time. But certainly for many, even while 'doing fieldwork', a separate personal life is maintained – going home in the evenings, keeping regular contact with supervisors, colleagues and departments, maintaining friendships, relationships and social contacts outside the field. For these researchers, fieldwork is more tightly framed and distinct from the rest of their lives. While fieldwork can still be a personal experience, the boundaries between fieldwork and a personal perspective are more tightly drawn on a day-to-day basis. This is not to say that such boundaries are not blurred or open to redefinition. Nor should it imply that, unless we completely immerse ourselves in the field for an extended and unbroken period of time we are immune to the formation of deeply personal *or* meaningful *or* sexual relations. The very nature of fieldwork implies a personal dimension. However, few sociologists, or educationalists for example, have written about actual sexual encounters in the field. That may be because they are less likely to occur in fieldwork with strong home/work, in the field/out of the field boundaries. When there is a sense of a reality outside the field, it may be possible to establish and maintain personal and sexual boundaries. This may be less easily achieved where the fieldworker is getting all of their personal and social, as well as professional, stimulation from the field place and people. Of course the possibility of sexual encounters may simply be more readily accepted by social anthropologists, and hence more easily confessed, although as Dubisch (1995a) notes, celibacy is considered the norm during anthropological fieldwork, and accounts of exceptions to this are still rare.

> I think it is safe to say that I and most of my fellow graduate students absorbed the idea that sexual relations with members of the community in which we were working would be neither appropriate nor wise . . . It is difficult to know the extent to which all of us followed this implicit directive in our own fieldwork. (Dubisch, 1995a: 30)

As Dubisch implies, it is difficult to analyse fully and understand sexual relations that occur during fieldwork as we do not really know the extent of such relations. There are some published accounts, although these are by no means common, or cross-disciplinary. There is also a strong oral culture within the ethnographic community generally. In that oral tradition there are tales and anecdotes of sex in the field. While this does not necessarily imply that sexual encounters during fieldwork are particularly common experiences, it does indicate that the possibilities of sex exist. The possibilities and realities can be used reflexively to examine the place of intimacy and the personal in fieldwork. There are a number of different contexts within which sex in the field can occur. It would be nonsense here to try to homogenize a wide and diverse range of experiences and emotions. But the possibility (and actuality) of sexual encounters in the field relates personal intimacy to the fieldwork experience. Where sex does occur, the field is eroticized. This has consequences for the ways in which fieldwork is conducted, data are collected and experiences remembered.

There is a tradition of married (or cohabiting) couples going into the field together and jointly participating in fieldwork (see for example Corbin and Corbin, 1984, 1987; Oboler, 1986; Scheper-Hughes, 1992; Schrijvers, 1993; Vera-Sanso, 1993; Wolf, 1992). In some instances both partners are explicitly involved in fieldwork. Perhaps more usually the partner is accompanying the fieldworker and to a lesser or greater extent both become involved in the fieldwork and subject to scrutiny by the local, field community. The marital status and relationship can be an important aspect of the identity work and the establishment of relations in the field. The status of 'couple', and with this the implicit assumptions about sexuality, establishes and maintains a fieldwork boundary. The fieldworker 'couple' come to the field with a distinct, collective identity already in place. While this may be exposed, challenged or modified over the course of fieldwork, nevertheless this sort of (sexual) relationship locates the fieldworker in a social world beyond the field. It serves as a physical and emotional marker, placing the fieldworker into a distinct personal context. Whether or not both partners are engaged in actual fieldwork, the fact that they are participating together in the everyday life of the setting helps to place them as distinctive from, though positioned within, the local socio-cultural setting.

These relationships have existed prior to fieldwork and are taken to the field intact. There are other examples of romance and marriage which occur *in situ*, during fieldwork. Fieldwork can provide the opportunity for the establishment of intimate, and in some cases long-lasting, commitments between the ethnographer and a significant 'other' in the field. Gearing (1995), for instance, fell in love and eventually married her *best informant* (*sic*) during fieldwork in the West Indies. What began as a productive, professional relationship became personal and sexual:

> As we spent more time together, discussing our respective family histories, I came to trust him and began to see him as a person I cared for deeply, as well as a person to whom I was strongly sexually attracted. I was also impressed by the sacrifices E.C. made to help me, and his refusal to take any money in return, even

though I explained to him how valuable his help was to me. E.C. was always considerate, was concerned about my safety, and often brought me small gifts of food or flowers.

The combination of personal and professional attractions was incredibly appealing, and actually impossible to resist. My intellectual excitement kept pace with my physical attraction as I learned more and more. (Gearing, 1995: 199)

For Gearing, her relationship and eventual marriage to 'E.C.' was personally fulfilling *and* fruitful ethnography. Gearing describes her fieldsite as a potentially sexually dangerous setting. Prior to her relationship with E.C., she frequently encountered sexual harassment and intimidation. Though she is absolutely clear that fear did not propel her into the relationship (and indeed she still received unwanted sexual advances even after marriage), her marriage did make it safer to visit places, and to collect data that would otherwise have been problematic. E.C. helped her gain access to men's perceptions of gender and sexuality. Gearing argues that she was also able to gain an 'intimate view of the erotic dimension of Vincentian life' (1995: 202). Her sexual relationship in the field became an important aspect of the fieldwork. While a rewarding and sexually compatible relationship, her marriage was also central to the construction of her self-identity within the field. It provided an opportunity for making sense of the sexual and cultural context in which she was living.

I came to appreciate the favourable attitude and sense of entitlement that many Vincentian women expressed about women's sexuality. From knowing one Vincentian man very well and by meeting others through him, I also learned about the wide diversity present among Vincentian men. (Gearing, 1995: 209)

There are other examples of romantic encounters in the field. Not all of them last beyond the fieldwork. Blackwood (1995) describes how her lesbian relationship ended on her return to North America, where there were no legal provisions in place for a lesbian to be joined by her foreign partner. However, despite the end of the relationship with Dayon, Blackwood provides an account of the relationship as loving, sexual and meaningful. It is difficult to separate her fieldwork experience and identity from this personal encounter. The fieldwork, and her memories of it, are interwoven with/in the relationship.

Long-term (and emotionally committed) relationships are one outcome of sex in the field, though they are by no means the only or indeed commonest experience of sexual liaisons during fieldwork. As I have noted elsewhere in this chapter sex can be part of the field setting, and entered into as part of the fieldwork (as in the case of Bolton, 1995). Our sexuality, and its expression in the field, is not confined to the negotiation of romantic or permanent intimacy. Sexual encounters do not need to be long term in order to be identified as epistemologically significant. Dubisch (1995a, 1995b) provides a good example of how her sexual encounters in the field were part of her ongoing identity work. During fieldwork trips to Greece, Dubisch had sexual relationships with two local men. The sexual encounters were part of a fieldwork process of locating herself within the field. Whether or not one has sex in the field, Dubisch argues that sexuality is an aspect of the self which may be particularly challenged by fieldwork. Her relationships with Nikos and Yanis were part of a process of realizing the complexity of the self. She suggests that Nikos and Yanis did not solve her confusion about identity during fieldwork. Rather her sexuality, and her sexual relationships, made her more aware of the complexity of identities and relationships that we bring to and take from the field. Dubisch's sexual experiences during fieldwork problematized and complicated her identity construction in the field. At the same time they made explicit some of the aspects of identity work that often remain hidden. Wade's account of his lovers in the field further illustrates this point.

> My motives for forming these relationships were not essentially about gaining access to information in a simple sense, but rather about a desire to transcend the separateness that I perceived as distancing me from a constructed otherness of black culture, by participating in a relation classed as the most intimate in my own culture, one not just of sex, but of 'love'. (Wade, 1993: 203)

Sexual intimacy is one sort of intimacy which can be experienced during fieldwork. It can symbolize one of the most intimate of relationships between researcher and researched (which is not to deny that sexual encounters can be casual, and far from intimate). While most of us do not experience sexual relations during fieldwork, many of us are faced with decisions over the level of intimacy and closeness with our informants and research participants. El-Or's (1997) account of intimacy and friendship with a woman during fieldwork in a suburb in Tel Aviv, near to her home, questions the scope for intimacy in fieldwork:

> Intimate relationships between researcher and informants, blur the subject–object connection they actually maintain. Being able to communicate on equal levels of everyday life, sharing feelings and thoughts, revealing anxieties, dreams or desires obscure the working bond they've agreed to preserve. Intimacy thus offers a cosy environment for the ethnographic journey, but at the same time an illusive one. (El-Or, 1997: 188)

While El-Or is not describing a sexually intimate relationship, her general point about the limitations of intimacy may be equally valid in such cases. El-Or questions the endurance of intimacy and reciprocal relations precisely because at the heart of fieldwork is the quest for information. Sexual relations during fieldwork blur the boundary between subject and object in emotional and physical ways. There is therefore a contradiction in discussing and *confessing* such relations. On the one hand it may be both ethno-graphically productive and personally important to be reflective about sexual encounters in the field. On the other hand by writing about these intimate relations in the context of fieldwork, the sexual encounter becomes part of the analysis of fieldwork. Sexual intimacy clarifies the boundaries between object and subject, researched and researcher, and helps us make sense of them. Knowing and writing about sex in the field simultaneously reveals the intimate possibilities of fieldwork and denies that intimacy as purely personal.

The sexual encounters I have discussed above have been framed in terms of personal gratification and, in some cases, ethnographic payoff. The relationships have been recounted as reciprocal and certainly as ones to which the fieldworker was consenting. In the literature on gender and fieldwork there are accounts of sexual harassment. These are usually, though not exclusively, told by women (see for example Gurney, 1985; Warren, 1988). Tales of sexual intimidation and harassment are usually referred to in terms of sexist language, gender joking, innuendo and inappropriate, unwelcome touching. On a few occasions this actually results in physical and emotional sexual assault. Moreno (1995) provides an account of sexual intimidation during fieldwork, which resulted in her being sexually and emotionally raped. Her example is highly illustrative of the fragility of field relations, and as such has significance beyond the immediacy of a sexual attack. Writing under a pseudonym she tells how her professional relationship with Yonas ended in rape. Yonas was employed by Moreno as a local research assistant. While clearly distressing, physically and emotionally scarring, the rape highlighted, for Moreno, the false dichotomy between professional and private. Moreno (1995: 243–4) remembers her feelings immediately following the violation of her sexual self: 'overwhelmed by a flood of information on gender relations and sexuality . . . I was in no position to record, understand, or utilise the material. I felt naked, a simple civilian, a deserter from the anthropological field'.

The violation of her body meant that for a while she was, understandably, unable to analyse the meanings of the encounter. However, on reflection, Moreno was able to use her experience to renegotiate her field identity:

> In the field the false division of time and space between the 'professional and the private' that underpins the supposedly gender-neutral identity of the anthropologist collapses completely. In the field it is not possible to maintain the fiction of a genderless self. In the field, one is marked. (1995: 246–7)

The violation of her sexual, physical self held, for Moreno, personal and ethnographic significance. The complexity of issues raised by sexual encounters during fieldwork are rife with both personal and professional concerns. As Moreno herself notes, time and space between professional and personal is not an absolute, nor necessarily a useful dichotomy in such contexts. As a sexualized, gendered self, the fieldworker is open both to the pleasure of sexual intimacy and to the violence of sexual intimidation. Both are deeply affective at the personal, private level of the individual self.

The positionality of the sexual self within the field is something to which several authors have turned their attention. In relation to sexuality, and more specifically to sexual encounters, a debate ensues over the relationship between the self and sex in the field. Wengle (1988), for example, has argued that in order for the anthropological self to remain whole and secure in his (*sic*) identity, celibacy is crucial. Celibacy in the field forces desire and sexual need to be located outside the field, at home and thus in a private sphere (and separate from fieldwork). Kulick (1995), among others, has expressed concern with this, arguing that the psychological argument put forward by Wengle effectively 'silences' sexual relationships and partners in the field. To deny our sexuality, sexual identity, partners and lovers is, in effect, to render ourselves asexual. It serves to reinforce a false dichotomy between the fieldworker self and other selves. This in itself denies the reality and complexity of fieldwork and the identity work that it entails. The self is positioned in a range of contexts – cultural, historical, political, gendered and sexual. As partial (Haraway, 1991; Strathern, 1991), positioned selves, the identity work we engage in during fieldwork cannot help but draw on these contexts of the self. Desire and sex in the field enables the fieldworker to experience a positionality at first hand. The fieldworker is able to locate him/herself as a partial, yet knowing self. Whether the desire originates from them, or whether they are the objects/subjects of that desire, they are able to use their experiences to locate the self and the fieldwork. Sexual encounters can be viewed as both personally and ethnographically productive. Sexual encounters and relationships can, in themselves, be illuminating. They allow for reflections on the fieldwork, relationships, people, the sexuality of others, the nature of self and the production of knowledge.

I have said little about the ethics of sexual encounters in the field. Most of the authors who have discussed their experiences of desire and sex in the field are all too aware of the ethical issues these involve. At one level there are lessons that emerge from Said's (1978) critique of sustained Orientalism. The erotic is quickly associated with the exotic, and in studying 'other' cultures ethnographers have been accused of exploiting and 'otherizing'. This is, of course, part of a more general ethical problem of power and exploitation in fieldwork. Sexual encounters perhaps crystallize these ethical dilemmas – cutting across the personal and the professional, as well as genders, sexualities, cultures, ethnicities, ages. Dubisch observes that as an intimate encounter, sex is not of itself bad or any worse than other fieldwork activity.

> We do almost everything else with our 'informants': share their lives, eat with them, attend their rituals, become part of their families, even become close friends, and sometimes establish life-long relationships. At the same time, we 'use' them to further our goals, writing and speaking in public contexts about personal and even intimate aspects of their lives, appropriating these lives for our own professional purposes. Could a sexual relationship be any more intimate,

committing, or exploitative than our normal relations with the 'natives'? (In some societies, it might even be less so.) (Dubisch, 1995a: 31)

Simply stopping with a crude consideration of sex in the field to some extent misses the point. The physical act of sex is positioned alongside emotion, desire, gender, culture, time, space and so on. Many ethnographers who have told of their sexual encounters are women, and even where the relationships have been long term and rewarding, they are often recounted in the context of the 'fear' of being a woman in a different culture/place/space. The point is, as Dubisch argues, that sex is but one aspect of the positionality of the self and the relationships that are formed in the field. Like other aspects it can be revealing and epistemologically valuable (as well as personally rewarding) if it is reflected upon critically and honestly. Gearing (1995) argues for an emotionally aware ethnography – and in doing so she recognizes that emotions can include fear, intimidation and hurt as well as desire, attraction, caring and love. The point she makes is that by ignoring our emotions we are denying they exist and hence denying that they do have an impact on the knowledge we produce. As she argues:

> I do not think that effective ethnographic research can be done without emotional engagement, and the pursuit of a methodology that ignores what we learn from our emotions is undermining the validity of the resulting information . . . in fieldwork as in all of life, sensation, emotion and intellect operate simultaneously to structure and interpret our experience of the world. Our emotional reactions, and those to which we interact, guide our analysis of life 'at home' as well as 'in the field'. (Gearing, 1995: 209)

Conclusion

I return here to the issue of talking and writing about 'sex in the field'. Should sexual encounters during fieldwork be counted as data and do they have impact on our ability to conduct fieldwork? Freeman's (1991) attack on Mead because of the affairs 'she might have had' during her fieldwork addresses the second of these points. Responding to what Landes (1970) describes as gossip about Mead's relationships, Freeman argued that Mead's personal sexuality discredited her ability as an ethnographer (see Bryman, 1994 for a summary of the Mead/Freeman controversy). While Mead's relationships are largely unsubstantiated, the accounts that I have presented in this chapter suggest this is at best a simplistic view and at worst a gross misunderstanding of the issues. There is, however, little evidence that they unequivocally hinder fieldwork. On the contrary in some instances they clarify and aid a better understanding of the process.

There are still relatively few 'confessions' which overtly refer to sexual encounters or desire in the field. *Yet* when they do, a lot of what is said does strike home. We are emotional beings engaged in fieldwork so it is perhaps surprising that there are not more emotional and sexual attachments in the field. Perhaps there are, perhaps we just do not talk about them. There is still perhaps the myth of the neutral, semi-detached, 'scientific' and 'objective' ethnographer in operation, in theory if not in practice. We should certainly not automatically privilege the accounts of ethnographers who 'confess' to sexual relationships in the field. The epistemological productiveness of such fieldwork relationships is dependent not on the sex act in itself, but on the ways in which the erotic subjectivity and experiences of the ethnographer can be harnessed to further understand the field and the self, and the boundaries and connectedness between the two. Accounts of sexuality and desire do have potential for an exploration of fieldwork relationships, their nature, basis and consequences. Whether we choose to talk and write about desire and sex will always be a matter of individual choice. Regardless, the sexual self is part of our being and part of the way we experience our lives. Not reflecting upon that silences the people with whom we forge relationships, engage in sexual encounters with, fall in love with, are sexually intimate with (and indeed intimidated by). Dubisch (1995a) suggests that sexuality is one dimension of the self, which may be particularly challenged in the field. Consequently it is both realistic and epistemologically valuable at least to confess and have the conversation with ourselves.

6   Romancing the Field

The concept of romance is not one readily associated with ethnographic fieldwork. Yet 'romance' conjures up many of the feelings and positions experienced in and beyond the field. Romance and fieldwork both encompass multiple personal dimensions. These include the erotic and the exotic; sexualities and physical desire; emotional commitments; long-standing friendships; deeply entrenched antagonisms; joy and pain. The personal and emotional qualities of fieldwork serve to emphasize the diversity of biographies and identities that shape and are shaped by the ethnographic encounter.

Personal relationships and commitments are pervasive in the ethnographic and the romantic project. Both exemplify the complexities of engagement with, and separation from, people, places and memories. In exploring the romance of fieldwork we are engaging directly with the emotionalism inherent in the qualitative endeavour (Gubrium and Holstein, 1997). Emotional sociology adopts the received sensibilities and methods of romanticism, going beyond rationalized analytic linguistic devices for understanding social experience. The desire and commitment to engage with the emotions in qualitative research has worn a number of guises. Gubrium and Holstein (1997) use the term 'emotionalism' to refer to the existential sociology of the 1970s (Douglas and Johnson, 1977), qualitative studies of emotion particularly prominent during the 1980s (Hochschild, 1979, 1983) and more recent calls for self-conscious emotional engagement (Ellis and Flaherty, 1992). As a research idiom, emotionalism has theoretical and practical meaning:

> it alludes both to the topic of 'studies of emotionality' and to many of its practitioners' commitment to convey, even embody, the very personal depths and passions of lived experience within their texts. (Gubrium and Holstein, 1997: 58)

The new idiom of emotionalism establishes the view that the fieldworker is cognitive and emotional. It has contributed to a new vocabulary for talking about fieldwork. For some, the re-enactment of fieldwork emotionality has become central to the development of alternative representational forms (see Chapter 8). The new emotionalism of qualitative enquiry thus captures a long-standing commitment to convey the affect of lived experience, while not separating the cognitive and the emotional.

The notion of the emotional fieldworker is not a new one. It has long been argued that conceiving fieldwork as a series of rational steps – access, rapport, field roles, self-management, writing fieldnotes, analysis and so forth – does little to capture the emotional contours of the experience (Johnson, 1975; Wolff, 1964). Indeed many autobiographical accounts of fieldwork (see Chapter 7) stress the deeply personal effect of fieldwork on the relationships, lives and understanding of the self. The metaphor of romance is a useful way of exploring some of these issues.

In this chapter I suggest that romance can be conceptualized as a process, a relationship and a collection of emotional feelings. Some of the characteristics of protracted research in a social setting compare with a conventional notion of romance. To illustrate this I have set out below a retrospective account of a romantic encounter. Imagine this being spoken as a love letter or a private diary entry. It is a way of reflecting upon the good and the bad of a deeply personal and protracted relationship.

Our courtship was slow and difficult. We stumbled into each other quite by accident and knew immediately that there was something there. It was difficult to describe at first. An attraction, no, more a curiosity. I was interested yet cautious about what I would find. I desired commitment yet was scared of over-involvement. I was concerned about rushing things, of it all going along too quickly. I needed to get to know you, to understand you.

We met briefly at first. I watched, observed you. We shared stories and pasts. We began to explore each other's feelings. I began to become emotionally attached, yet I remained slightly aloof. I was still cautious about getting in too deep, about losing myself, about our identities blurring, about losing my sense of independence.

At times being with you was so special. It was exciting and exhilarating. We shared new experiences, you made me laugh, you made me feel good about myself. You let me get close to you. I was so proud of you and of our relationship. I think in your own way you were proud of me too. You never told me but when you looked at me sometimes I could tell. I remember the time we first decided that we loved each other, although we were both unsure of what that meant. Being with you was fun, yet much, much, more than that. It was fast yet slow, vibrant yet calming. When we had been apart I could not wait to get back to you. I began to dread our times apart more and more. I needed to be there with you, to be part of you.

We did have our 'downs' too. I never thought of our relationship as stormy, yet there were times of disagreement. I would sometimes get angry over silly things. Sometimes I felt let down when perhaps I should not have done. I wanted to be the centre of your life, your existence, and yet I knew I could never be. Sometimes that was difficult. You had a rich, vivid existence of your own. I was important but I was not the totality of your existence. Perhaps the way it should have been. You shared and existed with others too. That hurt sometimes, especially as I gave up so much for you. At least it seemed like I did at the time. Despite my initial caution I did throw myself into the relationship. I wanted so much to be a part of your life, I gave up most of mine. I did so willingly. I was there for you all of the time. I stopped existing in separation from you. You were not part of my life, you were my life. I would have done anything for you, to be part of you.

Living with you was good, exciting and challenging; fun and rewarding. You taught me so much. You made me feel whole. You gave me a purpose and a place. But your indifference sometimes scared me. There were times when I felt angry, hurt and even physically sick. Your violation of my space, my body and my mind sometimes left me numb, confused, alone. On balance I could not have asked for anything more or less. I know I too was demanding and difficult; all consuming and, dare I say it, difficult to live with.

Eventually we both knew it had to end. Neither of us really wanted it to, yet we both admitted, privately at first and then publicly to each other, that we had gone as far as we could. I remember thinking that I did not know how I could ever live without you. You and I were so closely entwined I did not know who I was any more. I was 'we'. But we were tired of trying to make it work. You were feeling trapped and I was feeling more and more unhappy. I knew you so well I had stopped knowing myself. I expected more than you could give and I needed to move on, get out, find myself again. We had what is called a mutual separation of the ways. We told each other, and others, that we would remain friends. We would still see each other occasionally, we would 'keep in touch'. Yet we both knew that would not really happen. 'Mutual' meant mutual loss, anger and loneliness.

Too much had gone on between us; too much liking and sharing and then disappointment, but not hate. I never hated you and I know you felt the same. At least I think you did. We always said we would remember the good times. I was no longer in love with you, but I would always love you. I can still recall the good times (and alas some of the bad). Memories change and fade, but they still remain. I remember our first meeting (and our last). I still keep the images (both the real photographs and the pictures in my mind), the notes and letters we shared. 'Us' was a special part of my life and I hope of yours too.

The story told above is a reminiscence about a relationship beginning, maturing and eventually coming to an end. It is a purely fictional, and indeed clichéd, account of a romantic encounter. In writing it I have exaggerated the text, drawing on a genre often found in trade novels of love and romance. Although many of us would not choose to write such a letter or account, the experiences and reflections contained within it are ones with which anyone who has had a romantic attachment may identify. The account sets out the career of a romance, drawing on memories of the process and the emotions. From first meeting and courtship, through the highs and lows of intimacy, to the difficulties and joys of living together, and the ending of the relationship. In constructing the narrative of this romance I drew upon familiar aspects of a romantic genre, as well as exaggerated aspects of my own memories and experiences. As it stands the account refers to a romantic personal relationship. My aim was to give a flavour of the variety of emotional and physical feelings that such a relationship can bring. But the *same* account could refer to a relationship an ethnographer has with the field.

On rereading the account I am certainly able to conjure up memories and emotions relating to my own fieldwork in the accountancy firm (Coffey, 1993). On the surface this setting would not strike one as especially, or even marginally, romantic. Yet early encounters with the setting and the people were fraught with the awkwardness that might characterize the beginnings of a romance. Over the course of the fieldwork I became more confident of my place within the organization and more emotionally attached to individuals. I wanted to be part of the setting and felt hurt and embarrassed on occasions when I was not included in social activities. At other times I experienced feelings of belonging and warmth. Deciding to leave the field was not especially fraught, although consequently I found it hard to maintain some and sever other relationships I had made. The career of my fieldwork contained, therefore, a number of elements equally identifiable as aspects of a romantic career. Initial access to the field and the establishing of field roles can be fraught and exciting – it is a courtship of sorts. Relations with the field can be exhilarating and disappointing; joyful and painful. Over-involvement is an issue for many engaged in fieldwork *and* is cautioned against in texts on the conduct of fieldwork (see Hammersley and Atkinson, 1995; Lofland and Lofland, 1995). Yet this is countered by the reality that we do become physically and emotionally embroiled in the places and the people. To coin a phrase more readily associated with a love affair, fieldwork can be difficult to live with and to live without.

One of the essential commitments and working concepts of ethnography is participation or real engagement in the field. Ethnographic fieldwork works, and is meaningful precisely because we have a physical and emotional presence in the field. The way I remember my own fieldwork is with both fondness and regret – about things going right and wrong, about events being fun and disappointing. But the crucial point is that *I do remember*. I have very strong, long-lasting memories of what fieldwork was like, what happened, when, and how. Of course my memories and feelings have not remained static or constant – in the same way that our memories of romantic encounters develop and change through time and space. Over time and in different contexts people, places, interactions and events are remembered differently. Reminiscences are socially and temporally framed, but nevertheless are very real to the teller, can be made real to others. With romance come stories and memories. And our stories and memories imbue our fieldwork experiences with romantic overtones. We rely on our memories and reminiscences to reconstruct versions of the relationship we forge within the field. Moreover the commitment and feelings we had, have and remember are imbued with romantic connotations, emotional and physical meanings. This concept of romancing fieldwork provides a mechanism for further exploring the relationship between fieldwork, the personal and the self. In remembering and reconstructing fieldwork we romanticize and emotionalize the field, the people and ourselves.

First Love

There is a saying that you never forget your first love – and like a first 'romance' there is something very special and long-lasting about first fieldwork. For some ethnographers, particularly (but not exclusively) those working within the social anthropological discipline, 'first' fieldwork symbolizes the beginning of a lengthy, even lifelong relationship with a fieldsite and a people. Some devote their whole working lives to the study of one place or culture or one group of people. The collection edited by Fowler and Hardesty (1994) contains reflections on ethnographic careers by a number of anthropologists who have undertaken long-term fieldwork with particular sites. They note the ways in which long-term study enables history (and memories) to be created and documented:

> Long-term study also affords the opportunity for the development of a truly ethnohistoric perspective – one that covers the observer's own life as well as those of the people studied. It becomes possible to see the direction of individuals' lives as they grow up and play out different life-roles. This, in turn, allows a better understanding of the central values and practices of the culture as they structure and influence the lives of individuals within it. (Fowler and Hardesty, 1994: 4)

First fieldwork and protracted research experiences are symbolized by a ritual of 'courtship' whereby the ethnographer begins to get to know a culture, in which they will spend significant portions of the rest of their life. Ottenberg recalls this process:

> As graduate students we do not usually plan, before our first field trip, to devote our research life, or a good part of it, to the study of one people. Certainly I did not. Frequently, toward the end of his or her first research trip, the budding scholar considers returning perhaps to complete some unfinished projects, to probe in new directions, or because he or she has fallen in love with the people and the country. (Ottenberg, 1994: 93)

First fieldwork is not always a step along the way to a lifelong project. Yet even where it is not, first fieldwork can have a significance which lasts over and beyond the fieldwork, and the production of the text of the field. Ethnographers remember (often with a mixture of fondness and cringing embarrassment) their first major piece of fieldwork. Researchers often become known and remembered by their first major ethnographic project. It is relatively easy to think of social anthropologists who have become associated with specific places and peoples, from Malinowski's autonomous association with the Trobriand islands (Malinowski, 1922), and Mead's fieldwork in the Pacific islands (Mead, 1986), to Kenna's (1992) long-standing relationship with the Greek islands and Ottenberg's (1990, 1994) long-term fieldwork among the Igbo of Nigeria.

In other disciplines too, fieldworkers have become associated with particular places, often where they have conducted their earlier fieldwork. First fieldwork, especially where it becomes the subject of a major monograph or other piece of scholarly writing, is taken as an especially significant moment in the career of the ethnographer. Take for example the association between educational ethnographers and 'their' schools. There are many examples of school-based ethnography which can be seen as marking out the early careers of educational sociologists. Although many have subsequently gone on to undertake studies in other settings (individually or with others) we tend to remember and relate certain educational ethnographers to their early fieldwork. Ball (1981) will always be associated with 'Beachside' Comprehensive in the same way as Burgess (1983) is with 'Bishop McGregor', Delamont (1984) with 'St Lukes', Gillborn (1990) with 'City Road' and Lacey (1970) with 'High Town Grammar'. Similar patterns of long-term association can be identified in other fieldwork disciplines: for example, within the sociology of health and medicine, Dingwall (1977) and health visitors, Olesen and Whittaker (1968) and nurses, and Atkinson (1981, 1997) with the Edinburgh Medical School. Such associations do not mean that this is the only fieldwork conducted by particular researchers, nor the only fieldwork by them that is memorable. But their memories (and our associations) of that fieldwork are caught up with images of the special qualities of that early experience.

The memories of early fieldwork, whether or not it turns out to be the start of lifelong or protracted fieldwork, are particularly significant. First experiences of fieldwork often mark the *rite de passage* into a discipline and can symbolize the beginnings of relationships and research commitments. Burgess's study of Bishop McGregor school (1983), for instance, established a lifelong connection between Burgess and that particular school. Unusually for an educational ethnographer Burgess did return to the school on a number of occasions to conduct further fieldwork after his initial ethnography. In that sense his early fieldwork was symbolically the beginning of a longer-lasting relationship. However, Burgess 'interrupted' fieldwork in Bishop McGregor for other studies and other projects. His commitment to fieldwork in the school was not all encompassing or lifelong. Yet Burgess's reflections on his association present a particularly strong bond between the ethnographer and the school. In a discussion of that relationship Burgess (1987) begins with an almost fictionalized (and indeed romanticized) reflection. He writes in a particularly storied genre:

It all began under the fireplace in the Merston teachers' centre in October 1972, for this was my initial encounter with the headmaster of Bishop McGregor school. As we sat beneath the fireplace at the back of a crowded meeting we briefly chatted about what we both did and I was invited to visit Bishop McGregor school. Little did I think that this casual conversation was an important research encounter which could result in research projects, a research career and a research relationship. (Burgess, 1987: 67)

This narrative contains elements which could just as easily be found in a personal reflection on a new relationship, or a romantic novel. One does not need to undertake a detailed narrative analysis (for example as advocated by Cortazzi, 1993 or Riessman, 1993) to see how the structure of Burgess's account follows a specific narrative form. 'It all began', the evocative feature of the fireplace, an initial encounter in a crowded room, a casual conversation, the exchange of 'face sheet' information, the reflection that this (retrospectively) was the start of something. All of these aspects of the narrative are characteristic of the fictional genre of the romance novel. Yet Burgess uses them here to begin a reflection on his relationship with a secondary school in the UK and a headmaster. Not on the face of it a particularly romantic setting or encounter!

Others have similarly reflected upon how first fieldwork stands out in the memory as a significant moment and personal encounter. Kenna (1992) describes the ways in which we often remember early fieldwork experiences:

> [this] inevitably involves making a fool of ourselves, facing up to apparently overwhelming difficulties, and unravelling clues which lead to some sort of satisfactory explanation . . . it is no accident that it is the experiences of the novice which are so easily represented by standard fictional genres: the funny story, the fairy tale, the detective puzzle. Incidents of my 1960s fieldwork ('the night the well overflowed', 'how a hen pecked my bottom') have become set pieces to be retold to friends in Britain or in Greece, or used as anecdotes in lectures. (Kenna, 1992: 150)

As a social anthropologist, Kenna sets her fieldwork experience within a particular disciplinary framework. Fieldwork is an important status passage, contributing to an anthropological career (Coffey and Atkinson, 1996). First fieldwork is the apprenticeship in becoming a fully fledged member of that scholarly community. In that sense early fieldwork encounters may have personal career as well as emotional significance. First fieldwork can mark a crucial aspect of the scholarly apprenticeship. It often serves to demarcate a temporal phase in the ethnographer's biographical history. It may evoke memories of youth, or a career change (in the case of mature entrants to ethnography). For example Kenna's long anthropological association with Greece began as a young, single, postgraduate student. Memories of her first fieldwork combine anthropological data with personal memories of youth, status, relationships, dress, physicality and the body. First fieldwork marks not only anthropological and ethnographic time but also biographical and bodily time. She reflects that 'What I remember most clearly about that first experience of fieldwork, and what was consciously omitted from all my writings, was its extremely physical nature. Fieldwork memories are nearly all bodily ones' (Kenna, 1992: 155).

Kenna's body narrative is not romantic as such, yet the memories of how her body felt during first fieldwork, absent from her earlier writings but vividly encompassed in this later reflection, give her early fieldwork in rural Greece meaning above and beyond the collection of anthropological data. The *rite de passage* was not only disciplinary but also bodily and biographically located in time and place. Such memories take the ethnographer back to an earlier life, earlier feelings, a younger (and more resilient) body, a different status and a different time. While individual memories might not necessarily be happy ones, the overall picture locates the ethnographer simultaneously in the past and in the present – reflecting on physical and emotional change and continuities. Burgess (1987) continued to be drawn back to Bishop McGregor school, partly because it was associated with early fieldwork experiences and emotions. He returned both physically and emotionally to the field on a number of occasions. Burgess conducted his initial ethnographic study of Bishop McGregor School in the 1970s, and returned to study the school's transition to community college status in the early 1980s. He returned a third time during the mid-1980s to interview the headteacher on a regular basis as the head was preparing for retirement. It is clear that Burgess is and was reflective about restudying the school, and aware of the potential problematics of being over-familiar with a setting under study. Burgess justifies his continued involvement in terms of maintaining consistency in the research as the school undergoes change. However, his involvement with the school and its inhabitants goes beyond that purely methodological justification. Burgess felt he had a special bond with the school, one in which he was reluctant to let others join. When the opportunity arose for further fieldwork Burgess was not keen on sharing his school with other researchers.

> [Another fieldworker] would need not only to be acceptable to me but also to the head and teachers in McGregor school. Furthermore, what kind of person would need to be selected? Someone like me? Someone like I was ten years ago? Someone with similar sociological skills and educational interests to me or someone with different skills and interests? (Burgess, 1987: 88)

Burgess was aware of his ambivalence about disconnecting from the field. His long association with Bishop McGregor had become important to him professionally and personally.

> My involvement with McGregor school has been more than a brief encounter in a research career, for my association with the school, the head, and many of the staff has been a major part of my life. This poses a problem that other researchers engaged in short-term studies have identified, namely the problem of 'getting out'. But I have often asked myself, do I really want to 'get out' of McGregor school . . . ? (Burgess, 1987: 89)

While, unlike Kenna, Burgess is not so vivid in his account of first fieldwork, his reluctance to let go and his emotional commitment to the school and the teachers remain significant to the construction of his ethnographic career, and more generally his life.

It so happens that the two examples I have used here both represent long-term relationships with a fieldsite. First fieldwork symbolizes the beginning of a long-lasting relationship between an ethnographer, a place and a people. However, for many ethnographers first fieldwork remains significant to our biography and memory, but not a physical place to which we return. The first experiences of protracted fieldwork are experiences that we remember and reflect upon, as disciplinary and personally significant.

Our early experiences of fieldwork symbolize both socialization into an academic research discipline and a more personal status passage. They may become what we are best known and remembered for. Even where this is not so, early fieldwork usually represents a personal journey which we always remember and retell. The correspondence of first fieldwork to a sort of first love is significant in itself in trying to make sense of fieldworkers' sense of attachment to a field. Moreover it is highly demonstrative of the depth of personal involvement in fieldwork. Gubrium and Holstein (1997) highlight the metaphors regularly used in emotionalist methods talk – such as the 'pressure cooker' (portraying constrained feelings), and the 'tornado' (feelings bursting forth out of control). The metaphor of first love evokes long-standing memories of early fieldwork – of excitement and trepidation, fondness and sadness, personal growth and quiet reflection. In recalling and remembering we often romanticize the field and our place within it. Not all our memories of romance may be happy or fulfilling ones. Though usually they are personally significant.

Endings

To continue with the clichéd sayings, all good things come to an end. Certainly like many romantic encounters, fieldwork evolves, develops, changes and in most cases comes to an end. Sometimes that ending is planned for and expected. At other times leavings and endings are unexpected, sudden and unprepared for. There has been little systematically written about leaving the field. Two notable exceptions to this are Delamont (1992) and the collection edited by Shaffir and Stebbins (1991). Where individual researchers have documented and shared their leaving, the fieldwork has often been particularly emotionally charged. For example Cannon (1992) describes the difficulties of ending fieldwork. Her informants were women suffering from cancer, and leaving the field had enormous personal connotations for Cannon. She had built up personal friendships she felt she could not and did not want to walk away from.

Advice that is usually offered on leaving the field tends to be pragmatic rather than personal, concerned with the necessity of ending fieldwork, saying goodbye and keeping research 'doors' open. Lofland and Lofland give practical advice on the etiquette of leaving the field, in which they draw parallels with saying goodbye in everyday life. They offer the following guidelines (Lofland and Lofland, 1995: 63):

- Inform people of your plans ahead of time and try to avoid leaving or appearing to leave abruptly.
- Explain why and where you are going.
- Say your goodbyes personally.
- Promise to keep in touch.
- Where appropriate, keep in touch.

Easy! From this advice it would appear that ending fieldwork is a necessity to be skilfully managed, rather than an experience to be lived through. However, like personal goodbyes, leaving the field is not necessarily straightforward or unproblematic. Even where the research site is not especially emotionally charged, protracted fieldwork means investing personal time and emotions in a place and a people. Leaving the field usually also means leaving people and perhaps a part of yourself. It certainly marks the closing of a chapter of one's life. For some, the end of fieldwork symbolizes deep personal loss (see for example Loizos, 1981). Stebbins (1991), for one, is sceptical as to whether we ever truly leave the field. He suggests that we always remain in some way connected and involved. For many of us fieldwork is by no means an easy or straightforward task. We may indeed be relieved that we can get back to a life – separate from the lives of those we have chosen to study. Yet the 'place' of fieldwork cannot help but hold memories for us – good and bad – and hence leaving the field means leaving a personal and a shared space. That may involve physically moving or giving away possessions, and for some the loss of a home (in the case of social anthropologists who chose to 'live' in the field). For others it simply means not going there any more, and that in itself can be an emotional as well as a physical severing. The significance of the ending is not diminished by the physical location of the field. Even the best-planned goodbyes (and the most amicable) can be difficult and complex for a number of reasons.

The ending of fieldwork and leaving the field usually represents the end of a particular phase of an ethnographer's life and career. It may mark one stage of a disciplinary career, which in and of itself is emotionally charged. For example, doctoral students in social anthropology describe a post-fieldwork phase in their apprenticeship, often associated with a sense of strangeness or loss (Coffey and Atkinson, 1996). Leaving the field is also returning from it, signifying that fieldwork has been completed and an apprenticeship served. It signifies the beginning of a new phase; perhaps the analysis and writing up of the fieldwork, or the moving on to new sites and new people. Whether or not the end of fieldwork is so closely associated with a disciplinary marker, leaving the field signifies the end of an era, a distinctive time in our lives. It can mean a stopping or a moving on. It may bring relief or sadness, or both. The end of a period or phase of fieldwork is a temporal boundary of lives changing. Leaving the field often invokes the remembering of events, activities and interactions which have occurred in or during the fieldwork. Leaving may also mean writing about the field, rereading fieldnotes and transcripts, getting to know the field again, in a more physically distant, but not necessarily a less emotionally charged way. Leaving enables us to reflect upon the place of fieldwork, the people and the self; how they have interacted, engaged, identified and changed over the course of, and indeed beyond, fieldwork.

Ending fieldwork is a distinctive part of the process of ethnography. It provides a temporal and physical boundary between the field and the self. It heralds the start of a new sort of relationship with a site and a people – based upon the reconstruction and retelling of lives and experiences. For many, leaving is particularly difficult because it means leaving people, collectively and individually. Fieldwork is essentially relational and inter-actional. It is about making acquaintances, making friends (and occasionally enemies), getting to know individual social actors, often on a deeply personal level. Exiting the field involves ending these relationships, or at least altering the intensity and nature of them. Cannon's fieldwork with women dying from and living with breast cancer is an exemplar of the difficulties of completely leaving the field. The personal quality of the rela-tionship she had struck up with these women was extremely strong.

> Long before the fieldwork ended it became clear to me that I would not be able to completely 'leave the field'. That is, I knew that I could not (nor did not want to) say 'thank you and goodbye', and tell the women that I would not be seeing them again. Many told me that they 'could not say these things to anyone else' and Liz said 'But you won't be finished with *me* then will you?' (that is after the fieldwork was completed). (Cannon, 1992: 175–6)

While Cannon ended her fieldwork (in the sense of no longer undertaking research) she could not emotionally disengage from these women whose lives she had touched. Arguably it is right that this is so. Certainly, alongside well-rehearsed arguments of not getting over-involved, and maintaining an ethnographic distance, are the realities of fieldwork, often predicated on trust and personal commitment. Further there are important issues of trust and reciprocity associated with the practical, emotional and textual accomplish-ment of fieldwork (see the collection edited by Bretell, 1993 on the politics of ethnography which includes several examples on the issues of trust and reciprocity in fieldwork). For some, leaving the field may also involve leaving real romance, as Blackwood (1995) experienced. By leaving Indonesia and ending her fieldwork, Blackwood was also leaving Dayon, a woman with whom she had had a love affair.

> It has been five years since I returned to the U.S. alone, unable to bring my love with me because she had no legally recognised relationship to me. Although some of my heterosexual colleagues have returned from the field with their partners, I was forced to leave Dayon behind, effectively severing our relationship, because the U.S. embassy would not grant her a tourist visa. (1995: 70)

Disengagement from fieldwork is often more messy and drawn out than the advice we are offered suggests. Emotional disengagement from people may be particularly difficult, although simply not being part of a place any more can also be disorientating. Fieldwork provides us with a place, a purpose and a structure. The characteristics of fieldwork are not dissimilar to those of romance. Personal relationships provide us with emotional commitment, but also physical structures and social processes – perhaps a routine, a social life, material possessions. Likewise fieldwork also offers us a place to work (and often to live), rituals and routines. Ending my fieldwork in the accountancy firm did mean modifying some relationships and ending others, although I did not have the same emotional ties as Cannon or Blackwood. Yet my life had become interwoven with the people and the place. Among other things leaving meant clearing a cupboard and retrieving a coffee cup. Relatively small tasks in themselves, these symbolized leaving a place as well as a people. Once I had ended my fieldwork I came to realize that I had forged personal friendships in the field that could not survive unaltered on leaving the field and then writing up the fieldwork (see Chapter 3 for a more detailed discussion of friendship and fieldwork).

Furthermore, re-establishing a work and social routine which did not involve the accountancy office and its inhabitants was far from easy. In many ways I was glad to have finished fieldwork, and was at last able to reclaim my time and my previous life. Yet in parallel I felt sad at the ending (or changing) of friendships I had forged; guilty that I was no longer 'interested' in the people whose lives I had shared; confused as to what my future relationships with them should and could be. Lastly I felt physically disorientated without the daily routine of the fieldwork and the familiar setting of the field.

Lofland and Lofland (1995) suggest that on leaving the field one should promise to stay in touch where appropriate. Thus far, I have described the ending of fieldwork as a discrete and final happening where relationships simply stop. This is often not the case, and indeed it is a rare occurrence for fieldwork to abruptly end. Even where no further commitments or engagement are planned, most endings are phased. Indeed the ending of fieldwork is often rather hazy and blurred, not tightly defined or bounded. For some, leaving the field is temporary, rather than a permanent position, though this by no means excludes emotions, nor the rethinking of field relations. As I have already indicated, social anthropologists in particular revisit the same fieldsite over a lifetime of research. They spend substantial periods of their careers and lives studying and restudying one fieldsite. The goodbyes in this context are often transitional rather than absolute, marking the ends of phases of study rather than the ending of a relationship with place and people. The ethnographer will be returning. This may mean the refining and recasting of relationships but does not mean the end of the ethnographer's connection to the field. Even where this is the case, however, each goodbye, each leaving of the field may be physical and emotional, encapsulating many of the aspects I have already discussed. In addition, long-term fieldwork – where the ethnographer goes back and reviews fieldwork over a number of years – compounds the problems of endings.

Fowler (1994) undertook fieldwork among Great Basin Indian peoples in North America over a 28-year period. She notes that social anthropology is biographical from two perspectives, that of the fieldworker and that of the 'hosts'. From her own autobiographical perspective Fowler connects her biography with that of key individuals with whom she forged close personal relationships during her fieldwork. She notes that at times she would have stopped fieldwork altogether had it not been for those personal relationships and commitments. When she was not 'actively' engaged in fieldwork she continued to visit and telephone. 'Endings' in this context were forced by the death of these friends rather than her periodic leaving of the field.

> Long term relationships in fieldwork are not without difficulties. In long term relationships, especially when the people with whom you work are already elderly, you unfortunately also must watch the slow, painful process of their personal deterioration. Ultimately you witness their deaths. You reach a point in your fieldwork when you can no longer gather data from them as they are unable to give any longer. (Fowler, 1994: 163)

The ending of fieldwork coinciding with the dying of friends (and informants) occurs rarely. Yet such a final ending of fieldwork poignantly illustrates the connectedness of ethnographic data collection with the lived realities of the people we study (with). Like Fowler, Myerhoff (1978) experienced the fragility of life and death, during her study of elderly Jews. As they died they would be taking their memories of the Holocaust with them. The data Myerhoff was engaged in collecting relied upon both memory and life.

We invest ourselves in fieldwork, so it is inevitable and indeed proper that we will continue to have feelings, both good and bad, about that period of our lives. Through 'remembering' fieldwork – in analysing, thinking, writing, reproducing – we are remembering a shared past. We draw on our memories of what the place was like – how it felt, looked, smelt, tasted – and what the people were like – how they felt, looked, talked, laughed, cried, acted, worked, played, lived (and in some cases died). Quite properly, leaving the field never happens completely, as that would be leaving ourselves, our pasts and our memories. Endings, and leavings are important aspects of the process of ethnographic fieldwork. Whether as a temporary or permanent measure all of us who engage in fieldwork experience the physicality and emotionality of leaving a place and a people we have come to know well. It almost does not matter whether those experiences and memories are good or bad, and most of us will have some of each (even good things are less good some of the time). The significance of leaving the field is much more bound up with what that symbolizes. Leaving implies that we were there in the first place. In rethinking the emotional and personal context of fieldwork, leaving is symbolic of the reality of the fieldworker – physically and emotionally located in the research process.

Memories

Conceptualizing the romantic qualities of fieldwork, such as remembering first times and managing endings, highlights the centrality of memory to the whole research endeavour. Our memories are what enable us to reflect upon and locate our fieldwork experiences. Romancing the field is part of a more general argument that ethnographic fieldwork draws upon memory and reminiscence as craft skills. We rely upon our memories in the reconstruction and reproduction of the field and our place within it. Our memories are sometimes helped by other mementoes of fieldwork – such as audio tape recordings, video footage, still photography, visual or material artefacts and documents of the field. Our fieldnotes, and analyses, draw upon our collected memories and souvenirs. The craft skills of reconstructing and reproducing the field pivot on how we remember and what we remember. Our (re)construction is temporal and evokes the past in the present. Fieldwork is dependent upon the memories and reminiscences of our experiences, feelings, thoughts, actions, interactions and relationships. We know that the 'field' is not a pre-given entity, not naturally bounded in time and space. Fields are not discovered, so much as made through a recurrent process of transaction, interaction and remembrance. This is not to argue that the fieldworker or ethnographer 'conjures' up a false reality or constructs the field in a radical sense. Rather, ethnography is in itself an act of collective and individual memories. Texts of the field are constructed from data that are the memorabilia of fieldwork, and which are read with the imagination of memory. Fieldwork experience is a unique biographical episode which is retrospectively transformed by our memories and reminiscences of it (Atkinson and Silverman, 1997). Ethnography can be conceptualized in this context as an act of collective memory. The memories collected during fieldwork, and reproduced consequently, go beyond a private capacity to remember. The personal experience of autobiographical memory is understood and organized through socially shared resources, such as culture, language and conventional storied genre. These give shape to what is memorable and provide a more general set of principles for how it is remembered and retold. Memory is dependent upon and mediated by the social world. Moreover, the field and our connections to it are the outcomes of the devices of shared memory and the culturally defined means of framing memory. The accounts of the field are produced, and understood through the interpretive frameworks of memory and reminiscence.

Fieldwork and memory are linked on a number of levels. Our data are constructed through our memories of happenings *and* the memories of our informants. The people whose lives we share during fieldwork are just as influenced by cultural understandings and modes of memory telling and sharing. The collection of data through the construction of fieldnotes is the documenting of memories. We also have a much longer-term memory of the field, the people and our own position in relation to them. Many fieldworkers will retell and remember fieldwork experiences for years or decades afterward. We continue to write about and talk about particular fieldwork relationships, instances, events or feelings. Indeed it is quite common to see both reanalyses of fieldwork data and autobiographical accounts published a considerable time after the original fieldwork was conducted (and ethnographic monograph or text produced). At worst, most of us have funny or traumatic stories of the field that remain with us and which we continue to share with others. The very fact that the fieldworker was there, and part of the field, enables such reminiscing. This is perhaps less noticeable when we are writing up fieldnotes, yet here too we are remembering 'what happened' from a perspective of being there, thinking about, and then retelling (to ourselves). Fieldwork and ethnographic writing are, then, tied to the autobiographical and by definition the memorable. Both are framed and reframed by our own biography and lives, feelings and emotions, memories, stories and reminiscences. The (re)construction of fieldwork is an intertextual event. Remembering the field merges fieldnotes, memories, written accounts, memorabilia and personal biography.

I suggested earlier in this chapter that first fieldwork is evocative because it enables us to remember and capture a particular temporal moment of our lives – as first fieldwork is often done when we are young – academically and/or chronologically. Our memories of first fieldwork are hence often memories of our comparative youth. This has a more general point; that is our memories (and hence our fieldwork experiences) are always tied to and interconnected with our own lives and biographies. Returning to an example used earlier in this chapter, Kenna (1992) describes her 20-year anthropological association with the Greek island of Nisos, and reflects upon the changing nature of her relationship with the island and its people. At the same time she locates this relationship within her own biography:

> This long term association of mine with the same places and with people who regard themselves as in some sense members of the same community provides an opportunity to assess the significance of my own gender, age, stage in the life cycle, personal history and other factors for my fieldwork and writing. (Kenna, 1992: 147)

Kenna marries her memories of the field with memories of her personal history and biography. She first visited as a young, unmarried woman, she returned as a newly married woman, then later (and following fertility treatment) with her husband and a son. Her relationship with the place and the people, and her reflections on her analysis, is bounded by her particular place in the life cycle, her academic status and her physical age. As she reflects, 'changes in age, status and stage in the life cycle have altered my own perspectives and affected both fieldwork experience and analysis' (1992: 161). In her essay (Kenna, 1992) she presents two photographs of her fieldwork. One is a 'family shot' taken in 1966 of Kenna with three Nisos village children, a small boy perched on her knee. The four figures are smiling. The second photograph is of Kenna at the harbour in Nisos in 1989, with the same 'small boy' that was perched on her knee in the early photograph. The boy is now an adult man. While Kenna does not herself reflect upon this in detail, the juxtaposition of the photographs is in itself a powerful image of the connectedness of fieldwork, age, biography and memory. The photographs provide a visual memory of a personal, temporal relationship with a fieldsite.

Obviously Kenna's fieldwork makes it relatively easy to see the connections between the life cycle, personal history and our memories of the field. Where there is a long-term ethnographic commitment to a place and a people our lives and theirs are fundamentally interconnected, as Ottenberg suggests:

> In one time research the anthropologist does fieldwork, leaves and writes of that time. In long term research one is always writing of the new and relationship to the old, seeing people one knows change, mature, die, notching one's life experiences against theirs. (Ottenberg, 1994: 114–15)

We do not have to undertake long-term or lifelong research to establish the links between our own lives and the memories of fieldwork. Schrijvers (1993), for example, explicitly discusses her fieldwork in Sri Lanka and its relationship to her motherhood status. In undertaking fieldwork with two young children, her memories are also memories of motherhood. Indeed her relationships in the field are intimately connected to her status as a mother. In her narrative account she suggests that her experiences and friendships formed in the field, particularly with other mothers, were (almost) part of the reason for having two other children. It is at least difficult to disengage her memories of the field from her personal biography and experiences.

The interconnections of the personal and the academic, the biographical and the autobiographical, the emotional and the intellectual are played out particularly pertinently when we consider the craft skill of memory – and how that relates fieldwork as work and fieldwork as lives. Memories and reminiscences are always personal and biographical even when they are disguised as ethnographic *work*. The prompts and props we may use to help us 'remember' – audio and video tape, notes, artefacts, documents, photographs – can only give a partial picture of places, people and happenings. Our personal memories are also our ethnographic memories. As one informs the other, so too are they part of each other.

Our romance with the field, and indeed with fieldwork, is also then about romancing ourselves. The intertexuality of field, text and memory establishes the centrality of our own situatedness, not only in the social interactions of the field, but also in the shared understandings of its meanings. Romance in this sense is not necessarily memorable, but is remembered and understood in terms of our individual, and shared, temporal positioning and biographical moments. In the sense that our representations of the field are evocative of a past, they are also fragments of our present and future. For as romance fades, it remains in our consciousness – as a representation of aspects of our life remembered.

Conclusion

Romancing the field captures aspects of fieldwork which have been discussed in other contexts – the intensity and emotions, the attachments, the difficulties of separation, the thrill of the chase and the hurt of the ending; the relationship between ethnography and memory. Moreover by evoking the idea of romance, we can make sense, or understand why we cannot make sense, of the *feelings* many of us have about our fieldwork experiences, both at the time and for years afterwards. While there is much about romance which is tangible and accessible, exemplified by the genre of the romantic novel, there is also much that remains mysterious and inexplicable. The rush of the heart can, of course, be explained in pure physiological terms but that never really captures the preoccupation of romance at the time. Nor does such an explanation deal with the full extent and implications of what and how we remember those feelings as time moves on.

With the seemingly insatiable growth of texts on qualitative methods it has become more and more possible to describe fieldwork, qualitative analysis and writing in terms of *craft* skills, to be learnt, interpreted and practised. In a sense the craft skill of collective memory fits into such an approach. How we remember and the cultural frameworks within which we remember are in themselves craft knowledge. We have progressed far in the demystification of qualitative methods, passing on skills to new scholars and stressing the parity with quantitative methods in terms of academic credibility, the need for systematic approaches and so on. Such steps forward are welcome and have done much to establish the credibility of qualitative enquiry. That said, we should not lose sight of the romantic qualities of conducting fieldwork and writing about our experiences. This does not imply that fieldwork is blurry, less than serious or not real. Such an argument responds to the passion, anxiety and long-standing attachments that make fieldwork simultaneously transparent and mysterious.

7 Writing the Self

The relationship between observer and observed has always been the subject of debate and scrutiny. In recent years attention has turned to the interactional nature of that relationship. Our analyses of *others* result from interactional encounters and processes in which we are personally involved. Qualitative methods texts have always, as a matter of course, offered advice on personal field roles, the effects of context and guarding against over-familiarity or other potential biases. But increasingly, attention has been paid to how we make sense of and reflect on our own experiences, interactions and positions in the field. The self has been re-examined, written about, and to some extent celebrated in this process. Personal narratives have developed as a major preoccupation for many contemporary sociologists and anthropologists who espouse qualitative methods (Atkinson and Silverman, 1997). There is a widespread assumption that they offer uniquely privileged data, grounded in biographical experiences and social contexts. In parallel, the personal narratives *of the researcher* have been collected, told and celebrated; offering data on the autobiographical as well as the biographical work of field research.

It has long been recognized that ethnographic fieldwork has a biographical dimension. We are, after all, concerned with the observing, reconstructing and retelling of people's lives. In seeking to understand a particular social world we attempt to people that world. In writing and representing the social world we are primarily analysing and producing lives (Stanley, 1993). Conventionally this view of ethnographic practice has emphasized the *other* lives that are being observed, analysed and produced. The ethnographer serves as a biographer of others. In conventional accounts of the field considerably less emphasis is placed on the autobiographical practices of the researcher-self. Yet the ethnographer is simultaneously involved in biographical work of their own. Fieldwork is a site for identity work for the researcher. The aim of this chapter is to explore how this identity work is achieved through the textual products of ethnography, and how the self gets written into accounts of fieldwork.

Field journals of social anthropologists have often included a personal narrative. Private field journals have been used to record the personal place of the field worker; the feelings, emotions and personal identity work that come with prolonged engagement. The field diaries of Malinowski, which were eventually published (Malinowski, 1967), serve as a classic example of this sort. There has been a number of collections by anthropologists, that reflect a more sustained attempt to document the self in the process of documenting the field. For example, Okely and Callaway (1992) address the relationship between anthropology and autobiography. By presenting detailed autobiographical accounts of fieldwork, the collection emphasizes the role of the researcher as active participant and author. In Fowler and Hardesty's (1994) collection senior anthropologists present personal portraits of their discipline, their long-term fieldwork and their reformulations of the self over time and space. The essays demonstrate the simultaneous outcomes of fieldwork: learning about other cultures and learning about the self. In sociology and allied disciplines the presence of the researcher self has also gained prominence in recent years. The collection by Hammond (1964), while not specifically about fieldwork, was an early contribution to the 'uncovering' of the sociologist. Since then other collections (for example, Bell and Encel, 1978; McKeganey and Cunningham-Burley, 1987) have heralded a renewed visibility for the social researcher. Ethnographers have embraced a particular style of personal writing to produce autobiographical accounts as confessional tales (cf. Van Maanen, 1988). The 'confessional' has been coined as a mode of ethnographic representation that emphasizes the writing of the self into the process of research. Atkinson (1990, 1996) has noted that as a genre, the ethnographer's confessional tale encompasses and draws on literary conventions of the narrative or story, in order to construct a specific sort of text.

There is now a range of examples of those engaged in ethnographic fieldwork reflecting upon and rewriting the self into the texts of the field. These include accounts of how the research was carried out as well as personal reflections of participating, analysing and writing (see Van Maanen, 1988). Some recent collections recapitulate many of the general themes of the confessional in ethnography (for example Hobbs and May, 1992; Lareau and Shultz, 1996). Lareau and Shultz (1996) collect together well-known accounts to demonstrate the personal and social side of fieldwork. Many confessional tales like these deal with problematic aspects of fieldwork, such as the difficulties of access, immersion, departure, the collecting of field-notes and the maintenance of field roles. The conceptualization of ethnographer as hero and the conduct of fieldwork as a personal quest or voyage of discovery is a noted characteristic of the ethnographic confessional (see Atkinson, 1990, 1992, 1996). The ethnographer is often represented as a castaway or naive explorer; a social intruder who must learn to come in from the margins; an anti-hero who engages in a sort of 'pilgrim's progress', embarking on a quest to be accepted – along the way perhaps learning something about themselves. The confessional allows the ethnographer the opportunity to be self-revelatory and indiscreet about the practical accomplishment and problematics of fieldwork. This sort of text of the self is now relatively accepted by ethnographers and ethnographic audiences. They can be perceived as methods texts, serving to demonstrate the reality and unevenness of the research process.

They provide clarity of how methodological goals such as building rapport are translated into action. They provide insight into the kinds of factors other researchers considered when they stumbled into difficulty and the strategies – for example, of reflection and data analysis – that researchers used to extract themselves from their temporary woes. More to the point, they highlight the uncertainty and confusion that inevitably accompany field research. (Lareau and Shultz, 1996: 2–3)

While ethnographers have embraced the spirit of writing themselves into the process and practice of research (through the confessional, reflexive account) it is unusual for fieldwork accounts to centre or privilege the self. Many tales of the field are told in order to emphasize the social side of research, but not necessarily to prioritize it. There have been few explicit attempts to write about particularly personal aspects of ethnographic field-work experience, for example sexual relationships forged in and beyond the field (the Kulick and Willson, 1995, collection on sex and erotic subjectivity in fieldwork being a notable exception). Feminist scholars have engaged with the emotional dimensions of research in general, and ethnography in particular (Stanley, 1993; D.L. Wolf, 1996). Feminist epistemology specific-ally addresses the emotional dimension of the research enterprise and the tacit linkage between the production of knowledge and lived experience (Funow and Cook, 1991). This implies a fluid boundary between the self, the field and the outcomes of fieldwork. Writing the self into the ethnographic process can be seen as an attempt to present a more realistic account, although it may serve to do so in a crafted, self-conscious and even artificial way. The autobiographical mode of ethnographic writing reflects wider cultural emphases on self-revelation and confession, and an appeal to subjectivity and lived experience. Placing the biographical and the narrated self at the heart of the analysis can be viewed as a mechanism for establishing authenticity. In identifying the advent of what they term the interview society, Atkinson and Silverman (1997) point out the increasingly important role of the self-revelatory narrative. They identify this as a trend within sociological enquiry, but also note that it captures a more general trend in social, literary and cultural studies. The ethnographic confessional, and writing of the self, is highly illustrative of this trend. The confes-sional voice and the biographical devices of personal revelation serve to reveal and restore the self.

The narrative is therapeutic not only for the teller but also for the audience(s). Viewing, hearing, or reading a confessional interview invites complicity with the penetration of the private self. The dramaturgy of revelation and (auto)bio-graphical narration affirms the interiority of the self. It displays the emergence of a true self that escapes the bonds of private reticence. Reminiscence incorporates past experiences into the present performance. It also integrates the selves of memory into an essential and timeless self. Revelation displays a number of techniques of selfhood. Equally, they include affirmations of the essential continuity of the abiding self. (Atkinson and Silverman, 1997: 313)

It is still relatively common practice to separate the narratives of the field and the self. The variety of confessional tales and personal 'self' stories are still more usually written as parallel yet separate texts from the monographs of ethnographic research. The conventions of writing about the self often present the ethnographer as a split subject. There is an authorial monograph as well as a personal narrative. So while it is acceptable and deemed desirable to reconstruct and rewrite the self, there is still some ambivalence about how far such practices should divert the telling of the field.

The interconnectedness of the writing of other lives (the biographical aspect of conventional ethnography) and the writing of one's own life (autobiographical ethnography) is met with caution by some. The authorial purity of the ethnographic text has been questioned, as texts have become more messy and infused with the personal narrative of the explorer-author-ethnographer. Again this is not a uniformly held opinion. For example Atkinson (1990) argues that while a separation of the 'personal' and the 'ethnographic' keeps the account of fieldwork simpler and more straightforward, including the personal narrative does not threaten the purity or conviction of the ethnographic text. On the contrary Atkinson argues that by incorporating, fragmenting and mingling these texts, and by reinforcing the intertextuality of ethnography, the claims to authenticity may be strengthened rather than weakened. Writing the self into the ethnography can be viewed as part of a quest toward greater authenticity, and as part of a biographical project. It can also be seen as part of a movement towards the representation of voices in social research. In recent years attention has been drawn to the polyvocality of social life, and previous generations of scholars have been criticized for appropriating and effectively silencing the voices of others. There has been a revolt against monologic modes of authorship, toward an emphasis to 'give voice' – to others (and indeed to the author as present rather than as silent, though authoritative). Equally, and somewhat ironically, confessional or autobiographical ethnography may actually serve to privilege the self-revelatory speaking subject (the ethnographer). This leads to a different, though by no means more authentic reflection of the field and the self, grounded in an uncritical castigation of the personal narrative as 'real', rather than crafted and 'conventional'.

These general issues about (auto)biographical ethnography are explored in more detail in the course of this chapter, where I examine some of the ways in which we can and do write of ourselves in the context of our fieldwork. I draw attention to the ways in which the biographical and the autobiographical are connected in fieldwork and ethnographic representation. The intertextuality of fieldwork and auto/biographical practice are used as a platform for engaging with both conventional and new forms of personal narrative writing.

(Auto)biographical Writing

The products of ethnographic fieldwork take a variety of textual, and indeed, non-textual forms. Here, I concentrate on the different ways in which ethnographic textual forms have enabled a writing of the self. All ethnographic writing is to some extent autobiographical. We author texts from a perspective of having been to, and lived in, the field. Texts are written, crafted, shaped and authored by a knowing subject who has experienced the field. More specifically there have been self-conscious attempts to author a personal narrative of fieldwork and the fieldwork self. In order to facilitate an analysis of these I concentrate on some of the contrastive strategies and devices which have been used to accomplish a writing of the self. These examples offer a variety of mechanisms and approaches, though they are by no means exhaustive. Rather they serve to illustrate that autobiographical ethnography encompasses a variety of objectives and literary styles.

Before proceeding further, I should deal with an explicit omission of this chapter. While the intention is to engage with the variety of strategies for writing the self into the ethnographic text, I do not deal with alternative forms of ethnographic representation *per se*. By that I mean specifically formats such as ethnotheatre (cf. Mienczakowski, 1995) or ethnopoetics (Richardson, 1992). The literary turn in ethnography, set alongside a so-called crisis in ethnographic representation (see Atkinson and Coffey, 1995, for a summary), has broadened the ways in which some authors have conceptualized the ethnographic text. With this has come new styles of textual representation: poetry, dialogue, theatrical scripts. Embraced by these approaches has been a concern with the representation of voice and self as part of the rewriting of ethnography. I have chosen to deal with these approaches and attendant claims in the next chapter, under the more general auspices of the re-presentation of the field. In this chapter I concentrate more on the ways in which the self has been written about as part of the process and the products of fieldwork. In that sense this chapter deals with the more conventional approaches to writing the self into the ethnographic text.

Fieldnotes

> At times they are seen as 'data' – a record – and at times they are seen as 'me'. I create them but they also create me, insofar as writing them creates and maintains my identity as a journeyman [*sic*] anthropologist. (Jackson, 1990: 22)

The fieldnotes which we collect and *write* have always embraced the personal. Fieldnotes describe places and people and events. They are also used as textual space for the recording of our emotions and personal experiences. Often these different roles for fieldnotes are kept physically distinct. For example, it is not unusual for the fieldworker to keep separate sets of notes – in the form of descriptive or analytical notes and a more personal diary or journal. This is perhaps indicative of the uncomfortableness that we feel about including the personal as part of the fieldwork process. Maintaining a textual distance is a strategy for including, while at the same time distancing the self. Nevertheless fieldnotes are the textual place where we, at least privately, acknowledge our presence and conscience. The self is part of the reality of fieldnotes (Hastrup, 1992). Like any other text, fieldnotes are themselves literary creations, authored and crafted. And like other literary forms there are conventions about what we write and how we do so. In taking and making fieldnotes we are involved in the construction and production of textual representations of a social reality of which we are a part. At the same time as 'producing' a field, we use fieldnotes as a way of documenting our personal progress. Fieldnotes serve as private records, documents of a personal journey and diaries of our experiences.

While many of us will include a personal narrative in our fieldnotes, this does not necessarily imply any sort of public reading of the self. Although the production of fieldnotes, as the core of ethnographic work (Emerson et al., 1995), has always contained autobiographical elements, fieldnotes themselves are very private texts. Most of us will refer to them or quote from them during a writing of the field, but the notes themselves are rarely made available for public scrutiny. The extracts of fieldnotes which become part of a published text are selected by the author, and have usually been 'tidied up' in some way or another. For example, Geertz (1960) produced a compendium of his fieldnotes from field research in Java. This contained an appendix which describes how the notes were constructed, typed up and cleaned up for publication. In making his fieldnotes available at all, Geertz is relatively unusual. Audiences are not usually privy to original fieldnotes, as they were taken in the field. Even tidied up ones. Exceptions stand out, to prove rather than disprove this general rule. For example, the medical sociologist Julius Roth made his fieldnotes available to a small corpus of scholars, and Weaver and Atkinson (1996) made use of them in their detailed exploration of the possibilities of computerized and qualitative data analysis software.

In many analyses and finished ethnographic products fieldnotes are referred to and used – but remain somewhat elusive in themselves.

> While fieldwork (the typification of anthropological practice in the popular mind) has been a focus of disciplinary attention and while ethnography (anthropology's official public medium) is now also an object of unsettling critical analysis, fieldnotes remain largely obscured from view, even among practitioners. They are a 'muted' medium, seeming to be merely a means to an end or an end to the day. One wonders whether fieldnotes constitute a topic worth writing about at all and casts about for a proper analogy: are they like historians' archives, or like the notes historians take when they are in the archives? In view of the obvious

centrality of fieldnotes to our work, professional silence on the matter ought at least to raise suspicions. (Lederman, 1990: 72)

Fieldnotes provide a structure and a purpose to day-to-day field experiences. They are a step along the way to a published account of the field. At times, writing fieldnotes can be an unwelcome, time-consuming though necessary end to a day in the field. They provide a temporal and tangible reality to what might otherwise appear a never-ending and rather obscure form of social research. Despite this matter-of-factness, they can be very personal texts and therefore difficult to share. Fieldnotes are highly evocative. They serve as textual memories of fieldwork. It is notable that the Sanjek (1990) collection on anthropological fieldnotes contains essays that cover a wide range of issues including: the making of fieldnotes; how fieldnotes are used and changed; the reading of fieldnotes; and identity work. Yet there are remarkably few actual fieldnotes presented and shared by the contributors. Lederman, for example, finds the prospect of sharing her personal fieldnotes difficult:

> Among my own notes, my personal journals are the most orienting and accessible because they contain long, synthetic passages on particular topics. But perversely, they are also the most private of my notes. They are, in fact, what I imagine I would never want to make public, since they are as much a diary 'in the strictest sense' as they are a record of reflections on my reading and my field observations and interviews. (Lederman, 1990: 75)

Fieldnotes can be perceived as personal and sacred objects. They provide private textual space for the self, but do not necessarily contribute to a public autobiographical ethnography. The self remains hidden and distinct from the texts that are consumed and read by others. In some instances, fieldnotes do have to be shared. For example research teams may need to pool their notes, students share their fieldnotes with supervisors, or in graduate class (see Strauss, 1987). During my own doctoral supervisions I was encouraged to bring my fieldnotes for discussion. Yet I was careful to bring tidied notes, rather than my field notebooks. The field data I presented to my supervisors were selected and worked up. I did not show 'raw' data, nor did I show my field diary, where I kept a record of my feelings and private thoughts during fieldwork. My sharing was both managed and partial.

Scholars working as a research team may also need to share or pool fieldnotes to analyse and write. Yet because of the elusiveness of fieldnotes such practical issues are rarely acknowledged in the design of team-led ethnographies, nor openly discussed in supervisions. In such instances the self may become fragmented or multiple. Personal diaries of fieldwork may still not be shared, while fieldnotes take on a collective status. This sharing will still be limited *and* may still be based on fieldnotes that have to some extent been 'tidied up' for consumption by those who must share them. What may well be created here is a tiering of selves within the notes.

Personal, private fieldnotes become journals for purely private consumption: the place where the self is most prominent. Other fieldnotes become shared, worked at and perhaps 'rewritten' by a group or team – whereby the privacy and selves in the text are shared and have collective meaning. The public sharing of fieldnotes in this context (and consequent published textual products) may mask the self, or reveal not one but several versions of the self. The very fact that fieldnotes and field journals remain obscured, private and elusive is highly demonstrative of the personal qualities they embrace. As the building blocks of ethnography, fieldnotes serve as a primary space for personal narratives. While there is now a greater tolerance or expectation of the explicitly personal in the ethnographic text, the personal has never been subordinate in the 'private' world of the fieldnote. Fieldnotes are often messy, fragmented and complex creations of ourselves and the other selves in the field. For most of us they remain sacred and secret, as a personal diary of the experience of fieldwork and the development of self. Yet the reluctance on the part of ethnographers to share 'raw' fieldnotes does not detract from the importance they have in connecting the self to the field.

Partial Autobiographical Accounts

One of the most common ways of writing about the self is in a personal account of the research process, whereby the self is presented as a medium through which the fieldwork was conducted. The resultant autobiographical account is firmly rooted in an exploration of the research strategy. It is only partially autobiographical as it does not take the self as the subject of study or analysis. Rather what is presented are insider accounts of how the research evolved and developed: how access and relationships were nego- tiated and managed; what went wrong; what was rewarding or challenging. These sorts of personal account are often written as separate stand-alone pieces, rather than interwoven into a fieldwork analysis. They are often written retrospectively or for some specific purpose, for example as part of an edited collection on the personal experiences of research, or as a 'methods' chapter for a higher degree thesis, or as a methodological appendix to the main text (see Whyte, 1981). Whyte, for example, included an autobiographical account of how his fieldwork evolved as an appendix to the third edition of *Street Corner Society*. This personalized account includes a discussion of how the research 'site' (gangs of young men who hung around the street corners of an Italian-American community) was chosen; how Whyte developed his research questions; how he met and developed a relationship with Doc (his key informant); and how he went about the day- to-day fieldwork. Whyte describes his mistakes and the struggles which he experienced over the course of his research, and locates his own background as a context to the study. In many ways Whyte's personal account of his fieldwork is a classic confessional tale (cf. Van Maanen, 1988). He admits to a lack of confidence, and to incompetence and ignorance. He presents a narrative of learning by trial and error, of getting by, learning from mistakes and of surviving in the field. Whyte presents himself as human, with no exceptional powers. Confessional tales and the personal account of the research process are not limited to ethnographers. Indeed the humanizing of the research process has been one way in which the authenticity has been assumed. The confessional presents a subjective account of the research process which appeals to the privileged authenticity of narrated experience. Social researchers, from a variety of methodological standpoints and disciplinary traditions, have provided personal narratives of the research process. See for example Burgess (1984) and Walford (1987) on educational research, Roberts (1981) and Stanley (1990) on the conduct and experience of feminist research, and McKeganey and Cunningham-Burley (1987) on the research experiences of sociologists. More generally, the characteristics and qualities of the ethnographic confessional tale have been dealt with at length elsewhere (see Atkinson, 1990; Van Maanen, 1988). It should, nevertheless, be emphasized that these semi-autobiographical accounts are still relatively cautious in the way they write about the self. Usually located as separate from the ethnographic text proper, they actually serve to isolate rather than integrate the self, keeping the self distinct from the ethnographic analyses. Moreover the confessional is usually a wholly descriptive, rather than analytic exercise. The presence of the ethnographer is as a research instrument. Difficulties and dilemmas are problems for the research, that have to be more or less overcome, managed and justified. The writing of the self can be critical and self-revelatory in such accounts, though more often than not it is revealed as consequential or problematic or mediating rather than as central, integral or as a unit of analysis. In that sense the self remains partial, fragmented and semi-detached.

Tales of the Self

The sorts of personal narrative described above only partially relate the self to the fieldwork and the field. There have been attempts to locate the self more centrally as part of the subject and context of the research, by treating the self as a unit of analysis. Tales of the field have become, in these instances, tales of the self. There are different ways in which these have been written and constructed, and no one particular genre into which they neatly fit. Tales of the self represent ways of combining ethnography and autobiography in explicit and self-conscious ways. They serve as exaggerated examples of the ways in which the self and the field are interwoven, illustrating how, as well as collecting and writing the biographies of others, we are engaged in biographical work of our own.

The autobiographical can be used as a basis for ethnographic analysis and understanding. Take, for example, Delamont (1987) and Beynon (1987) who both used their personal experiences of hospital and surgery as autobiographical fieldwork (see also Davis and Horobin, 1977 where sick sociologists use their illness narratives to explore aspects of medical sociology). Delamont and Beynon both kept fieldnotes during hospital stays, gave conference papers based on their experiences, and published their analyses. While neither entered the hospital setting with the specific intention of making it a fieldsite, by taking fieldnotes of their experiences and writing them up they used the ethnographic method to write about the self. (Delamont initially started to take fieldnotes to relieve boredom and stress, and to be 'professional rather than powerless': see Delamont, 1992: 146–7). However, while Delamont and Beynon both write of their experiences in a personal way, they remain cautious about their contributions to scholarship. Delamont, for example, notes the difficulty of compromising her personal preferences and her perceived fieldwork needs:

> As a good fieldworker I should have moved out of the single room three or four days after the operation onto the larger Nightingale Ward, but when the sister offered me a chance I stayed put alone. (1987: 141)

Similarly Beynon played down the authority of his account by stressing that 'it must be clear at the outset that this paper is not presented as a serious contribution to the ethnography of hospital life' (1987: 144). Beynon describes his 'fieldwork' as journalistic, rather than a serious attempt at research or the formulation of theory. Neither Delamont nor Beynon use their 'tales of the self' as reflexive pieces on the relationships between the self, the field and the text. Indeed the self remains strangely distant, almost something to be apologized for. The essays are definitely autobiographical, in the sense that they recount personal experiences. But they do not claim to be using ethnography to understand as well as write the self.

A very different approach to the writing of the self is taken by Sparkes (1996), also drawing on the theme of illness. His ethnographic body narrative is extremely personal and highly reflective. Sparkes is much more explicit about the body self in his narrative than either Delamont or Beynon. Using extended diary entries and personal conversations Sparkes reconstructs his failing body self over his biographical career. His body and self are not adjunct to the writing, but centrally positioned. Sparkes acknowledges that this gives a performative quality to the autobiographical-ethnographic project. The extract below is indicative of this:

> Stopping for a rest I turn toward Kitty, my wife, who is 6 months pregnant 'Déjà Vu' I say to her, 'It's happening again'. The tears well up in her eyes and we hold each other close in the corridor. I kiss her on the cheeks. I kiss her eyes. I want to drown and be saved by the blueness of those eyes. As the roundness of her stomach presses against me a wave of guilt washes over me. Kitty is pregnant, so tired, caring for Jessica our daughter (3 years old at the time) and now having to worry and cope with the stress of me and my body failure. My uselessness makes

me angry with my body. At that moment I *hate* it intensely. (1996: 468; emphasis
in original)

There is, of course, a debate as to whether these personalized accounts
actually constitute ethnographic writing, something to which I return in
Chapter 8. However, as Sparkes presents his text as ethnography I have
chosen to include it here. Sparkes presents a rather different, self-centralized
approach to ethnographic writing and tales of the body. His combination of
the personal and the ethnographic is explicit and foreshadowed – forming
the pivot rather than the apology in the text. The account can be located
within a new wave of autobiographical writing which focuses on the body
and the self. (For highly personalized ethnographic accounts of illness see
Kolker, 1996; Paget, 1993.) They are qualitatively different from the
confessional or semi-autobiographical accounts, though they may still be
presented as separate from an ethnographic monograph as conventionally
understood. These kinds of tales use ethnographic analyses and writing to
explore the self. They centralize rather than add the self. The emphasis is on
the analysis and the writing of the self, and the relationship between the self
and the field. These texts do not apologize for the presence of the self, nor
are they simply accounts of the research process. Engaged with viewing the
self as an integral part of the field, not easily separated from the analysis,
they take the idea of the confessional into relatively new territory. Collections of essays which attempt to engage with a recentring of the self in the
writing of the field include Okely and Callaway (1992), D.L. Wolf (1996)
and Kulick and Willson (1995). The participating self is an explicit vocality
in these texts and it becomes difficult to separate the personal narrative from
the narrative of the field. These are not accounts of the naive incompetent,
overcoming adversity and difficulty, in the quest for data. Rather the self and
the field are seen as symbiotic, and the writing seen as establishing the
interconnectedness of the two. The process of writing thereby adds 'critical
reflection to our ongoing task of making sense out of who we are and what
it is we do' (Agar, 1986: xi).

The movement towards more autobiographical ethnographic texts is in
some part due to the literary turn in the social sciences generally. Other
contemporary movements, such as postmodernism and feminism, have
contributed to an understanding that texts should be more emotional,
personal and complex. Earlier texts which claimed an autobiographical
aspect seem rather impersonal and guarded when placed against these new
forms of autobiographical-ethnographic writing. There has a been a movement away from emphasizing the personal aspects of the research process
towards viewing it as fundamentally personal. The positionality of the self is
the starting point for such accounts. The narratives of the self parallel, and to
some extent consume, the narratives of the field. The selves that are
constructed and written are complex and relational. They are not research
instruments, or props. Rather they are gendered, racialized, sexualized,

embodied and emotional. In contrast to fieldnotes (which are often private) and the partial autobiographical accounts (which are usually orientated to the research process), ethnographic writing which locates the self as central gives analytic purchase to the autobiographical.

I return to how the self is written, in terms of alternative writing styles in the next chapter. What I have done here, is to provide different ways in which the self is embedded in the ethnographic text. The three cases of fieldnotes, partial autobiographical/confessional and tales of the self represent contrastive approaches. Moreover they construct different selves. Fieldnotes construct a private self and the confessional presents a questing, working, research self. The more overtly autobiographical writings present fragmented and multiple selves, embedded in and connected to the field and the text, in often complex ways. What links them is the way in which they all point towards the (auto)biographical work that is inherent to the ethnographic project. In the next section I explore this further by returning to the relationship between autobiographical and ethnographic work and writing.

Connecting Lives

An emphasis on the autobiographical side of fieldwork and ethnographic writing can be a productive way of encapsulating ethnography. It enables a focus on the production and representation of lives which we engage in through fieldwork practices. I am not advocating that autobiography should somehow supersede ethnography, nor that our texts should be full of ourselves, to the neglect of others. At the very least, I am acknowledging that as we are part of the field, so we are involved in its authorship and representation. To remain silent is to deny our existence and our biographical place. Charmaz and Mitchell (1997) challenge the myth of silent authorship in ethnographic writing. They argue that as there is merit in humility and deference to subjects' views, and reasoned, systematic discourse, so too there is merit in 'a visible authorship' (1997: 194). They dismiss the view that the words of ethnographers are magical or necessarily authoritative. Of themselves they do not necessarily make an account any more authentic. Charmaz and Mitchell do not share the cynical belief that ethnography, *because* of the author's voice, is a biased irrelevancy. What they advocate is a middle position which calls for a vocal text. As healthy sceptics of so-called new representative forms (see Chapter 8), Charmaz and Mitchell argue that there is a need to put ourselves in the text; to be seen to be there as an active participant:

> We do ourselves and our disciplines no service by only telling half-tales, by only reporting finished analyses in temperate voice, by suppressing wonder or perplexity or dread. Alternatively, writing tricks and data transformations may distract us, but they do not guarantee a clearer tale or a greater truth. Turning Henry and Ric

into iotas of a path model or changing John and Patricia into stanzas of a song will not make their lives more vivid or true than candid description. Henry and Ric and John and Patricia have every right to expect us to represent their lives as something more than scientific artifacts or art objects. In ethnography, the emergent self is acculturated; it learns the limits of its own power. Fieldwork leavens immodesty but it does so imperfectly. And that is good. (1997: 212–13)

The general point here is that texts are authored and peopled by a participating self. From this perspective the self should be present and emergent in the text. Establishing an autobiographical voice in the text is not an excuse for an unattributed celebration of the self. On the contrary, writing in the self can be a strategy for a more reflexive practice. In order to explore this further I will now highlight some of the connections and commonalties between (auto)biographical practice and ethnographic representation.

Memory and Reminiscence

Ethnographic fieldwork is a lived reality and relies upon the experiences of being there. Like autobiographical practice, ethnography is about experiencing and remembering; ordering and giving frameworks to our memories. Our fieldnotes form part of our world of private memories (Bond, 1990), and are often used as triggers for memories we did not write down. Our memories of the field go beyond the textual and visual artefacts we collect. In much the same way souvenirs of our life (the schoolbook, the teddy bear, the piece of ribbon) help us to remember and reconstruct far more than is materially saved. Fieldnotes get combined with headnotes (Sanjek, 1990) – our ever-evolving memories of the field. Memories are individual and collective, the result of shared experiences and individual quests. In the process of ethnography we collect our own memories and the memories of social actors with whom we are sharing a field. Ethnography is an act of memory. Moreover, as Atkinson (1996) has noted, the memory that is brought to bear is both uniquely biographical *and* collective. The personal experience of autobiographical memory is organized through socially shared resources. We draw on cultural meanings and language to shape our memories and to provide a framework for remembering. Hastrup (1995) clarifies a distinction between recollection and memory, and in doing so helps to establish the centrality of memory to our ethnographic *and* autobiographic experiences. Recollections, she suggests, are imprinted: eternally present in one's life they cannot be erased.

> Memories on the other hand, are placed in the time they are remembered, narrated, reinterpreted, sometimes rejected and often forgotten. Recollections are immediately experienced. Memory makes a critical difference to these: in being remembered an experience becomes a memory. (Hastrup, 1995: 102)

Memory and reminiscence are pivotal to both autobiography and ethnography. Moreover they serve to directly link the two. We cannot separate fieldwork, and our consequent texts, from the memories that shape them. In turn, those memories are part of our own biographical work, giving temporal meaning to our experiences.

Narrative Themes

The narrative themes of biographical and autobiographical practice are also themes which are present in ethnographic texts. Although relatively little systematic attention has been paid to the narrative qualities of the data that ethnographers collect, the ethnographic text portrays the social world as a series of patterned and understandable events, actions and characters by virtue of a narrative approach. People's lives are narrated and arranged – conveying sequences, consequences, time, causality, structure and agency. There are a few ethnographies which are wholly and explicitly narrated (for example, see Festinger et al. *When Prophecy Fails*, 1964; Krieger's *Hip Capitalism*, 1979b or *The Mirror Dance*, 1983). More generally, all ethnographic writing draws on narrative conventions and the genre of story-telling to create and people the social world. Ethnographies contain and construct memorable, almost heroic, characters in the same way that life histories and biographical accounts centre and emphasize the character. Atkinson (1990) has remarked that *The Jackroller* (Shaw, 1966) is actually an (auto)biographical account of the central character. This life-history approach to ethnography provides a detailed understanding of an individual as well as the social setting. In more conventional ethnographies, individual social actors are not so prioritized, the life story is not the primary goal. However, characters are still narratively constructed, through episodes, events and the context of the setting. Lives still get constructed and told, but as exemplars of the social setting and social processes. So the 'corner boys' of Whyte (1981) or Liebow (1967) are characterizations of the street corner societies in which they are located, as the 'brotherhood boys' are to North American biker culture (Wolf, 1991), or the college freshman to college life (Moffatt, 1989).

These forms of peopled narrative can also be found in biographical writings. Alongside the singular hero, many biographies are exemplars – the footballer, the actor, the politician and so on. Episodes and events are used to construct a life or lives in terms of the social or cultural setting to which they belong. Ethnographies also draw on strategies of narration, in similar ways to biographical writing. In both we can identify accounts and stories of great achievement, adversity, fear, celebration, determination and so forth. For example the women lawyers of Pierce's study (Pierce, 1995) are presented as developing strategies to succeed 'against the odds' of gendered expectations and organizational dynamics, while Fordham (1996) chronicles the struggle of identity construction for African-American students in terms of success and failure, challenges and tribulations. The ethnographer's tale or confessional is loaded with the narrative props of the story. As a now well-established genre, the ethnographic confessional invites particular kinds of writing style, readings and responses. The confessional draws on the conventions of the good story. Atkinson (1996) in analysing the confessional accounts of urban ethnographers identifies a number of stock themes. Failure and success, heroes and helpers, tests and dangers, hardship and fortitude. These sorts of conventional narrative themes are the stock-in-trade of autobiographical and biographical writing, as well as ethnography.

Hastrup (1995) uses the concept of allegory to describe the processes of ethnographical and biographical writings. Allegory refers to a narrative practice in which the text continually refers to other patterns of ideas or events without assuming identity with them. The allegoric nature of ethno-graphy acknowledges the storied qualities inherent within it. In that sense ethnographic representation is creative. And with that, ethnographic pres-ence is a precondition for representation proper. Hastrup's (1995) experi-ences of her biography performed on stage highlight the creativity of ethnographic representation. Her experiences of being the subject of a play about a woman anthropologist were pivotal in linking the ethnographic with the biographic. The intersubjectivity of anthropology was revealed to her as she was both 'fieldworked' and performed.

> I could neither identify with nor distance myself from Kirsten on stage. She was neither my double nor an other. She restored my biography in an original way, being not me and not-not-me at the same time. I was not represented, I was performed. (Hastrup, 1995: 141)

Hastrup's 'performance' is a striking and unusual link between the narrat-ives of biography and ethnography, though indicative of a more general argument that it is often difficult to separate the two. Both share genres, conventions, and to some extent common aims.

Voicing the Text

The production and analysis of lives through ethnography and (auto)bio-graphy are concerned with the giving or restoring of voice. This may be the authoritative voice of a present narrator, or story-teller. Equally, the repre-sentation of lives can restore a polyvocality to the text – suggesting multiple versions of multiple realities; an understanding of lives and selves shaped by different and varied voices. Take for example Krieger's study of a radio station, *Hip Capitalism* (1979) and her ethnography of a lesbian community, *The Mirror Dance* (1983). In both of these, she explicitly creates and represents a multiplicity of voices in the text. The stylistic qualities of Krieger's work have been commented upon elsewhere (see Atkinson, 1990). What is very clear from her ethnographic monographs is her attention to the representation of social actors *accounts* and *reflections* (plural). Her resultant texts are fragmentary or 'messy', peopled by accounts and narratives, chopped up, selected and represented. In *The Mirror Dance* the voices of the women in the community interweave with each other and comment on one another. Krieger's writing rejected conventional ethnographic writing styles as she attempted to recreate and people her social worlds. As such her texts have a non-linearity and a complexity absent from some other ethnographic representations. In her later writings Krieger (1985, 1991) engages with her own voice in the text. Her self and her voice are subsumed back into the voices of the mirror dance community, hidden from view. Krieger's early dissatisfaction with her sense of estrangement during the fieldwork and writing of *The Mirror Dance* led her to call for a fuller recognition of the individual perspective in social science and a requirement for the writer to be present in the production of the text. Mykhalovskiy (1997), for one, has expressed reservations at Krieger's conclusions that a social science should and does reflect the unique personal selves of its writers. Mykhalovskiy argues that such a position relies on romantic notions of an inner self and promotes an individualization of knowledge. This is, of course, part of the much broader debate about the authenticity of the personal narrative, and the cultural significance of self-revelation, referred to in the introduction to this chapter. For our purposes here, however, the importance of voice (or voices) is in the ways in which ethnography and biography can both give and silence voice.

Exchange and Reciprocity

The practice of ethnography relies upon the exchange of lives, selves and voices. It is about personal communications, face-to-face interactions and encounters. And it is then about the writing and representing of these. Fieldwork involves the coming together of lives and biographies – those of ethnographers and others sharing the research endeavour – all involved in the negotiation of the telling of individual, collective and cultural lives. How this is achieved and how explicitly it is perceived as a shared activity is open to some debate and question. Yet, like biographical practices and writing, ethnography is implicitly about the sharing of lives and experiences. We share and help to tell the lives of others, while simultaneously sharing and constructing our own biographies. There is little question that, through our fieldwork and our representations of it, we are engaged in the construction of the lives of others. Those constructive practices are not always shared or agreed. Bretell's collection *When They Read What We Write* (1993) explores how the sharing of our writing and constructions can be both rewarding and harrowing. By taking our writing back to those we write about, the implied reciprocity of ethnography can be both challenged and confirmed.

It is less usual to acknowledge the ways in which we share our lives with others in the field. There are, of course, instances of personal friendship and private sharing. More generally though, the people and place of our studies are implicitly involved in the shaping, crafting and reconstructing of our lives and identities. Our own selfhoods are defined and interpreted by others in the field, as well as ourselves as biographical actors. The construction of self is, as I suggested in Chapter 2, a multiple and shared process, though it is relatively unusual for our lives to be written and reconstructed for a readership, other than ourselves. Yet this does not detract from the realization that biographical and autobiographical work is accomplished by all social actors in the field, all active in the interpretation and 'rewriting' of lives.

Embodied Auto/biography

The narrative construction of lives encompasses not only a social being but a physical being. Lives are embodied. Fieldwork involves placing our physical, embodied selves among the lives, selves and bodies of others. In responding to a need to rethink our lives as embodied experiences, we are recognizing the ways in which we experience and reconstruct our fieldwork selves and lives in bodily ways. Connecting and writing lives is also about connecting and writing about the embodiedness and physicality of the self. The peopling of biography and ethnography is physical as well as social and cultural. In writing ethnography, we are engaged in a practice of writing and rewriting the body. This does not only include the writing of other bodies, as performers and physical entities of the social world. We are also engaged in responding to and writing our own bodies – as well or sick or fit or hurting or exposed or performing. It is possible through autobiographical ethnography to capture and emphasize the physicality of fieldwork and the embodiedness of the fieldworker. Autobiography gives us the tools to connect emotionally with the field. It also connects the physical self to the place and representation of fieldwork. 'I was there' evokes physical as well as mental meaning and presence.

Conclusion

By exploring some of the relationships between autobiography and ethnography I am not arguing that they are the same practice, with the same ends. Rather in addressing the intertextuality of the two, I am advocating that there is merit in thinking creatively about how the self does, and whether it should, get written into ethnographic texts (see Reed-Danahay, 1997). There has been some sustained justification for the presence of the autobiographical in sociology, anthropology and related disciplines, especially related to claims over the authenticity of the self-revelatory personal narrative. This debate has had particular significance for those engaged in ethnographic fieldwork, where the production and analysis of lives is a central tenet, and where well-established forms of analysis (such as self, life course, career) sit readily alongside biographical practices. Biography, the telling and positioning of lives, has always been implicit in what field-workers do. Making the practice explicit allows for the discussion of its epistemological, methodological and theoretical justification and relevance. Locating autobiographical practice alongside ethnographic representation engages with a resocialization of the individual social actor. Biographical ethnography can aid the steering of a course 'between the over-determinism of some varieties of socialisation theory, and the opposite extreme of seeing selves as extremely unique individuals which are the product of inner psychological processes' (Stanley, 1993: 2). It allows for a view of the (ethnographic) author as an active creator or producer of knowledge, and in part a product of knowledge and social life produced by others. Hence it helps to conceptualize (1) the self as an analytical topic rather than an inert research resource; (2) the intertextual links between reality and representations of reality; and (3) life or 'lives' as the products of biographies that are inextricably interwoven and networked.

Hertz (1997) makes the distinction between reflexivity – having an ongoing conversation about experience while simultaneously living in the moment – and voice – presenting the author's self while simultaneously writing the respondents' accounts and representing their selves. I have been most concerned, in this chapter, with voice, and reflections upon how the presentation of self is accomplished alongside the accounts and representations of other selves. Hertz draws our attention to the ethical considerations of voice in qualitative writings and these should be part of our reflections on the relationship between autobiography and ethnography. The boundaries between self-indulgence and reflexivity are fragile and blurred. There will always be the question about how much of ourselves to reveal. Moreover there is a question of balance between the voice of ourselves, as knowing subject/object, and the desire to recognize and reveal the voices of others. As we seem to be moving towards more self-revealing, more explicitly (auto)-biographical texts, issues of permission (to use 'voices') and confidentiality are vexed. Hertz, for example, argues that the more we display the individual and the more we allow others to speak for themselves, the more difficult it becomes to guarantee anonymity. Equally, as texts become more personal and more vocal, the less meaningful categories of confidentiality and anonymity actually become.

I return to a central criticism levelled against the autobiography in the ethnographic. To some extent we cannot escape an autobiographical slant to all of our writing. In authoring we are responsible for the personal crafting of the text. Yet are we in danger of gross self-indulgence if we practise autobiographical ethnography? Should we endeavour to balance the visible authorship of the ethnography against becoming a distinctive part of its analytic content? Mykhalovskiy (1997) suggests that autobiographical sociology *per se* is not necessarily narcissistic or self-indulgent. His epistemological justification for denouncing such a challenge is based on a belief that autobiography can be productive in the ways we think about the process of writing and reading. Mykhalovskiy argues that the charge of self-indulgence levelled against autobiographical product is actually ironic, as it inevitably gives support to 'a solitary, authorial voice who writes a text disembodied from the individuals involved in its production' (Mykhalovskiy, 1997: 246). His argument is that personal experience *present* in the text can be a source of insightful analysis. Autobiographical writing reacts against the *insularity* of intellectual, academic or disciplinary writing. Rather than speaking only to itself, the autobiographical product has a wider appeal. Furthermore it works against, rather than contributing to, the alienation of the writer from the reader. Mykhalovskiy argues that his own autobiographical writing (see Peters, 1993) challenged him to actively think about and engage in relationships with his audience as readers. It enabled the problematizing of authorship, not its passive acceptance. Autobiographical texts can, just as with any text, allow for the possibilities of multiple and critical readings. Indeed revealing the self in the text can highlight the tensions and contradictions of dichotomies such as self/other, writer/reader, and author/audience. Individual and collective experiences are connected and linked in productively meaningful ways rather than denied or forgotten.

The position articulated by Mykhalovskiy implies a general dissatisfaction with texts which do not 'reveal' the ethnographer. Yet how far self-revelation goes is still a matter of some dispute. There is general agreement that 'silent' authorship – writing the text without a visible presence – works against the contemporary spirit of ethnography. Beyond that, however, there remains considerable debate over the degree to which texts should represent the field or the self or both. While it has not been my intention to resolve this dilemma, I have shown that the self can be revealed in the ethnographic text in a number of ways, and that there are meaningful connections that can be drawn between ethnography and (auto)biographical practice. In the next chapter I continue to explore the relationship between the self and the text by outlining contemporary debates around representation in ethnography, and examining some of the claims of the so-called experimental (or alternative) representational forms.

8   (Re)presenting the Field

The analysis and representation of qualitative data have gained considerable critical attention in recent years. The approaches to qualitative data analysis and the writing of fieldwork have become much more self-conscious, and written about, activities. Qualitative researchers have increasingly looked beyond the actual experiences of fieldwork, towards the production and reproduction of the field. The conventional advice for the novice ethnographer has tended to concentrate on the design and negotiation of fieldwork, and the pragmatic issues of recording data. Until relatively recently, little attention or advice has been afforded to the processes of analysing and writing. They were often characterized as unproblematic, though inevitable latter stages of fieldwork, requiring neither detailed advice nor critical reflection. There are now detailed guides to the processes and problems of qualitative data analysis (for example Coffey and Atkinson, 1996; Dey, 1993; Gubrium, 1988; Miles and Huberman, 1994; Silverman, 1993, 1997; Strauss and Corbin, 1990). Qualitative writing and representation have also spawned a number of advice manuals and practical texts. Some have been particularly concerned with the craft skills of putting pen to paper (for example Becker, 1986; Ely et al., 1997; Richardson, 1990; Wolcott, 1990). Others have provided more detailed analysis of the genres, consequences and nuances of ethnographic text production (for example Atkinson, 1992, 1996; Clifford and Marcus, 1986). Some have engaged with the rethinking of ethnographic textual production, through an exploration of alternative genres and forms (see for example Denzin, 1994; Ellis and Bochner, 1996).

The more generalist textbooks on 'how to do' ethnography or fieldwork have also expanded their discussions on analysis and writing in recent editions. Again this reflects a growing awareness of these issues as part of the process and problematic of ethnography. For example in their third edition Lofland and Lofland (1995) have greatly expanded their chapters on analysing and writing, providing more guidance than before, and paying attention to recent developments and trends. Similarly Hammersley and Atkinson's second edition (1995) contains new material. They have radically redrafted their chapters on the recording, analysing and writing of ethnography. This chapter aims to provide a summary of these recent trends and developments in the reconceptualization of ethnographic production. It is not my intention to rehearse them in depth. Nor is it my aim to provide a lengthy exegesis of how to analyse and write about ethnographic data (see Coffey and Atkinson, 1996, for a detailed summary of the analytic and writing strategies available to the ethnographer and suggestions for further reading). In this chapter I particularly consider the linkages between representational work and identity work in ethnography. Building on my discussion on writing the self (in Chapter 7), I explore the relationship between the production process *and* the products of fieldwork. Ely et al. (1997: 329) use the phrase 'ripples on the self' to capture how research writing reaches inward to include the self in the research process. They argue that writing changes, moves and affects the self, thereby causing 'ripples' on the surface of the self. In this chapter I explore and document this process.

There is general agreement that analysis and writing fieldwork are extremely personal and self-conscious aspects of the ethnographic enterprise. It is at these stages of our research that we manipulate, rethink and represent our endeavours, drawing upon our own ideas of what the data are saying. In practice, reflection should occur during both the conduct of fieldwork and in the consequent analysis and writing. Analysing and writing involve choices and decisions. These choices are partially dependent upon the place, visibility and voice afforded to the researcher (and author). In Chapter 7 I considered the relationship between ethnographical and autobiographical textual production. The texts of ethnography are often the storying of lives. From this perspective analysing and representing are not simply about coding and writing in some distant, depersonalized way. What we are actually concerned with is the reconstruction and reproduction of lives and experiences through critical engagement with our data. Analysis and writing help to situate the self and the field as interconnected and coexistent (Hastrup, 1992). Both are sets of craft skills and emotional activities.

Passionate Analysis

> The depths of experience pose a major challenge to qualitative method. For decades, many qualitative researchers have been pointedly concerned about the neglect of 'inner' realms, arguing that theory and methodology do not adequately take account of deep emotions or what some call 'brute being'. (Gubrium and Holstein, 1997: 57)

Gubrium and Holstein's discussion points to the ways in which a focus on emotionality and inner experience has contributed to a new language of qualitative method. Their argument encompasses both the ways in which settings and people get discussed *and* the emotional feelings and presence of the fieldworker. Emotional sociology, they suggest, is a question both of subject and of method. One of the most central aspects of reformulating ethnography as emotional is the analysis of qualitative data. Analysis is indicative of the pursuit of 'passionate engrossment' with the subject matter (Gubrium and Holstein, 1997: 59). It is also one of the central ways in which the emotionality and passion of the fieldwork are enacted. During analysis the researcher becomes ever more intimate with the data of the field.

Qualitative data analysis can be said to have two simultaneous yet contrastive tendencies. On the one hand analysis is principled and formulaic, subject to a level of prescription and instruction. Techniques can be described, taught and utilized to aid the process of data analysis. Such techniques and approaches have been documented and described at some length (see for example, Coffey and Atkinson, 1996; Dey, 1993; Miles and Huberman, 1994; Strauss and Corbin, 1990). On the other hand qualitative data analysis can be thought about as a personal activity which is elusive and difficult to document. It is often difficult to describe or discover how analysis is actually done. There are very few confessional accounts of 'doing' analysis. Methods texts pay disproportionately less attention to the mechanics of analysis than to other aspects of the research process. Analysis and writing up are often identified as part of the same, unproblematic process ('. . . and then you analyse and write up your data'). Discussions of reflection and the self in fieldwork rarely refer to analysis *per se*. It is often hard to describe or demonstrate the analytic movement from data to ideas. Or from ideas to theory. Both characterizations of qualitative data analysis are equally valid. There *are* demonstrable ways of analysing qualitative data. Like data analysis more generally *there are* strategies and techniques that can be employed in the analysis of qualitative data. Data can be coded, framed, diagrammed, memoed, patterned, collated and enumerated. Concepts and theories can be drawn, applied, induced and tested. Data can be analysed for content, or form, or structure, or a combination thereof. It is both appropriate and extremely useful for such strategies and techniques to be described and documented; written up in 'instruction' mode for students and researchers to read, teach and apply.

Authors have been more or less prescriptive in their application of these analytic methods. Key examples of the documentation and codification of analytic method are the approaches articulated by Dey (1993) and Strauss and Corbin (1990). Though from slightly differing analytic perspectives (Dey, for example, uses his approach to demonstrate the value of computer-aided analysis) these commentators suggest that there are tangible techniques which can be learnt and applied to undertake qualitative analysis. Authors such as Lofland and Lofland (1995), Hammersley and Atkinson (1995) and LeCompte and Preissle (1993) are less prescriptive about analytic techniques, preferring to concentrate more on process and concepts. But there remains an indication that there are tangible ways of analysing qualitative data that can be learnt, internalized and followed, reflectively and self-consciously. One way of thinking about these approaches is in terms of some broad establishment of principles of analysis. Although there is variety in techniques and approaches, analysis can be conceptualized as systematic and documentable (Coffey and Atkinson, 1996). From this perspective, while analysis is not about adhering to one approach or set of 'right' techniques it is about being methodical and intellectually rigorous.

By contrast, qualitative data analysis cannot only be thought of in terms of technique and strategy. In some respects making sense of the field is not just about analysing 'data': that is, the manipulating and analysing of fieldnotes, transcripts, documents and so forth. Analysis also involves the researcher in meaningful engagement, which can be both imaginative and creative. Preliminary and prolonged analysis involves getting to know data – familiarizing, playing, thinking and creating. The imaginative, artful and reflexive aspects of data analysis are far less easy to codify, describe and teach. Yet because analysis involves such aspects it is perhaps far more passionate and emotional an activity than methods texts generally allow for. The analytical stage of fieldwork can be both exciting and daunting. It can fill you with anticipation or dread or probably both. Making sense of the field can be extremely rewarding and simultaneously terrifying. The analytic process is a point of emotional involvement and personal investment. This emotionality is not especially well acknowledged in methods texts. Lofland and Lofland (1995) do refer to the open-endedness of the analytic task, and the emotional dimension that this creates. They describe the analytic process as an emergent one, where frustration and anxiety are both commonly experienced. The Loflands suggest that such feelings should be socialized and accepted as a normal part of the analytical process. They advise relaxation and patience, systematically working at analysis and maintaining faith that it will all come together in the end. To be fair, the Loflands also note that the analysis part of qualitative research can be exhilarating and joyful – as ideas come together, discoveries are made and theories emerge. The emotionality of analysis is particularly visible in Wolf's recollections of turning fieldnotes into ethnographic texts (Wolf, 1990). Although Wolf does not herself refer to doing 'analysis', her account of reading, rereading and getting to know her fieldnotes is implicitly about the processes of analysing. Alongside the more formal coding of observations that Wolf (and her husband) had recorded during fieldwork with a Chinese family, Wolf re-engaged with her journal and interview data. She comments that,

> In this almost casual re-sorting of our fieldnotes, I found things that astonished me. Some items I had recorded myself and totally misunderstood; of others, recorded by Arthur or members of the field staff and in many cases typed by me, I had failed to see the import. (Wolf, 1990: 346)

Wolf recognizes and remembers a long struggle with the analysis of her fieldnotes. She attributes her own personal intellectual growth and development – as an anthropologist and a feminist – in part to that struggle. Getting to know her fieldnotes intimately, revisiting her data, analysing and writing were all deeply personal, emotional processes. Fine (1987) has also acknowledged the personal dimension of ongoing data analysis, and consequent revisits to his data. Reflecting on his three years of field research with North American little league baseball, Fine links the process of analysis with a sense of personal growth. He could not readily disentangle the analysis of data from personal influences and incidences. His ideas were used to inform his analyses, and his 'mistakes' in the data collection affected the formulation of hypotheses. His own personal development was both influenced by the fieldwork and helped to shape its outcomes:

> While each year the field research began with certain hypotheses, often by the middle of the year these had become reformulated, altered, or discarded and new ones were considered. This book is the result of internal and external debates, endless changes, forgetfulness, mistakes in data collection and perhaps most of all my own education. (Fine, 1987: 260)

Where researchers do talk and write about analysis, the potential for personal reward and growth is evident. As too is a sense of struggle or dismay. What we do with our data in terms of reading, rereading and sense-making is most definitely an emotional activity and one where the ethnographer-self is central. Whether we hate or love our data (and most of us usually experience both emotions over the course of a project), the major tasks of data management and analysis can easily lead to paralysis and despair. It is easy to get so wrapped up in one's data, and feel so attached to them that one is loath to interfere with them, never mind gain some analytic purchase and begin to make sense of them. In-depth analysis is often put off, skirted around, or purposefully ignored. Unpacking, rereading and rethinking our data can be panic inducing as well as intellectually stimulating and personally rewarding.

Early stages of analysis can be particularly frustrating, as we start to make sense of our data and search for meaning. While we may worry about manipulating, refining and tinkering, in-depth analysis offers the opportunity for us to really get to know our data intimately, and in turn the self within the data. Thinking about analysis may provoke the reading of fieldnotes exhaustively for the first time. The process of analysis takes the relationship with our data on to a different level – we discover and rediscover people, places, events – as pictures, theories and ideas emerge and develop. There is a danger, here, of over-emphasizing the emotional qualities of analysis. Many people do get on with their analysis relatively straightforwardly, and seemingly without untoward emotional investment. Nevertheless there is productive purpose in acknowledging the emotionality of the experience. Analysis involves personal investment and can be a lonely enterprise. It usually brings the necessity or opportunity of being alone and intimate with field data, notes, journals and thoughts. We personalize fieldwork through our analyses. We are making decisions about and connections with the data we have collected. We are responsible for discovering themes and patterns, deciding what goes where in a narrative account, what is significant, important, salient or typical. Our analysis relates to how we feel about the data, the field, the people, and often ourself.

For some qualitative data analysis is also about the explicit analysis of self. The self is a potential, and for some a central, unit of analysis. Fordham's school ethnography, for example, presents an analysis of school processes, student and teacher experiences at Capital High School (Fordham, 1996). It also presents an analysis of the ethnographer-author as engaged social actor. She writes:

> the analysis presented here reflects the way I watched and was watched at Capital High and within the Capital community. It documents how I became implicated and even 'over implicated' in a network of relationships. My involvement is not laminated by textual claims of scientific objectivity or lack of engagement. I *was* engaged and in far more than classroom observations. (Fordham, 1996: 340; emphasis in original)

Fordham acknowledges that her ethnography took her well beyond participant observation. She became implicated and embodied in the community she was intent on studying. In turn, her ethnographic analysis reflected her own multiple subjectivities. She felt unable to avoid responsibility for her moods, images and actions as she was really a part of the data and hence the consequent analyses. Fordham is particularly concerned with implicating and embodying herself in the analysis while not giving centre stage to her own presence. This concern is not to be taken lightly. Indeed it is through a recognition of the personal and emotional dimensions of analysis that we can seek to acknowledge and critically reflect upon the balance of self-analysis and ethnographic analysis. As I have indicated, analysis cannot simply be thought of as systematic and prescriptive, devoid of personal investment and emotional qualities. Obviously it is also impossible really to think of analysis without referring to its inevitable outcomes – the production of ethnographic representation and texts. Later, I consider new, alternative forms of ethnographic representation, and their implications for the analysis and production of the field and the self. Before doing so I briefly summarize the contemporary debates over the nature, form and consequences of ethnographic texts.

Rethinking Ethnographic Texts

The representation of ethnography through textual production is especially contested and varied (for a detailed account of the background to this argument see Atkinson and Coffey, 1995; Coffey et al., 1996). Qualitative writing has always reflected a variety of sorts – encompassing different disciplinary styles, textual conventions and, of course, the subject matter itself. Yet it is fair to say that the conventions of ethnographic representation and authorship have recently undergone further diversification, change and contestation. Such dynamism has been a response to a number of temporal and textual movements, for example, postcolonialism, postmodernism and (post)feminism.

Despite a recognition that the production of the ethnographic text has never been wholly static or monolithic, it has only been of late that the production of texts and the reading of those texts have been the subject of detailed, critical and self-conscious scrutiny. At the centre of this movement have been debates over both the representation of the cultural, and the textual construction of reality (Atkinson, 1990, 1996). Emerging from social anthropology (but now becoming widespread in sociology and other related disciplines) these debates have subjected ethnographic writing and its textual production to a critical reappraisal. This has been described as a crisis of representation deriving from a general thrust of postmodernism and associated factors (as well as part of ongoing development in those disciplines in which ethnography is located). The range of influences on the diversification or crisis of ethnographic representation is wide, and these have been discussed elsewhere (see for example Atkinson and Coffey, 1995). What follows is a brief summary.

The so-called 'rediscovery of rhetoric' movement has re-established rhetoric as central to scholarly, textual production. This is a wide and diffuse intellectual movement, spanning a range of disciplines. For example history (Megill and McCloskey, 1987), economics (McCloskey, 1985), psychology (Bazerman, 1987) and science (Gilbert and Mulkay, 1980). It has long been accepted that the Enlightenment saw the separation of rhetoric and science. This implies a radical distinction between two contrastive sets of commitments and principles: on the one hand science, logic, reason, method and evidence; on the other hand persuasion, opinion and rhetoric. A consequence of such a distinction has been the consignment of rhetorical forms to the margins of legitimate scholarship, including ethnography. The aspirations of the modern ethnographic endeavour have been rooted in this stark duality. In the creation of disciplinary knowledge rhetoric is thus separated from logic. This dichotomy established the possibility and perceived reality of ethnographic observers armed with a neutral and scientific language of observation, untainted by rhetoric and opinion. This brought with it a distinction between observer and observed, whereby observations are viewed as objective and scientific.

The rediscovery of rhetoric as central, and not peripheral, to scholarly work has had a profound impact upon the way the production of disciplinary knowledge is conceptualized. 'Scientific' accounts and texts have been recast as containing rhetorical qualities and features (Law and Williams, 1982; Lutz and Collins, 1993; Lynch and Wolgar, 1990). Distance between subjects and objects has been questioned. 'Taken for granted' concerns of science and reason have been reassessed. Distinctions between scientific fact and textual production have been challenged. Moreover, the dichotomy between the 'reality' of the natural scientific world and the narrative accounts of the social world has been problematized. The distinction between reality and representation has particular resonance for qualitative research and the production of ethnographic texts.

Gubrium and Holstein (1997: 101) argue that qualitative enquiry is 'especially sensitive to representational matters because of its unique position at the *lived border* of reality and representation'. By conceptualizing a border they imply an empirical distinction between reality and representation.

> It is our position that a world of *possible* things – that is, objects, events, experiences, and the like – exists prior to its mediation by signs and signs of signs. But this world requires representation for it to take the shapes in which we recognise it, for example as obdurate or as invariable. It is at the lived border of reality and representation that meaning is attached to raw materials to make 'things' of experience. Interpretation makes reality come alive to us; interpretive work at the border constitutes social reality, producing what we comprehend and treat as meaningfully real. (Gubrium and Holstein, 1997: 101; emphasis in original)

The re-recognition of the rhetorical features of lived experience, and therefore its representation, emphasize the narrative qualities of social life. That is, the ways in which 'reality' is textually constructed to render it socially meaningful.

Alongside the attention given to the textual arrangements of ethnographic products have come more overtly ideological critiques. Such appraisals have highlighted the weakening of cultural boundaries within an explicit framework of power and powerlessness. For instance Said's (1978) sustained commentary on the orientalism of Western observation has served to strengthen the argument that traditional ethnographic texts are privileged and privileging. From a 'postcolonial' perspective, Said has argued that many cultures which have been observed and represented have been reduced to the subjugated and muted objects of dominating discourse (Ardener, 1975). The observer is cast as privileged – able to classify and write the exotic characteristics of an oriental 'other'. The authority of the observer/ author is established by the production of texts of exploitation, description and classification (Marcus, 1992). The critique of orientalism is reflected in contemporary accounts of social anthropology. For example Stack highlights the balance between ethnographic writing and social responsibility. In the writing of her monograph of the northward movement of African-Americans from Mississippi, Arkansas and Louisiana to Chicago during the 1960s (Stack, 1972) Stack was confronted by her position as young, white woman studying (and writing of) black family life:

> When I stepped out of the field to write *All Our Kin* . . . my 'skin burned, I felt my color'. I confronted my whiteness more absolutely as a writer than as a researcher. I felt more alone and color conscious as I began writing. I also felt what, looking back, I might call a 'white woman's burden'. Inside The Flats, folks devised ways to blunt, yet clarify, color differences in our everyday experiences. When I began writing the ethnography I became color/politically conscious. I felt a strong sense

of social responsibility to those I had studied, and I was convinced that I could get the study right. (Stack, 1996: 99)

Stack reflects that her early training as an anthropologist in the 1960s had taught her that anthropologists should weave a coherent story, where parts fit together to buttress the whole. Looking back, she recognizes that she paid little attention to the tensions and contradictions in people's lives and experiences. While she transcribed and presented narratives word for word, she did not critically address the discontinuities in the construction of the narrative itself nor the question of social responsibility in ethnographic writing.

Of course, the critique of postcolonialism is of more general significance than one of race or colour. It is not limited simply to the sustained observation and writing of the 'other': as exotic or conquered. The same set of issues is also relevant to observation and writing 'at home'. Ethnographic fieldwork at home has been similarly represented by texts of exploitation and classification. Therefore the issue of representing 'otherness' remains a salient one. Some ethnographic authors have commented on this. For example Fordham (1996) undertook fieldwork in a school. The non-exotic setting made her involvement and consequently her writing more rather than less complicated. She notes the situatedness of her research:

My research activities followed the guidelines and mirrored the practices anthropologists have traditionally followed, with possibly one exception. Mine did not take place in an exotic context among the exotic Other outside North America, but in the Capital community, where the 'stickiness' of crosscutting and shifty social relationships complicated my involvement. (Fordham, 1996: 341)

Fordham's concern with representation encompasses an understanding of the authority that ethnographic texts can convey:

Those empowered to use one of society's most powerful weapons – the pen – can permanently shape or transform our thinking. If this premise is accurate, our perceptions of an entire generation could be permanently altered as a result of these ethnographic images. (Fordham, 1996: 341)

The privileged position of the ethnographer-observer as author has also been acknowledged and challenged by feminist theory and research praxis. Stanley and Wise (1993), for example, locate social research writing within an hegemonic masculine framework:

Words, sentences, writing styles, ways of presenting arguments, arguments themselves, criticism, all these are part and parcel of masculinist culture. They are among the artefacts of sexism and their use structures our experience before we can even begin to examine it, because they provide us with how to *think* as well as how to *write*. (Stanley and Wise, 1993: 179; emphasis in original)

Representational issues have formed part of a sustained dialogue between feminism and ethnography. The feminist critique of ethnographic texts has considered the relationship between gender and ethnography at a level that goes beyond a straightforward appraisal of men and women as social actors and authors. Clough (1992), for example, has argued that many realist accounts of ethnography incorporate unconscious fantasies and desires concerning gender (as well as race). Clough argues that the ethnographic pursuit of a realist genre has served to disguise the exploitative processes. Wolf (1992) has also argued that feminist ethnographers have been exploring the issues of power, authority and representation for a long time, almost independent of the wider attention they have recently enjoyed. Feminist scholarship encourages a critical examination of power and powerlessness. A similar argument is articulated by Mascia-Lees et al. (1989) who suggest that ethnographic texts need to be rethought in terms of *representation* and power. Feminist research has brought to the fore a concern with voices, authority, accounts and experiences (Olesen, 1994; Smith, 1987). Further it has contributed to the view that conventional ethnographic discourse can render the 'observed' as mute (Ardener, 1975), deprived of a culturally legitimized means of expression; visible and audible only through the eyes, voices and consequent texts of a dominant group (the observers).

Outcomes

This so-called crisis of representation in ethnography has had a number of practical consequences for the ways we think about the ethnographic endeavour. More than ever before, we are aware of the 'craft' skills of ethnographic writing and the ways in which those skills stem from conventions of written language. This has been encapsulated by a number of texts which have specifically dealt with how we write and indeed read ethnography (Atkinson, 1996; Hammersley, 1991). A more self-conscious approach to writing has been encouraged (for example in texts such as Ely et al., 1997, which explores how we compose meaning from our data and how we make our data meaningful to others). At the very least, writing and representing ethnography are no longer taken-for-granted aspects of the research process. The articulation of the self in the products of field research has also become a matter of critical reflection (Pierce, 1995). The relationship between the research process, the writing process and the self reconceptualizes the emotional, personal dimension of fieldwork, as well as drawing attention more generally to issues around authorship and authenticity. The impersonal, all-but-invisible, narrator status of the ethnographic author has been questioned (Charmaz and Mitchell, 1997; Van Maanen, 1988). The dynamic nature of power relationships in field research and ethnographic production has been explored through a specific focus on the writing of fieldwork. In placing the observable into recognizable textual formats, the ethnographer's opportunity to make the social world readable has been re-evaluated, and located alongside issues of authorship, authenticity and responsibility.

The critical attention that has been given to the processes and products of ethnographic writing has led to a more self-conscious approach to authorship and audience. The sometimes regimented adherence to the realism of conventional writing styles has been criticized as resulting in a thin description, and to narratives and descriptions imbued with a single implicit viewpoint of observer-author. A parallel argument has been articulated that such texts have not done adequate justice to the multi- or polyvocality of social life and the complexity of social forms. Rethinking ethnographic representation on the back of such criticism enables an ethnographic project to be peopled by both the social actors of the field and a critical self-conscious, ethnographic self. An essential element of this rethink is how ethnographers people their own texts. A consciously critical approach questions how the self is represented in texts and how we go about making connections, and pathways between the self and the other. Indeed it enables a reclassification of self and other as subjects (or objects) of the ethnographic gaze.

Alternative Visions

A sustained critique of conventional ethnographic texts has prompted the articulation, practice and evaluation of new representational forms. The social production of the ethnographic is no longer, if indeed it ever was, confined to a sole conventional literary type. Other formats and sets of textual conventions have been used and adapted by ethnographic authors across a range of disciplines. Alternative representational forms for the production of scholarly work convey particular analytic and conceptual approaches to data and the production of knowledge. These alternative forms can be viewed as part of an avant-garde spirit of experimentation: they are creative responses to the sustained critiques of conventional ethnographic writing. They also reflect a more general postmodernist agenda of how research is translated into representations and forms of knowledge production. Conventional scholarly texts have tended to assume a single dominant voice (of the author) and have been held up as embodying an essentially 'modern' set of assumptions. That is, such texts are predicated on a discovery of social reality through selective, unproblematic, scientific even, acts of engagement, inspection and notation. Postmodern agendas treat the status of conventional texts in different ways – as representations of social reality that are uncertain and more problematic in nature. This recognizes that all representational conventions are precisely that – conventional – and, to some extent at least, arbitrary. This recognition makes it possible to transgress literary boundaries and willingly seek alternative forms of representation. Textual variety is welcomed, and even necessary, from such a perspective.

Textual variety can be linked to the postmodernist perspective, and to an aesthetic which does not celebrate, or call for, a consistency of form. The publication of *Writing Culture* (Clifford and Marcus, 1986) was a crucial moment for the realization that ethnographic writing incorporated both politics and poetics. This anthology fuelled the debates over cultural representation through ethnographic writing and asserted the need for more dialogic, reflexive and innovative approaches. It gave 'permission' to write more creatively and self-consciously. There has been a sustained feminist response to *Writing Culture* (see Babcock, 1993; Gordon, 1988; Mascia-Lees et al. 1989; Wolf, 1992), mainly taking issue with the ways in which masculine subjectivity remained unchallenged by the essays. Authors such as Gordon (1988) did not argue, necessarily, that the essays were malicious, but rather that they did a disservice to feminism.

> For feminists, particularly feminist anthropologists and ethnographers, an important problem with 'experimental' ethnographic authority is its grounding in a masculine subjectivity which encourages feminists to identify with new modes of ethnography, claiming to be decolonial while simultaneously relegating feminism to a strained position of servitude. (Gordon, 1988: 8)

The inclusion of only one woman in the anthology, and the lack of engagement with feminist writing and scholarship were aspects which received sustained criticism.

> No two pages in the history of anthropological writing have ever created as much anguish among feminist readers as did James Clifford's uneasy statements justifying the absence of women anthropologists from the project of *Writing Culture*. Pushed to account for this gap by the criticism of a feminist reader who reviewed the book in manuscript, Clifford made the now infamous claim that women anthropologists were excluded because their writings failed to fit the requirement of being feminist *and* textually innovative. To be a woman writing culture became a contradiction in terms: women who write experimentally are not feminist enough, while women who write as feminists write in ignorance of the textual theory that underpins their own texts. (Behar, 1995: 4–5)

As feminist writing has demonstrated, the feminist concern with the production and representation of knowledge provides an especially appropriate platform from which to question conventional styles of writing and representing (Wolf, 1992). Feminist epistemology challenges the traditional, masculinist and highly conventional forms of scholarly narratives. *Women Writing Culture* (Behar and Gordon, 1995) is a collection of essays which directly engages with this debate. Partially in response to the earlier Clifford and Marcus anthology, the authors engage in the dialogue between women, writing and cultural representation. Gordon concludes that while the title, *Women Writing Culture* accentuates women as writers of culture, its reverse emphasizes cultural inscription. Inscription highlights the way culture produces individuals, authors, with a sexed identity. It is in tacking back and forth between the sense of women as writers and the cultural inscription of women that this volume eschews the notion of writing as individual effort and essence. (Gordon, 1995: 429)

The arguments for a revision of ethnographic textual form have come from a variety of sources. A general case has been made that the mode of narrative and description from a single, implicit viewpoint does not do justice to the complexity of cultural forms or ethnographic authors. One outcome has been the utilization of various 'alternative' approaches to textual representation. These epitomize the diversity of recent ethnographic work and reflect the interpretive turn. Various commentators have argued for texts that are more open, fragmented and messy – both as a mechanism for challenging the conventionality of ethnographic writing *and* for allowing for the development of more creative, complex modes of representation (cf. Mulkay, 1985).

A variety of forms of textual practice may be considered alternative or experimental in this context. These can be viewed along a loose continuum: at the one end are texts which 'look like' the conventional monograph, but explicitly aim to give voice to researchers and researched, as multiple selves of the field. Here the focus has not been so much on what the text looks like, so much as the meanings and voices inherent and explicit in the text. At the other end of the continuum are texts which provide ways of representing data through alternative visual structures, as well as promoting alternative meanings (Chaplin, 1994). For example, ethnographers have turned to poetry, dialogue, diaries and scripts to re-present their data and themselves.

Conventional/Unconventional

Kondo (1990) locates her ethnographic monograph as unconventional, yet to the naked eye it seems conventional enough – with discussion, extracts of data, theory and analysis interwoven. She argues that the conventional ethnographic text relegates theory to beginnings and ends, and concentrates the main body of the text on analytic descriptions of empirical data. Kondo describes how she breaks with this convention by scattering theoretical discussion throughout the text. She utilizes ethnographic anecdotes, vignettes and quotes in an analytically sophisticated way and slides back and forth between analysis/theory and ethnographic data/ anecdote. In attempting this less conventional approach to the writing of ethnography, Kondo (1990: 304) 'meant in part to capture the shifting, multiple levels of discourse at work in my co-workers [researched] lives'.

Kondo's research explored how selves are created and crafted in a Japanese workplace. She made power a central theme of her discussions of the 'crafting of self' and experimented with 'rhetorical strategies that might be more compatible with "theoretical" emphasis on multiplicity, contextuality, complexity, power, irony and resistance' (Kondo, 1990: 43). It is difficult to capture the overall feel of Kondo's monograph. The subtle movements between personal and political, theory and data are not easily revealed without her framing narratives and overall structures. For example Chapter 8 (pp. 258–99) concentrates on gender ideology and the structural position of women in the Japanese factory. It begins with a number of vignettes of stories of work, told by Kondo as the women related them to her:

> In these stories, told on the run between tasks, narrated episodically as we walked home, begun and then cut off by the necessity to start up some new task somewhere else in our work space, we may see pattern, but the patterns do not reinscribe familiar conventions associated with maturational scenarios of increasing prowess and self fulfilment. (1990: 263)

Kondo inserts the vignettes in her text as whole tales, and then sketches a response to them. She presents the 'larger historical discursive field with which women's work histories are produced' (p. 63). This includes, for example, theoretical work on gender and the workplace, and song lyrics (see Tsurumi, 1984). Kondo then returns to the neighbourhood and factory (the 'field') and explores the meanings social actors gave to their work. This takes the reader back to individual selves, collective selves and stories of working lives. Gender, class, hegemony, and the structuration of work are all explored here, *but* from a personal and emotive perspective. Part-time work is then explored in detail by returning to the shop floor and giving a thick description of a day at work – with times and activities – demonstrating the spatial and temporal boundaries of work. The conclusion to the chapter brings together the fragments of the chapter and the fragments of self contained therein.

> How, in the end, do we make sense of the fragmented stories I heard in snatches on the shop floor? They must be understood within complex, multilayered, mobile discourses on gendered work identities, that throw into relief the complicated ironies of constructing selves within fields of power. (Kondo, 1990: 298)

Like the understanding of the stories of work and self which she presents, Kondo's text is complex, multilayered, mobile, complicated and ironic. The messiness of her writing is meaningful, especially when it is considered alongside the 'messy meaning' of the selves she is describing, exploring and creating. The move between theoretical discussion and data is not the only balance which Kondo strikes in her text. By moving back and forth to the first person voice (especially at the beginning and end of her book) she frames her account with a personal reflexive view of the self. The account is situated within her personal experiences and writing strategies, screened through the narrator's eye. Kondo's account is alternative in that she challenges the dichotomy between researcher and researched, data and theory. She presents a highly reflexive, yet authoritative account of the crafting of identities – in this case, of Japanese workers and the researcher as Japanese-American, woman-self.

Fordham's (1996) ethnographic account of the African-American school 'Capital High' is similar to the approach articulated by Kondo. Fordham acknowledges the debates around ethnographic writing, and notes the importance given to the production of ethnographic text, especially within the anthropological community (cf. Coffey and Atkinson, 1996). Again Fordham's text looks in many ways 'conventional', yet the meaning she gives to the representation of culture locates it as alternative. She writes of this.

> While this ethnography grows out of a widespread concern regarding the 'images of others inscribed in writing', it is also evoked by a growing preoccupation with the nature of ethnographic texts and with how what is written censures Blackness. Thus, a central feature of this ethnography is African-Americans' multiple responses to the primary ways they are represented in anthropological (and other) texts. (Fordham, 1996: 4)

As I have noted elsewhere, Fordham is also explicit in locating herself within the ethnography and the text. She re-presents herself and her own identities as she re-presents the field. Fordham's monograph is in many ways a conventional account of a school ethnography. Yet the style of writing and her concern with the construction of multiple selves (within the school, neighbourhood and text) locate it as alternative, though not necessarily experimental. The narrative account Fordham offers of young black students and their understandings of race, gender and academic achievement is set within a context of multiple voices. She turns the ethnographic issue of representation back on itself to consider the representations of American racialized perceptions and lives. By engaging herself as 'native' anthropologist and African-American black woman, she makes herself part of that representational process she is engaging in. She thus presents a text that is both multilayered and multi-voiced.

Other authors have taken a different approach to the representation of selves. In doing so they have attempted to place the voices of the researched as the primary text. There are accounts which have attempted to capture the stories of individuals in their own words. The oral histories of the individual women portrayed by Abu-Lughod (1993) and Tsing (1993) are examples of this. They take the voices of individual women and use them to reconstruct stories of their lives as written text. In such writings, so-called 'editing' by the ethnographic author is kept to a minimum, although of course this obscures the reality that all writing is to some extent edited by those who are putting the pen to the paper. These oral histories attempt to represent the voices and textual structures of the narrated women themselves, not guided by research questions and agendas. These accounts can be located as attempts at capturing and giving voice to (in particular) women. In so far as they privilege the 'voiceless' and give them physical and textual space and a written voice they are a particular strategy of ethnographic representation. The approach relates, in a general way, to recent sociological and anthropological concerns with a biographical project (Erben, 1993) and a life history perspective that promotes the role of the researcher as biographer working in partnership with research participants (Denzin, 1989).

Some commentators (for example Lal, 1996) have questioned the ways in which alternative texts, such as those so far described, actually succeed in relocating the balance of power in ethnographic authorship, despite an explicit aim to do so. D.L. Wolf (1996) argues that such experimentation usually fails to challenge conventionally derived power differentials:

> Despite important efforts to experiment with strategies of representation and authorship, the basic power differences and the distribution of benefits of research remain the same. Few practical changes that have been attempted translate into radically transforming the researcher's privileged position. While more theorising on these contradictions is needed, perhaps an acknowledgement of their irre-concilability is also necessary. (D.L. Wolf, 1996: 34)

These issues are, to some extent, addressed in the pursuit of alternative ways of visualizing ethnographic texts.

Unconventional/Experimental

There are more visually striking attempts to transform the researcher's position of privilege. These approaches have challenged the textual format of ethnographic representation (as exemplified in the collection edited by Ellis and Bochner, 1996 and described in Ely et al., 1997). They include scripts, poetry, performance texts and diaries. Many of these draw on a dialogic approach to text (Allan, 1994; Dwyer, 1977, 1979; Holquist 1990) and are natural extensions of the biographical/life history projects mentioned above. They promote a self-conscious auto/biographical approach, and exemplify the ways in which ethnographic representation is simultaneously the writing of lives and selves (Ely et al., 1997; Hastrup, 1992; Stanley, 1992).

A dialogical approach to ethnographic representation exploits the conventions of naturalistic theatre or conversation, to make real, social events and interactions. Such an approach draws on the poetical and theatrical qualities of everyday social life. A number of ethnodramas have been produced which aim to capture the multiple voices of complex social situations. For example, Bluebond-Langer (1980) used a dramaturgical approach to explore the social worlds of dying children. Ellis and Bochner (1992) produced a powerful piece based on a reconstruction of the events and process of abortion. Paget

(1990, 1993) gave ethnographic representation to her life with cancer. Fox (1996) experiments with a multi-voiced text to present the contested voices of herself (as ethnographer and victim), a male sex offender and a young female 'victim'. She thereby gives a subversive reading of child sex abuse. These examples use the conventions of drama, or theatrical scripting, to narrate personal, and often traumatic, experiences. Arguably such representations promote contexted and multiple versions of social reality, giving a deep, richly contested account. Some ethnographers have gone beyond the scripts of ethnodrama toward the re-performance of the ethnography itself. For example Mienczakowski (1995, 1996) has used ethnodrama extensively to 'performance' the experiences of people undergoing the processes of detoxification.

A variation on this theme is the use of poetic style and innovation to represent ethnography. It is argued that ethnopoetry offers a mechanism to capture the pauses, rhyme and rhythm of everyday life and conversation (Richardson, 1994). Richardson (1992) used the words of Louisa May (a 'Mountain' woman), derived from life history interview data, to (re)construct a poetic account of her life. She drew on the conventions of poetical writing to re-present the ethnopoetics of Louisa May's life and words. The resultant poetry is both striking and emotive, illustrating Richardson's argument that poetry provides a mode of evocative representation of qualitative data. Ely et al. (1997) share the poetry of their qualitative writing group and argue that poems provide ways of creating and sharing analyses and meanings. Poems, they suggest, can foreshadow, encapsulate and move a story forward, thus providing a breathing space or thinking space; a place to contradict and share emotions. Poetry can be a mechanism for including rather than alienating readers. McCoy's (1997) poetry as a way of exploring pre-service teachers' use of the discourses of cultural difference is a striking and seductive way of presenting what would otherwise be potentially difficult arguments and ideas.

Creative approaches to the production of ethnographic texts such as these have value for thinking about and with data and can aid and promote a reflexive and self-conscious approach to writing. Some, like Sparkes (1995), argue that they create the opportunity for more realistic pictures of events, and serve to blur the power boundaries between researcher and researched. This is not, however, a universally agreed view, even by those who have engaged in and practised different modes of ethnographic representation. Lather (1991), for example, has argued that alternative representative forms do not remove the issue of power from ethnographic production. Texts are still authored – and selected, collected, edited, presented, written, crafted and read. As such, alternative forms of writing ethnography may blur or question boundaries but do not remove the issues. Indeed the very artfulness of many alternative or experiential texts actually draws attention to the craft work of authorship. Ethnodrama, theatrical scripts and poetry emphasize the creative potential and power of the author by overtly manipulating the appearance and ordering of words and text. By foregrounding the ethnographer as author, they could be conceptualized as a means of increasing, rather than diminishing, the distance between ethnographer and the 'other'. Equally such textual practice exposes the ethnographer to new forms of critical scrutiny. In dealing with critiques about authority and authorship by presenting new forms of representation, such practices expose the ethnographer not only to 'getting it right' as a social researcher but also as a more or less successful poet, playwright or creative writer.

Alternative forms of ethnographic, textual practice have been particularly well utilized as a way of representing deeply personal, sensitive events, emotive voices and stories. They have also been seen as appropriate ways of writing the self as part of the ethnographic process. Authors have chosen alternative textual forms in order to give ethnographic purchase to their own experiences of illness (Kolker, 1996; Paget, 1993); trauma and distress (Fox, 1996; Tillman-Healy, 1996); and personal and familial relationships (Ellis, 1996; Quinney, 1996) as well as the experiences of writing (Bochner and Ellis, 1996; Richardson and Lockridge, 1991). It is clear that not being tied to a specific representational mode can be empowering, analytically and personally meaningful. Yet there is much to be done in thinking self-consciously and critically about the alternative ways of writing and representing that we utilize. All ethnographic work and writing encompasses the self (whether articulated or not). Ethnography is deeply personal and emotive. Finding satisfactory and meaningful ways of representing that is essential. Yet, by definition, ethnographers are also authors, albeit sometimes empowering ones. Issues of authorship and authority do not go away because we have new ways of writing 'about' and 'with'.

A Note on Technology

I have hitherto said nothing about the impact of computer software on ethnographic analysis and representation. I do not intend to prolong the debate here, although the potential offered by multimedia approaches is something which qualitative researchers could usefully explore. It has already been established that computer software may have contributed to something of a homogeneity of ethnographic practice (Coffey et al., 1996). Linked to, though not exclusively, a grounded theory approach, Computer Assisted Qualitative Data Analysis Software (CAQDAS) has been developed as a subfield of qualitative 'methods' expertise (Lee and Fielding, 1991). There is now a range of packages (of differing levels of sophistication) aimed at analysing qualitative data. Most adhere to an analytic model of data marking and retrieval, associated with a particular form of grounded theorizing. It is not my intention here to review the existing software or the now extensive literature on CAQDAS. This has been done elsewhere in some detail (see Burgess, 1995; Coffey and Atkinson, 1996; Fielding and Lee, 1991; Kelle, 1995; Tesch, 1990; Weaver and Atkinson, 1994; Weitzman and Miles, 1995). Criticisms have been levelled at the CAQDAS approach to qualitative analysis. In particular it can encourage an oversimplified and mechanistic application of analysis and grounded theorizing.

As well as helping with the tasks of data management and data analysis it is also possible to think of contemporary technology in terms of its representative potential for the ethnographer. Information technology also offers ways of increasing the representational diversity and flexibility available to the production of ethnographic text (Coffey et al., 1996; Weaver and Atkinson, 1994). The use of hypertext and hypermedia applications, for example, increases the ways in which ethnography can be represented, authored and read. Drawing on the ideas that writing and reading is about process and cycles, rather than a linear model, hypertext applications support a much more complex and messy representation of texts. The interactive relationships between author, reader and texts can be blurred and multidimensional. Similarly hypermedia applications can allow a more complex authoring and reading environment to be created – with audio as well as textual data, video, film, photographs and so forth. Hypermedia and hypertext approaches to ethnographic representation are relatively new. They, like some of the other alternative representational forms, offer the possibility of not imposing a single linear order on ethnographic data. Such approaches are capable of recognizing the complexity of social worlds. Dey (1993) has especially welcomed hypertext for the management, retrieval and analysis of qualitative data, though he does not discuss or illustrate the use of a hypertext/hypermedia strategy for the writing and representation of qualitative analysis more generally. One of the most exciting possibilities of hypertext software may lie precisely in its capacities to support new forms of representation.

In the spirit of creativity and self-conscious ethnography we might cautiously welcome such innovations. Yet, to date, debates over ethnographic representation have tended to focus on the written text. The avantgarde have had very little to say on audio-visual technologies. At the level of representing, hypertext and hypermedia applications may well offer ways of allowing multiple voices and multiple texts to be omnipresent. Visual imagery has always been part of the representation of ethnography (film, photographs, artefacts). Hypermedia compounds this by offering even more complex ways of representing the social world. Clearly there are opportunities also for the writing of the self in these more complex authoring packages. The blurred relationships between different experiences and selves could be more fully explored through applications where different levels of analysis, different stories and different voices could all be presented and used simultaneously.

Alongside such an enthusiastic model remains the caveat that computer technology may serve to alienate and depersonalize the writer (and reader).

A more general criticism levelled at CAQDAS is the way in which it forces qualitative process and experience into an homogenic framework of analysis. Hypermedia and hypertext strategies could well extend the possibilities for a multi-voiced, multi-visual, multi-authored text. Equally they could turn the process of representing the field into a set of mechanistic, data entry techniques. They *could* challenge the power relations between author, reader and the field. They could contribute to a more self-conscious approach to the ways in which the field is represented. Alternatively they could paralyse creativity, and contribute to 'texts' devoid of emotionality and authorship.

Conclusion: Beyond Ethnography

Ethnographic fieldwork and the texts that derive from it are concerned with the studying of lives and experiences. Further, the processes of analysis and writing are aspects of research which can privilege the self. Analysis and writing are two of the most passionate and personal aspects of the whole ethnographic research process. The recent attention paid to both may be seen as a contemporary recognition of the emotional investments they entail. There is a case to be made that ethnographic writing and the postmodern approaches to representational issues have served to empower or celebrate the ethnographic self. To the extent that this serves as a recognition of the intertextuality of the field, the text and the self, this movement is a welcome one. However, in conclusion I wish to caution against a view of ethnography and representation as wholly autobiographic practices. The representation of the field and the writing of the self are not necessarily the same enterprises, nor should they be. As I noted in Chapter 7, the relationships between the writing of ethnography and the writing of the self are multiple and have become increasingly significant for some authors.

The boundary between ethnography and autobiography has, at times, become difficult to draw and navigate. For example, in the previous chapter I referred to the work of Sparkes (1996) who uses the self as a unit of analysis and representation. Sparkes uses his own body narrative to represent a narrative of the self (Richardson, 1994).

> The narrative focuses upon my current 40 year old, white, heterosexual, 'middle class', male, 'failed' body and memories of an earlier elite, performing, working class body that had a 'fatal flaw' in the form of a chronic lower back problem that terminated, very early on, my involvement in top class sport. (Sparkes, 1996: 467)

The narrative is (re)presented in the first person, as an autobiographical account. In the course of the essay we are presented with notes, and part of a conversation. Sparkes also uses extracts from a diary. We learn something of Sparkes's family circumstances – the relationship with his father, his wife

Kitty, his children, his hospitalization and surgery. Sparkes creates a powerful and compelling narrative of the self and the body. He uses ethnographic writing as analysis, autobiography, diary and self-discovery. Different textual formats are employed to create a multi-layered narrative of his body, family, self and experiences.

> I become increasingly aware of the performative element of my telling and the opportunities this has provided me with for reliving, reshaping and realigning past events and experiences in order to give them new meaning in relation to the present. (Sparkes, 1996: 468)

What Sparkes is actually engaged in here is the production of auto-ethnography or ethno-autobiography. Others, too, have engaged in the creation of this ethno-autobiographical genre, most notably contributors to *Composing Ethnography* (Ellis and Bochner, 1996). Tillman-Healy (1996) and Kolker (1996), for example, have both written body-biographies. Tillman-Healy writes emotionally about her 'relationship' with the eating disorder, bulimia, while Kolker describes coming to terms with cancer (as earlier Paget, 1990, 1993 had done). Others have used ethnographic writing to analyse and share autobiographical experiences and memories. Through poetry Austin (1996) describes and celebrates her friendship with a fellow student. Ronai (1996), Ellis (1996) *and* Quinney (1996) all recall and retell, in various innovatory ways, their relationship with a parent, drawing on ethnographic insights to re-present personal narratives of difficult, painful and rewarding relationships.

Ellis and Bochner (1996) argue that ethnographic writing can be a form of creative non-fiction, where data are connected to experiences and to an audience. That is, ethnography is also about writing *to* rather than simply writing *about*. Indeed many of the recent alternative forms of ethnographic writing do attempt to do both. The authors are writing to, as well as about, family, friends, informants and themselves. Many of the examples drawn upon in this chapter place the self firmly in the text and the ethnography. In these contexts it is less than clear when ethnography stops and autobiography begins. The preoccupation with the writing of self, and the writing to significant others of the self, can be conceptualized as both. The literary forms which are described above stand on the boundary between ethnography and autobiography. What we are witnessing may be a new form of ethnographic practice, more firmly rooted in a social context and the situatedness of author-self. This may have positive consequences for the representation of peopled, polyvocal social worlds. Yet some would argue that such texts are not 'doing' ethnography at all, but are self-indulgent writings published under the guise of social research and ethnography. Rather than utilizing literary and autobiographical devices to write ethnography we may be witnessing the use of ethnographic devices to write autobiography. It is uncertain whether this has any long-term benefit

for the development of ethnographic research and text, beyond the central-
izing of the researcher-self as omnipresent, something which critics have
argued ethnography needs to move away from. In Chapter 7 I argued that
commentators have engaged with this debate and have concluded that autobiographical ethnography (Reed-Danahay, 1997) has much to commend it
analytically and representationally, above and beyond a self-indulgent writing of the self. That said, it remains debatable as to whether utilizing
ethnographic strategies to write autobiography really 'counts' as ethnography at all. This may be especially the case where the only 'field' which is
being researched and presented is the researcher-self. From this perspective,
the so-called crisis in ethnographic representation and its textual outcomes
may have greater long-term impact on the rewriting of the self than on the
(re)writing of ethnography.

9 Consequences and Commitments

There is always a danger that 'methods' books are read with prescription in mind, and that the conclusion will somehow reveal the 'answers'. It seems that there is a continuous search for advice and recipes on how to do qualitative research. While various texts give concrete descriptions on issues of methodology and research strategy, this book is not one of them. It was never my intention to replicate existing guides to the conduct and writing of qualitative or ethnographic research. As I outlined in the introduction to the volume, it should be read as an addendum to, rather than a replacement for, the more generic texts on the ethnographic method.

It is not difficult to speculate that some readers may misinterpret the messages of the book, or criticize it precisely for a lack of explicit prescription. I have not attempted to convey prescriptive messages about key aspects of the research process – such as choosing the research setting, the conduct of the fieldworker, establishing roles and relationships, gauging levels of emotional attachment, writing and representation. Nor was the presentation of an uncritical case for autobiographical ethnography ever part of my agenda. Yet I am sure that it is possible to construct a reading of my text that focuses on self-indulgence, sexual intercourse, nudity and experimental forms of representation! I certainly do not wish to convey that autobiography and personal intimacy are the only valid contexts from which to undertake fieldwork. I would not wish to see the variety of analytic strategies, paradigms, theoretical perspectives, writing styles and foreshadowed research problems unduly limited by such a narrow reading of the text.

In attempting to clear up any misunderstandings that the book may incur, I take the opportunity here to draw together some of the recurrent themes of the book. In doing so, my aim is to highlight the relevance of topics and issues discussed for qualitative fieldwork in general (rather than a recapitulation of the substantive points of each chapter). I do not limit my discussion here to the especially evocative, emotional, sexual or physical fieldwork settings and experiences. Rather I draw on these to present a more general agenda for making sense of the ethnographic self and the experiences of fieldwork. My intention is not to be prescriptive of how to 'do' ethnographic work. But my comments do indicate a kind of prescription for how we *think about* fieldwork, representation and the ethnographic self.

Fieldwork as Biographical Work

It is not necessary to make the self the explicit focus of fieldwork, for biographical work to be accomplished. Detailed and prolonged ethnographic work inevitably involves the researcher in various sorts of autobiographical practice, and rightly so. The self is shaped by relationships, interactions and experiences which are not suspended for the duration of fieldwork. To deny the impact of fieldwork on the construction of the self rather misses the point. The ethnographic self cannot be separated out from the facets and phases of qualitative fieldwork. The self should not be viewed in isolation; as tangential to the practical and intellectual processes of fieldwork. I am not advocating that the only merit of ethnographic fieldwork is a better, or more complex understanding of the self. Nor am I making the case for fieldwork which is purely self-referential or autobiographical. No field interaction should be seen solely in terms of how it constructs or impacts on the self. The point is that we cannot separate the researcher from the social and intellectual context of fieldwork. In recognizing that we are constructed, shaped and challenged by fieldwork, we can become more attuned to what is actually going on in the specific cultural setting. The biographical work of managing the self in the field has consequences for the ways we come to understand the data we collect and seek to analyse. Fieldwork always starts from where we are. We do not come to a setting without an identity, constructed and shaped by complex social processes. We bring to a setting disciplinary knowledge and theoretical frameworks. We also bring a self which is, among other things, gendered, sexual, occupational, generational – located in time and space. This does not imply an uncritical celebration of the self. It does imply a self-conscious and self-critical approach to fieldwork.

Fieldwork is Physical and Emotional Work

We should never take for granted the physical and emotional demands of ethnographic work. Further, the physicality and emotionality of fieldwork should be seen as strengths, rather than burdens to be endured. Fieldwork does not need to be conducted in especially arduous or physical settings for us to 'feel' it in real, bodily ways. Moreover our emotional feelings about fieldwork are often connected to our physical state. As well as a distinctively physical activity, fieldwork is about emotions. We always have feelings about our research setting, peoples and experiences. We can and do feel joy, pain, hurt, excitement, anger, love, confusion, satisfaction, loss, happiness and sadness. Emotional connectedness to the processes and practices of fieldwork, to analysis and writing, is normal and appropriate. It should not be denied, nor stifled. It should be acknowledged, reflected upon, and seen as a fundamental feature of well-executed research. Having no emotional connection to the research endeavour, setting or people is indicative of a poorly executed project.

Recognizing the Relational

It is impossible to undertake fieldwork without entering into interactions with significant others. Moreover it is wrong to assume that the input and output of those interactions will be one-way. We should not even think about undertaking qualitative fieldwork without being prepared to become part of the interactions of the setting. At a basic level this reinforces an underlying perspective that everyday life is enacted through social interaction. While this is a guiding principle of qualitative fieldwork, we can easily lose sight of the fact that those relations and interactions implicitly include the researcher, as well as the researched. We should be prepared to enter into, as well as documenting, social interaction in the field. This does not mean that the field relations we engage in will always be positive and fulfilling, though they can often be so. Rarely, however, are the relations of fieldwork epistemologically and personally insignificant.

Documenting Decisions, Reflections and the Self

The process of fieldwork can be understood as a series of real and virtual conversations and interactions with informants and significant others; particular places; ideas; family and friends; lovers; memories; and self. All of these dialogues enable us to navigate pathways and understandings through the research. Fieldwork and its outcomes develop in the course of these transactions. Critically reflecting on these can unfold and enhance the processes and experiences of research. It is central to qualitative research practice that these interactions, and the reflections that develop from them, are recorded and documented. This can be for purely private or for public consumption. Documentation is part of a double transformation. On the one hand it aids the transformation from personal experience to public and accountable knowledge. On the other hand documentation helps to transform the public and social experience of fieldwork into a personal journey of self-discovery. Both are important aspects of the qualitative research project, and should be seen as coexisting.

Representation Matters

This book has fundamentally been concerned with the processes and practices of writing and reading. The examples that have been used to illustrate the chapters all originate from written (though not always published) accounts of fieldwork. To that end the whole text can be viewed as an exercise in rewriting selves. The ways in which we author ethnographic texts, and write the self into (or out of) the text, is a recurrent theme. An explicit focus on the self makes issues of representation even more central and pertinent to the ethnographic enterprise. There is no neutral medium for representing the social worlds we seek to understand. Our writing is implicated in how we reconstruct the settings we have researched, and in how we reconstruct ourselves. Authorship is an activity which we need to be aware that we are engaging in. This does not imply that our texts should necessarily be autobiographical or experimental, though these genres have their place and are part of the variety of representational forms that we have at our disposal. What I am advocating is an awareness of the fact that we are responsible for the reconstruction and telling of the field. Writing is not only a practical accomplishment of literary conventions. It is also an important mechanism through which we express, construct and represent ourselves. This is so, whether or not we explicitly choose to write about ourselves as part of the public process of documenting the ethnography.

Recognizing the Importance of Memory

Over the course of the book I have made reference to the relationship between fieldwork and memory. Our memories inform our data collection, analyses and the reconstruction of the field. We draw upon the conventions of memory – including the narrative construction of lives – in order to make sense of a field setting. Moreover, the ways in which we remember and share our memories are important to the contextualization of the self through fieldwork. Recognizing that our memories, and the collective memories of others, shape our field data, analyses, representations and emotions is central to an understanding of how ethnography, and indeed everyday social life, gets practically and intellectually accomplished. For a research method to evoke and rely upon memory should certainly not be seen as a weakness. The conventions and significance of memory should be both acknowledged and critically engaged with, as part of the process of ethnography.

Recognizing the Commitment to Others

Many of the preceding chapters have developed and discussed the idea that fieldwork is actually about peopled social worlds. Qualitative research involves the sharing of life experiences, biographies, places, times, family and friends This can be immensely rewarding, as well as emotionally and personally challenging. What one needs to remember, however, is that this sharing is predicated on a commitment *by* others to the pursuit of our research. In turn we must continue to recognize and demonstrate our commitment *to* others. This, of course, refers to well-versed issues of confidentiality, privacy and advocacy. But for many of us, our commitment does not and should not stop there. We incur debts during fieldwork that can never be fully repaid. We are, by and large, the greater beneficiaries of our research endeavours. We develop intimate and personal friendships and, even when we do not, we remain dependent upon others for our data and our ethnographic careers. This does not imply an uncritical celebration of the field. Our commitment to the *others* who are involved in the fieldwork endeavour is actually about realizing the intimate relations between our social world and theirs; ensuring we create the opportunities for appropriate polyvocality, reciprocity and acknowledgement.

Understanding the Commitment to Yourself

Finally, ethnographic work requires a high level of personal commitment. One should not embark upon this sort of research light-heartedly, nor without an understanding that it is based on long-term, emotional and even intimate involvement. Our research commitment is not only to the field setting, our informants, the academic discipline and academic scholarship. We should also have and enforce a commitment to ourselves. As the ultimate in research instruments we owe it to ourselves to undertake fieldwork that is ethical in our own terms; is reflective of and sensitive to our needs and emotions; aims at personal development as well as scholarly reward. Moreover, fieldwork is not only about the lives and privacy of others. It is also fundamentally about our own lives, intimate relations and privacy. And while we do not always have to write about it, we should not be afraid to recognize that this is so.

Ethnographic fieldwork has contributed substantially to the self-understanding of contemporary society. This looks set to continue, given the growing interest in qualitative methods across a range of disciplines. It is my contention that the continuing development of ethnographic methods can only benefit from a greater understanding of the processes and products of fieldwork. A critical awareness of the ethnographic self should not be seen as a mechanism by which ethnographic fieldwork, or qualitative methods more generally, can be undermined or dismissed. As importantly, this book should not be seen as a project in making fieldwork appear impossible, or the representations of fieldwork invalid. In rendering the ethnographic self both visible and problematic I hope to have provided the opportunity for fieldwork to take on new dimensions, complexities and fascinations.

References

Abramson, A. (1993) 'Between autobiography and method: being male, seeing myth and the analysis of structures of gender and sexuality in the eastern interior of Fiji', in D. Bell, P. Caplan and W.J. Karim (eds), *Gendered Fields: Women, Men and Ethnography*. London and New York: Routledge. pp. 63–77.

Abu-Lughod, L. (1986) *Veiled Sentiments: Honor and Poetry in a Bedouin Society*. Berkeley, CA: University of California Press.

Abu-Lughod, L. (1988) 'Fieldwork of a dutiful daughter', in S. Altorki and C.F. El-Solh (eds), *Arab Women in the Field: Studying Your Own Society*. Syracuse, NY: Syracuse University Press. pp. 139–61.

Abu-Lughod, L. (1990) 'Can there be a feminist ethnography?', *Women and Performance: A Journal of Feminist Theory*, 5 (1): 7–27.

Abu-Lughod, L. (1993) *Writing Women's Worlds: Bedouin Stories*. Berkeley, CA: University of California Press.

Acker, J. (1990) 'Hierarchies, jobs, bodies: a theory of gendered organizations', *Gender and Society*, 4 (2): 139–58.

Adkins, L. and Merchant, V. (eds) (1996) *Sexualizing the Social: Power and the Organisation of Sexuality*. Basingstoke: Macmillan.

Agar, M. (1986) Foreword to T.L. Whitehead and M.E. Conway (eds), *Self, Sex and Gender in Cross-Cultural Fieldwork*. Urbana, IL: University of Illinois Press. pp. ix–xi.

Allan, S. (1994) '"When discourse is torn from reality": Bakhtin and the principle of chronologoplicity', *Time and Society*, 3: 193–218.

Allison, A. (1994) *Nightwork: Sexuality, Pleasure and Corporate Masculinity in a Tokyo Hostess Club*. Chicago: University of Chicago Press.

Ardener, S. (ed.) (1975) *Perceiving Women*. London: J.M. Dent.

Atkinson, P. (1981) *The Clinical Experience: The Construction and Reconstruction of Medical Reality*. Farnborough: Gower.

Atkinson, P. (1990) *The Ethnographic Imagination*. London: Routledge.

Atkinson, P. (1992) *Understanding Ethnographic Texts*. Newbury Park, CA: Sage.

Atkinson, P. (1996) *Sociological Readings and Re-readings*. Aldershot: Avebury.

Atkinson, P. (1997) *The Clinical Experience: The Construction and Reconstruction of Medical Reality*, 2nd edn. Aldershot: Ashgate.

Atkinson, P. and Coffey, A. (1995) 'Realism and its discontents: on the crisis of cultural representation in ethnographic texts', in B. Adam and S. Allan (eds), *Theorizing Culture: An Interdisciplinary Critique after Post-Modernism*. London: UCL Press. pp. 41–57.

Atkinson, P. and Silverman, D. (1997) 'Kundera's *Immortality*: the interview society and the invention of the self', *Qualitative Inquiry*, 3 (3): 304–25.

Austin, D.A. (1996) 'Kaleidoscope: the same and different', in C. Ellis and A.P. Bochner (eds), *Composing Ethnography: Alternative Forms of Qualitative Writing*. Walnut Creek, CA: Altamira Press. pp. 206–30.

Babcock, B. (1993) 'Feminism/pretexts: fragments, questions and reflections', *Anthropological Quarterly*, 66 (2): 59–66.

Ball, S.J. (1981) *Beachside Comprehensive: A Case Study of Secondary Schooling.* Cambridge: Cambridge University Press.

Barnard, M. and McKeganey, N. (1995) *Sex Work on the Streets: Prostitutes and their Clients.* Buckingham: Open University Press.

Baudrillard, J. (1975) *The Mirror of Production*, trans. M. Poster. St Louis, MO: Telos Press.

Bazerman, C. (1987) 'Codifying the social scientific style: the APA Publication Manual as a behaviorist rhetoric', in J.S. Nelson, A. Megill and D.N. McCloskey (eds), *The Rhetoric of the Human Sciences.* Madison, WI: University of Wisconsin Press. pp. 42–69.

Becker, H.S. (1971) Footnote to M. Wax and R. Wax, 'Great tradition, little tradition and formal education', in M. Wax, S. Diamond and F.O. Gearing (eds), *Anthropological Perspectives on Education.* New York: Basic Books. pp. 3–27.

Becker, H.S. (1986) *Writing for Social Scientists.* Chicago: University of Chicago Press.

Behar, R. (1995) 'Introduction: out of exile', in R. Behar and D.A. Gordon (eds), *Women Writing Culture.* Berkeley, CA: University of California Press. pp. 1–29.

Behar, R. and Gordon, D.A. (eds) (1995) *Women Writing Culture.* Berkeley, CA: University of California Press.

Bell, C. and Encel, S. (eds) (1978) *Inside the Whale: Ten Personal Accounts of Social Research.* Oxford: Pergamon.

Berik, G. (1996) 'Understanding the gender system in rural Turkey: fieldwork dilemmas of conformity and intervention', in D.L. Wolf (ed.), *Feminist Dilemmas in Fieldwork.* Boulder, CO: Westview pp. 56–71.

Beynon, J. (1985) *Initial Encounters in the Secondary School.* London: Falmer.

Beynon, J. (1987) 'Zombies in dressing gowns', in N.P. McKeganey and S. Cunningham-Burley (eds), *Enter the Sociologist: Reflections on the Practice of Sociology.* Aldershot: Avebury. pp. 144–73.

Blackwood, E. (1995) 'Falling in love with an-other lesbian: reflections on identity in fieldwork', in D. Kulick and M. Willson (eds), *Taboo: Sex, Identity and Erotic Subjectivity in Anthropological Fieldwork.* London and New York: Routledge. pp. 51–75.

Bluebond-Langer, M. (1980) *The Private Worlds of Dying Children.* Princeton, NJ: Princeton University Press.

Bochner, A.P. and Ellis, C. (1996) 'Talking over ethnography', in C. Ellis and A.P. Bochner (eds), *Composing Ethnography: Alternative Forms of Qualitative Writing.* Walnut Creek, CA: Altamira Press. pp. 13–45.

Bolak, H.C. (1997) 'Studying one's own in the Middle East: negotiating gender and self–other dynamics in the field', in R. Hertz (ed.), *Reflexivity and Voice.* Thousand Oaks, CA: Sage. pp. 95–118.

Bolton, R. (1995) 'Tricks, friends and lovers: erotic encounters in the field', in D. Kulick and M. Willson (eds), *Taboo: Sex, Identity and Erotic Subjectivity in Anthropological Fieldwork.* London and New York: Routledge. pp. 140–67.

Bond, G.C. (1990) 'Fieldnotes: research in past occurrences', in R. Sanjek (ed.), *Fieldnotes: The Makings of Anthropology.* Ithaca, NY: Cornell University Press. pp. 273–89.

Bowen, E.S. (1954) *Return to Laughter.* London: Gollancz.

Bowen, E.S. [Bohannan, L.] (1964) *Return to Laughter.* New York: Doubleday.

Bretell, C.B. (ed.) (1993) *When They Read What We Write: The Politics of Ethnography.* Westport, CT: Bergin and Garvey.

Briggs, J. (1986) 'Kapluna daughter', in P. Golde (ed.), *Women in the Field: Anthropological Experiences*, 2nd edn. Berkeley, CA: University of California Press. pp. 19–44

Bryman, A. (1994) 'The Mead/Freeman controversy: some implications for qualitative researchers', in R.G. Burgess (ed.), *Studies in Qualitative Methodology 4: Issues in Qualitative Research*. London: JAI Press. pp. 1–28.

Burgess, R.G. (1982) *Field Research: A Sourcebook and Field Manual*. London: Allen & Unwin.

Burgess, R.G. (1983) *Experiencing Comprehensive Education: A Study of Bishop McGregor School*. London: Methuen.

Burgess, R.G. (1984) *In the Field: An Introduction to Field Research*. London: Allen & Unwin.

Burgess, R.G. (1987) 'Studying and restudying Bishop McGregor school', in G. Walford (ed.), *Doing Sociology of Education*. London: Falmer. pp. 67–94.

Burgess, R.G. (ed.) (1995) *Studies in Qualitative Methodology (Vol. 5): Computing and Qualitative Research*. Greenwich, CT: JAI Press.

Butler, I. and Shaw, I. (eds.) (1996) *A Case of Neglect? Children's Experiences and the Sociology of Childhood*. Aldershot: Avebury.

Cannon, S. (1992) 'Reflections on fieldwork in stressful situations', in R.G. Burgess (ed.), *Studies in Qualitative Methodology (Vol. 3): Learning about Fieldwork*. Greenwich, CT: JAI Press. pp. 147–82.

Carter, K. (1995) 'The occupational socialisation of prison officers: an ethnography'. PhD dissertation, University of Wales, Cardiff.

Chaplin, E. (1994) *Sociology and Visual Representation*. London: Routledge.

Charmaz, K. and Mitchell, R.G., Jr. (1997) 'The myth of silent authorship: self, substance and style in ethnographic writing', in R. Hertz (ed.), *Reflexivity and Voice*. Thousand Oaks, CA: Sage. pp. 193–215.

Clifford, J. and Marcus, G.E. (eds) (1986) *Writing Culture: The Poetics and Politics of Ethnography*. Berkeley, CA: University of California Press.

Clough, P.T. (1992) *The End(s) of Ethnography: From Realism to Social Criticism*. Newbury Park, CA: Sage.

Coffey, A. (1993) 'Double entry: the professional and organizational socialization of graduate accountants'. PhD dissertation, University of Wales, Cardiff.

Coffey, A. and Atkinson, P. (1996) *Making Sense of Qualitative Data: Complementary Research Strategies*. Thousand Oaks, CA: Sage.

Coffey, A., Holbrook, B. and Atkinson, P. (1996) 'Qualitative data analysis: technologies and representations', *Sociological Research On-Line*, 1, <http://www.socresonline.org.uk/socresonline/1/1/4.html>

Corbin, J.R. and Corbin, M.P. (1984) *Compromising Relations: Kith, Kin and Class in Andalusia*. Aldershot: Gower.

Corsaro, W.A. (1981) 'Entering the child's world – research strategies for field entry and data collection in a preschool setting', in J.L. Green and C. Wallat (eds), *Ethnography and Language in Educational Settings*. Norwood, NJ: Ablex. pp. 72–83.

Corsaro, W.A. (1985) *Friendship and Peer Culture in the Early Years*. Norwood, NJ: Ablex.

Corsaro, W.A. and Streeck, J. (1986) 'Studying children's worlds: methodological issues', in J. Cook Gumperz, W.A. Corsaro and J. Streeck (eds), *Children's Words and Children's Language*. Berlin: Mouton de Gruyter. pp. 13–36.

Cortazzi, M. (1993) *Narrative Analysis*. Lewes: Falmer.

Crick, M. (1992) 'Ali and me: an essay in street-corner anthropology', in J. Okely and H. Callaway (eds), *Anthropology and Autobiography*. London: Routledge. pp. 175–92.

Davies, R.M. (1988) 'The happy end of nursing: an ethnographic study of initial encounters in a midwifery school'. MSc. Econ. dissertation, University of Wales, Cardiff.

Davies, R.M. (1994) 'Novices and experts: initial encounters in midwifery', in A. Coffey and P. Atkinson (eds), *Occupational Socialization and Working Lives*. Aldershot: Avebury. pp. 99–115.

Davis, A. and Horobin, G. (eds) (1977) *Medical Encounters: The Experience of Illness and Treatment*. New York: St Martin's Press.

Delamont, S. (1984) 'The old girl network: recollections of fieldwork at St Lukes', in R.G. Burgess (ed.), *The Research Process in Educational Settings: Ten Case Studies*. Lewes: Falmer. pp. 15–38.

Delamont, S. (1987) 'Clean baths and dirty women', in N.P. McKeganey and S. Cunningham-Burley (eds), *Enter the Sociologist: Reflections on the Practice of Sociology*. Aldershot: Avebury. pp. 127–43.

Delamont, S. (1992) *Fieldwork in Educational Settings*. Lewes: Falmer.

Delamont, S. (1998) 'You need the leotard: revisiting the first PE lesson', *Sport, Education and Society*, 3 (1): 5–17.

Delamont, S. and Atkinson, P. (1995) *Fighting Familiarity*. Creskill, NJ: Hampton.

Delamont, S. and Galton, M. (1986) *Inside the Secondary Classroom*. London: Routledge.

Denzin, N.K. (1989) *Interpretive Biography*. Newbury Park, CA: Sage.

Denzin, N.K. (1994) 'The art and politics of interpretation', in N.K. Denzin and Y.S. Lincoln (eds), *Handbook of Qualitative Research*. Thousand Oaks, CA: Sage. pp. 500–15.

Denzin, N.K. (1997) *Interpretive Ethnography: Ethnographic Practice for the 21st Century*. Thousand Oaks, CA: Sage.

Denzin N.K. and Lincoln, Y.S. (eds) (1994) *Handbook of Qualitative Research*. Thousand Oaks, CA: Sage.

Dey, I. (1993) *Qualitative Data Analysis: A User Friendly Guide for Social Scientists*. London: Routledge.

Dingwall, R. (1977) *The Social Organisation of Health Visitor Training*. London: Croom Helm.

Douglas, J.D. and Johnson, J.M. (eds) (1977) *Existential Sociology*. New York: Cambridge University Press.

Douglas, J.D., Rasmussen, P.K. and Flanagan, C.A. (1977) *The Nude Beach*. Beverley Hills, CA: Sage.

Dua, V. (1979) 'A woman's encounter with Arya Samaj and untouchables: a slum in Jullunder', in M.N. Srinivas, A.M. Shah and E.A. Ramaswamy (eds), *The Fieldworker and the Field: Problems and Challenges in Sociological Investigation*. Delhi: Oxford University Press. pp. 115–26.

Dubisch, J. (1995a) 'Lovers in the field: sex, dominance, and the female anthropologist', in D. Kulick and M. Willson (eds), *Taboo: Sex, Identity and Erotic Subjectivity in Anthropological Fieldwork*. London and New York: Routledge. pp. 29–50.

Dubisch, J. (1995b) *In a Different Place: Pilgrimage, Gender and Politics at a Greek Island Shrine*. Princeton, NJ: Princeton University Press.

Dwyer, K. (1977) 'On the dialogic of fieldwork', *Dialectical Anthropology*, 2: 143–51.

Dwyer, K. (1979) 'The dialogic of ethnology', *Dialectical Anthropology*, 4: 205–41.

Ellis, C. (1996) 'Maternal connections', in C. Ellis and A.P. Bochner (eds), *Composing Ethnography: Alternative Forms of Qualitative Writing*. Walnut Creek, CA: Altamira Press. pp. 240–3.

Ellis, C. and Bochner, A.P. (1992) 'Telling and performing personal stories: the constraints of choice in abortion', in C. Ellis and M.G. Flaherty (eds), *Investigating Subjectivity: Research on Lived Experience*. Newbury Park, CA: Sage. pp. 79–101.

Ellis, C. and Bochner, A.P. (eds) (1996) *Composing Ethnography: Alternative Forms of Qualitative Writing*. Walnut Creek, CA: Altamira Press.

Ellis, C. and Flaherty, M.G. (eds) (1992) *Investigating Subjectivity: Research or Lived Experience*. Newbury Park, CA: Sage.

El-Or, T. (1997) 'Do you really know how they make love? The limits on intimacy with ethnographic informants', in R. Hertz (ed.), *Reflexivity and Voice*. Thousand Oaks, CA: Sage. pp. 169–89.

Ely, M., Vinz, R., Downing, M. and Anzul, M. (1997) *On Writing Qualitative Research: Living by Words*. London: Falmer.

Emerson, R.M., Fretz, R. and Shaw, L.L. (1995) *Writing Ethnographic Fieldnotes*. Chicago: University of Chicago Press.

Enslin, E. (1994) 'Beyond writing: feminist practice and the limitations of ethnography', *Cultural Anthropology*, 9 (4): 537–68.

Erben, M. (1993) 'The problem of other lives: social perspectives on written biography', *Sociology*, 27 (1): 15–25.

Farrell, S.A. (1992) 'Feminism and sociology, introduction: the search for a feminist/womanist methodology in sociology', in S. Rosenberg Zalk and J. Gordon-Kelter (eds), *Revolutions in Knowledge: Feminism in the Social Sciences*. Boulder, CO: Westview. pp. 57–62.

Favret-Saada, J. (1980 [1977]) *Deadly Words: Witchcraft in the Bocage*, trans. C. Cullen. Cambridge: Cambridge University Press.

Featherstone, M. and Turner, B. (1995) 'Body and society: an introduction', *Body and Society*, 1 (1): 1–12.

Festinger, L., Riecken, H., and Schachter, S. (1964) *When Prophecy Fails*. London: Harper and Row.

Fielding, N.G. and Lee, R.M. (eds) (1991) *Using Computers in Qualitative Research*. London: Sage.

Fine, G.A. (1987) *With the Boys: Little League Baseball and Preadolescent Culture*. Chicago and London: University of Chicago Press.

Fleuhr-Lobban, C. and Lobban, R.A. (1986) 'Families, gender and methodology in the Sudan', in T.L. Whitehead and M.E. Conway (eds), *Self, Sex and Gender in Cross-Cultural Fieldwork*. Urbana, IL: University of Illinois Press. pp. 152–95.

Fordham, S. (1996) *Blacked Out: Dilemmas of Race, Identity and Success at Capital High*. Chicago: University of Chicago Press.

Fowler, C.S. (1994) 'Beginning to understand: twenty-eight years of fieldwork in the Great Basin of Western North America', in D.D. Fowler and D.L. Hardesty (eds), *Others Knowing Others: Perspectives on Ethnographic Careers*. Washington and London: Smithsonian Institution Press. pp. 145–66.

Fowler, D.D. and Hardesty, D.L. (eds) (1994) *Others Knowing Others: Perspectives on Ethnographic Careers*. Washington and London: Smithsonian Institution Press.

Fox, K.V. (1996) 'Silent voices: a subversive reading of child sexual abuse', in C. Ellis and A.P. Bochner (eds), *Composing Ethnography: Alternative Forms of Qualitative Writing*. Walnut Creek, CA: Altamira Press. pp. 330–56.

Frank, A.W. (1990) 'Bringing bodies back in', *Theory, Culture and Society*, 7 (1): 131–62.

Frank, A.W. (1991) 'For a sociology of the body', in M. Featherstone, M. Hepworth and B.S. Turner (eds), *The Body: Social Process and Cultural Theory*. London: Sage. pp. 36–102.

Freedman, D. (1986) 'Wife, widow, woman: roles of an anthropologist in a Transylvanian village', in P. Golde (ed.), *Women in the Field: Anthropological Experiences*, 2nd edn. Berkeley, CA: University of California Press. pp. 335–58.

Freeman, D. (1991) 'There's tricks i' th' world: an historical analysis of the Samoan researches of Margaret Mead', *Visual Anthropology Review*, 7 (1): 103–28.

Freilich, M. (ed.) (1970) *Marginal Natives: Anthropologists at Work*. New York: Harper and Row.

Friedl, E. (1986) 'Fieldwork in a Greek village', in P. Golde (ed.), *Women in the Field: Anthropological Experiences*, 2nd edn. Berkeley, CA: University of California Press. pp. 195–236.

Funow, M.M. and Cook, J.A. (eds) (1991) *Beyond Methodology: Feminist Scholarship as Lived Research*. Bloomington and Indianapolis, IN: Indiana University Press.

Gearing, J. (1995) 'Fear and loving in the West Indies: research from the heart (as well as the head)', in D. Kulick and M. Willson (eds), *Taboo: Sex, Identity and Erotic Subjectivity in Anthropological Fieldwork*. London and New York: Routledge. pp. 186–218.

Geer, B. (1964) 'First days in the field', in P.E. Hammond (ed), *Sociologists at Work*. New York: Basic Books. pp. 322–44.

Geertz, C. (1960) *The Religion of Java*. New York: Free Press.

Geertz, C. (1988) *Works and Lives: The Anthropologist as Author*. Cambridge: Polity Press.

Gilbert, G.N. and Mulkay, M. (1980) *Opening Pandora's Box: A Sociological Analysis of Scientists' Discourse*. Cambridge: Cambridge University Press.

Gillborn, D. (1990) *'Race', Ethnicity and Education: Teaching and Learning in Multi-Ethnic Schools*. London: Unwin Hyman.

Goffman, E. (1959) *The Presentation of Self in Everyday Life*. New York: Doubleday.

Gold, R.L. (1958) 'Roles in sociological fieldwork', *Social Forces*, 36: 217–23.

Golde, P. (ed.) (1986) *Women in the Field: Anthropological Experiences*, 2nd edn. Berkeley, CA: University of California Press.

Gordon, D.A. (1988) 'Writing culture: writing feminism – the poetics and politics of experimental ethnography', *Inscriptions*, 3 (4): 7–24.

Gordon, D.A. (1995) 'Conclusion: culture writing women – inscribing feminist anthropology', in R. Behar and D.A. Gordon (eds), *Women Writing Culture*. Berkeley, CA: University of California Press. pp. 429–41.

Goulet, J.G. (1994) 'Dreams and visions in other lifeworlds', in D.E. Young and J.G. Goulet (eds), *Being Changed by Cross Cultural Encounters: The Anthropology of Extraordinary Experience*. New York: Broadway Press. pp. 16–38.

Gubrium, J.F. (1988) *Analyzing Field Reality*. Newbury Park, CA: Sage.

Gubrium, J.F. and Holstein, J.A. (1997) *The New Language of Qualitative Method*. New York and Oxford: Oxford University Press.

Guedon, M.F. (1994) 'Dene ways and the ethnographer's culture', in D.E. Young and J.G. Goulet (eds), *Being Changed by Cross Cultural Encounters: The Anthropology of Extraordinary Experience*. New York: Broadway Press. pp. 39–70.

Gurney, J.N. (1985) 'Not one of the guys: the female researcher in a male-dominated setting', *Qualtitative Sociology*, 8: 42–62.

Hammersley, M. (1991) *Reading Ethnographic Research: A Critical Guide*. London: Longman.

Hammersley, M. and Atkinson, P. (1995) *Ethnography: Principles in Practice*, 2nd edn. London: Routledge.

Hammond, P.E. (ed.) (1964) *Sociologists at Work: Essays on the Craft of Social Research*. New York: Basic Books.

Haraway, D. (1991) *Simians, Cyborgs and Women: The Reinvention of Nature*. London and New York: Routledge.

Harding, S. (1987) *Feminism and Methodology*. Bloomington and Indianapolis, IN: Indiana University Press; Milton Keynes: Open University Press.

Hastrup, K. (1992) 'Writing ethnography: state of the art', in J. Okely and H. Callaway (eds), *Anthropology and Autobiography*. London: Routledge. pp. 116–33.

Hastrup, K. (1995) *A Passage to Anthropology: Between Experience and Theory*. London: Routledge.

Hearn, J. and Parkin, W. (1987) *Sex at Work: The Power and Paradox of Organisation Sexuality*. Brighton: Wheatsheaf.

Hearn, J., Sheppard, D.L., Tancred-Sheriff, P. and Burrell, G. (eds) (1989) *The Sexuality of Organization*. London: Sage.

Hendry, J. (1992) 'The paradox of friendship in the field: analysis of a long-term Anglo-Japanese relationship', in J. Okely and H. Callaway (eds), *Anthropology and Autobiography*. London: Routledge. pp. 163–74.

Hertz, R. (ed.) (1997) *Reflexivity and Voice*. Thousand Oaks, CA: Sage.

Heyl, B. (1979) *The Madam as Entrepreneur: Career Management in House Prostitution*. New Brunswick, NJ: Transaction Books.

Hobbs, D. and May, T. (eds) (1992) *Interpreting the Field: Accounts of Ethnography*. Oxford: Clarendon Press.

Hochschild, A.R. (1979) 'Emotion work: feeling rules and social structure', *American Journal of Sociology*, 85: 551–75.

Hochschild, A.R. (1983) *The Managed Heart*. Berkeley, CA: University of California Press.

Hockey, J. (1986) *Squaddies: Portrait of a Subculture*. Exeter. University of Exeter Press.

Hockey, J. (1996) 'Putting down smoke: emotion and engagement in participant observation', in K. Carter and S. Delamont (eds), *Qualitative Research: The Emotional Dimension*. Aldershot: Avebury. pp. 12–27.

Holquist, M. (1990) *Dialogism: Bakhtin and his World*. London: Routledge.

Homans, R. (1991) *The Ethics of Social Research*. London: Longman.

Hughes, A. and Witz, A. (1997) 'Feminism and the matter of bodies', *Body and Society*, 3 (1): 47–59.

Humphreys, L. (1970) *Tearoom Trade: A Study of Homosexual Encounters in Public Places*. Chicago: Aldine.

Humphreys, L. (1975) *Tearoom Trade: Impersonal Sex in Public Places* (enlarged edition with a retrospective on ethical issues). New York: Aldine de Gruyter.

Hunt, S.C. (1987) 'Take a deep breath in: an ethnography of a hospital labour ward'. MSc. Econ. dissertation, University College, Cardiff.

Hutheesing, O.K. (1993) 'Facework of a female elder in a Lisu field, Thailand', in D. Bell, P. Caplan and W.J. Karim (eds), *Gendered Fields: Women, Men and Ethnography*. London and New York: Routledge. pp. 93–102.

Jackson, J.E. (1990) '"I am a fieldnote": fieldnotes as a symbol of professional identity', in R. Sanjek (ed.), *Fieldnotes: The Makings of Anthropology*. Ithaca, NY and London: Cornell University Press. pp. 3–33.

Jennaway, M. (1990) 'Paradigms, postmodern epistemologies and paradox: the place of feminism in anthropology', *Anthropological Forum*, 6 (2): 167–89.

Johnson, J.M. (1975) *Doing Field Research*. New York: Free Press.

Jules-Rosette, B. (1978) 'The veil of objectivity: prophecy, divination and social inquiry', *American Anthropology*, 80 (3): 549–70.

Junker, B. (1960) *Fieldwork*. Chicago: University of Chicago Press.

Karim, W.J. (1993) 'With *moyang melur* in Carey Island: more endangered, more engendered', in D. Bell, P. Caplan and W.J. Karim. (eds), *Gendered Fields: Women, Men and Ethnography*. London and New York: Routledge. pp. 78–92.

Karp, D.A. (1980) 'Observing behaviour in public places: problems and strategies', in W.B. Shaffir, R.A. Stebbins and A. Turowetz (eds), *Fieldwork Experience:*

Qualitative Approaches to Social Research. New York: St Martin's Press. pp. 82–97.

Katz, C. (1996) 'The expeditions of conjurers: ethnography, power and pretence', in D.L. Wolf (ed.), *Feminist Dilemmas in Fieldwork.* Boulder, CO: Westview. pp. 170–84.

Kelle, U. (ed.) (1995) *Computer Aided Qualitative Data Analysis: Theory, Methods and Practice.* London: Sage.

Kenna, M.E. (1992) 'Changing places and altered perspectives: research on a Greek island in the 1960s and in the 1980s', in J. Okely and H. Callaway (eds), *Anthropology and Autobiography.* London: Routledge. pp. 147–62.

King, R.A. (1978) *All Things Bright and Beautiful.* Chichester: Wiley.

Kolker, A. (1996) 'Thrown overboard: the human costs of health care rationing', in C. Ellis and A.P. Bochner (eds), *Composing Ethnography: Alternative Forms of Qualitative Writing.* Walnut Creek, CA: Altamira Press. pp. 132–59.

Kondo, D.K. (1990) *Crafting Selves: Power, Gender and Discourses of Identity in a Japanese Workplace.* Chicago: University of Chicago Press.

Krieger, S. (1979) *Hip Capitalism.* Beverly Hills, CA: Sage.

Krieger, S. (1983) *The Mirror Dance: Identity in a Women's Community.* Philadelphia: Temple University Press.

Krieger, S. (1985) 'Beyond subjectivity', *Qualitative Sociology*, 8(4): 309–24. Reprinted in A. Lareau and J. Schultz (eds) (1996) *Journeys through Ethnography: Realistic Accounts of Fieldwork.* Boulder, CO: Westview. pp. 179–94.

Krieger, S. (1991) *Social Science and the Self: Personal Essays as an Art Form.* New Brunswick, NJ: Rutgers University Press.

Kulick, D. (1995) 'The sexual life of anthropologists: erotic subjectivity and ethnographic work', in D. Kulick and M. Willson (eds), *Taboo: Sex, Identity and Erotic Subjectivity in Anthropological Fieldwork.* London and New York: Routledge. pp. 1–28.

Kulick, D. and Willson, M. (eds) (1995) *Taboo: Sex, Identity and Erotic Subjectivity in Anthropological Fieldwork.* London and New York: Routledge.

Lacey, C. (1970) *High Town Grammar: The School as a Social System.* Manchester: Manchester University Press.

Lal, J. (1996) 'Situated locations: the politics of self, identity and "other" in living and writing the text', in D.L. Wolf (ed.), *Feminist Dilemmas in Fieldwork.* Boulder, CO: Westview. pp. 185–214.

Landes, R. (1970) 'A woman anthropologist in Brazil', in P. Golde (ed.), *Women in the Field: Anthropological Experiences.* Berkeley, CA: University of California Press. pp. 119–42.

Langellier, K. and Hall, D. (1989) 'Interviewing women: a phenomenological approach to feminist communication research', in K. Caiter and C. Spitzack (eds), *Doing Research on Women's Communication: Perspectives on Theory and Method.* Norwood, NJ: Ablex. pp. 193–200.

Lareau, A. and Schultz, J. (eds) (1996) *Journeys through Ethnography: Realistic Accounts of Fieldwork.* Boulder, CO: Westview.

Lather, P. (1986) 'Issues of validity in openly ideological research: between a rock and a soft place', *Interchange*, 17 (4): 63–84.

Lather, P. (1991) *Getting Smart: Feminist Research and Pedagogy with/in the Postmodern.* New York: Routledge.

Law, J. and Williams, R.J. (1982) 'Putting the facts together: a case study of scientific persuasion', *Social Studies of Science*, 12: 535–58.

LeCompte M.D. and Preissle J. (with R. Tesch) (1993) *Ethnography and Qualitative Design in Educational Research*, 2nd edn. San Diego: Academic Press.

Lederman, R. (1990) 'Pretexts for ethnography: on reading fieldnotes', in R. Sanjek (ed.), *Fieldnotes: The Makings of Anthropology*. Ithaca, NY and London: Cornell University Press. pp. 71–91.

Lee, R.M. and Fielding, N.G. (1991) 'Computing for qualitative research: options, problems and potential', in N.G. Fielding and R.M. Lee (eds), *Using Computers in Qualitative Research*. London: Sage. pp. 1–13.

Lees, S. (1986) *Losing Out*. London: Heinemann.

Lewis, L.A. and Ross, M.W. (1995) *A Select Body: The Gay Dance Party Subculture and the HIV/AIDS Pandemic*. London: Cassell.

Liebow, E. (1967) *Tally's Corner*. London: Routledge & Kegan Paul.

Lincoln, Y.S. and Denzin, N.K. (1994) 'The fifth moment', in N.K. Denzin and Y.S. Lincoln (eds), *Handbook of Qualitative Research*. Thousand Oaks, CA: Sage. pp. 575–86.

Lindisfarne, N. (1994) 'Variant masculinities and variant virginities: rethinking "honour and shame"', in A. Cornwall and N. Lindisfarne (eds), *Dislocating Masculinities: Comparative Ethnographies*. London and New York: Routledge. pp. 82–95.

Lofland, J. and Lofland, L.H. (1995) *Analyzing Social Settings: A Guide to Qualitataive Observation and Analysis*, 3rd edn. Belmont, CA: Wadsworth.

Loizos, P. (1981) *The Heart Grown Bitter*. Cambridge: Cambridge University Press.

Lutz, C.A. and Collins, J.L. (1993) *Reading National Geographic*. Chicago: University of Chicago Press.

Lynch, M. and Wolgar, S. (eds) (1990) *Representation in Scientific Practice*. Cambridge, MA: MIT Press.

Mac an Ghaill, M. (1988) *Young, Gifted and Black: Student–Teacher Relations in the Schooling of Black Youth*. Milton Keynes: Open University Press.

McCloskey, D.N. (1985) *The Rhetoric of Economics*. Madison, WI: University of Wisconsin Press.

McCoy, K. (1997) 'White noise – the sound of epidemic: reading/writing a climate of intelligibility around the "crisis" of difference', *International Journal of Qualitative Studies in Education*, 10 (3): 333–48.

Macintyre, M. (1993) 'Fictive kinship or mistaken identity? Fieldwork on Tube Island, Papua New Guinea', in D. Bell, P. Caplan and W.J. Karim (eds), *Gendered Fields: Women, Men and Ethnography*. London and New York: Routledge. pp. 44–62.

McKeganey, N.P. and Cunningham-Burley, S. (eds) (1987) *Enter the Sociologist: Reflections on the Practice of Sociology*. Aldershot: Avebury.

Malinowski, B. (1922) *Argonauts of the Western Pacific*. London: Routledge and Kegan Paul.

Malinowski, B. (1967) *A Diary in the Strict Sense of the Term*. London: Routledge and Kegan Paul.

Malinowski, B. (1987 [1929]) *The Sexual Life of Savages*. Boston, MA: Beacon Press.

Marcus, J. (1992) *A World of Difference: Islam and Gender Hierarchy in Turkey*. London: Zed.

Mascia-Lees, F.E., Sharpe, P. and Cohen, C.B. (1989) 'The postmodernist turn in anthropology: cautions from a feminist perspective', *Signs*, 15: 7–33.

Maynard, M. (1994) 'Methods, practice and epistemology: the debate about feminism and research', in M. Maynard and J. Purvis (eds), *Researching Women's Lives from a Feminist Perspective*. London: Taylor & Francis. pp. 10–26.

Maynard, M. (1996) *Feminist Social Research: Pragmatics, Politics and Power*. London: UCL Press.

Mead, M. (1949) [1928]) *Coming of Age in Samoa: A Psychological Study of Primitive Youth for Western Civilization*. New York: Mentor Books.

Mead, M. (1986) 'Fieldwork in the Pacific islands 1925–1967', in P. Golde (ed.), *Women in the Field: Anthropological Experiences*, 2nd edn. Berkeley, CA: University of California Press. pp. 97–116.

Measor, L. (1985) 'Interviewing: a strategy in qualitative research', in R. Burgess (ed.), *Strategies of Educational Research*. London and Philadelphia: Falmer. pp. 55–78.

Megill, A. and McCloskey, D.N. (eds) (1987) *The Rhetoric of the Human Sciences*. Madison, WI: University of Wisconsin Press.

Mienczakowski, J.E. (1995) 'The theatre of ethnography: the reconstruction of ethnography in theatre with emancipating potential', *Qualitative Inquiry*, 1: 360–75.

Mienczakowski, J.E. (1996) 'The ethnographic act: the construction of consensual theatre', in C. Ellis and A.P. Bochner (eds), *Composing Ethnography: Alternative Forms of Qualitative Writing*. Walnut Creek, CA: Altamira Press. pp. 244–64.

Miles, M.B. and Huberman, A.M. (1994) *Qualitative Data Analysis: An Expanded Source Book*, 2nd edn. Thousand Oaks, CA: Sage.

Moffatt, M. (1989) *Coming of Age in New Jersey: College and American Culture*. New Brunswick, NJ and London: Rutgers University Press.

Moreno, E. (1995) 'Rape in the field: reflections from a survivor', in D. Kulick and M. Willson (eds), *Taboo: Sex, Identity and Erotic Subjectivity in Anthropological Fieldwork*. London and New York: Routledge. pp. 219–50.

Mulkay, M.J. (1985) *The Word and the World: Explorations in the Form of Sociological Analysis*. London: Allen & Unwin.

Myerhoff, B. (1978) *Number Our Days*. New York: Simon & Schuster.

Mykhalovskiy, E. (1997) 'Reconsidering "table talk": critical thoughts on the relationship between sociology, autobiography and self-indulgence', in R. Hertz (ed.), *Reflexivity and Voice*. Thousand Oaks, CA: Sage. pp. 229–51.

Nielsen, J.M. (ed.) (1990) *Feminist Research Methods*. Boulder CO: Westview.

Oboler, R.S. (1986) 'For better or worse: anthropologists and husbands in the field', in T.L. Whitehead and M.E. Conway (eds), *Self, Sex and Gender in Cross-Cultural Fieldwork*. Urbana, IL: University of Illinois Press. pp. 28–51.

Okely, J. and Callaway, H. (eds) (1992) *Anthropology and Autobiography*. London: Routledge.

Olesen, V. (1994) 'Feminisms and models of qualitative research', in N.K. Denzin and Y.S. Lincoln (eds), *Handbook of Qualitative Research*. Thousand Oaks, CA: Sage. pp. 158–74.

Olesen, V. and Whittaker, E. (1968) *The Silent Dialogue: A Study in the Social Psychology of Professional Socialization*. San Francisco: Jossey-Bass.

Ottenberg, S. (1990) 'Thirty years of fieldnotes: changing relationships to the text', in R. Sanjek (ed.), *Fieldnotes: The Makings of Anthropology*. Ithaca, NY and London: Cornell University Press. pp. 139–60.

Ottenberg, S. (1994) 'Changes over time in an African culture and in an anthropologist', in D.D. Fowler and D.L. Hardesty (eds), *Others Knowing Others: Perspectives on Ethnographic Careers*. Washington and London: Smithsonian Institution Press. pp. 91–118.

Paget, M.A. (1990) 'Performing the text', *Journal of Contemporary Ethnography*, 19: 136–55.

Paget, M.A. (1993) *A Complex Sorrow: Reflections on Cancer and an Abbreviated Life*. Philadelphia: Temple University Press.

Parry, O. (1982) 'Campaign for respectability: a study of organised British naturism'. MSc. Econ. dissertation, University College, Cardiff.

Parry, O. (1987) 'Uncovering the ethnographer', in N.P. McKeganey and S. Cunningham-Burley (eds), *Enter the Sociologist: Reflections on the Practice of Sociology*. Aldershot: Avebury. pp. 82–96.

Patrick, J. (1973) *A Glasgow Gang Observed*. London: Eyre Methuen.

Peshkin, A. (1985) *God's Choice: the Total World of a Fundamentalist Christian School*. Chicago: University of Chicago Press.

Peters, E. (1993) 'Table talk', in T. Haddad (ed.), *Men and Masculinities: a Critical Anthropology*. Toronto: Canadian Scholars Press. pp. 77–90.

Pettigrew, J. (1981) 'Reminiscences of fieldwork among the Sikhs', in H. Roberts (ed.), *Doing Feminist Research*. London: Routledge & Kegan Paul. pp. 62–82.

Pierce, J.L. (1995) *Gender Trials: Emotional Lives in Contemporary Law Firms*. Berkeley, CA: University of California Press.

Pollard, A. (1985) *The Social World of the Primary School*. London: Holt, Rinehart and Winston.

Punch, M. (1986) *The Politics and Ethics of Fieldwork*. Beverly Hills, CA: Sage.

Quinney, R. (1996) 'Once my father travelled west to California', in C. Ellis and A.P. Bochner (eds), *Composing Ethnography: Alternative Forms of Qualitative Writing*. Walnut Creek, CA: Altamira Press. pp. 357–82.

Reed-Danahay, D. (ed.) (1997) *Auto/Ethnography: Rewriting the Self and the Social*. Oxford and New York: Berg.

Richardson, L. (1990) *Writing Strategies: Reaching Diverse Audiences*. Newbury Park, CA: Sage.

Richardson, L. (1992) 'The consequences of poetic representation: writing the other, writing the self', in C. Ellis and M.G. Flaherty (eds), *Investigating Subjectivity: Research on Lived Experience*. Newbury Park, CA: Sage. pp. 125–37.

Richardson, L. (1994) 'Writing: a method of inquiry', in N.K. Denzin and Y.S. Lincoln (eds), *Handbook of Qualitative Research*. Thousand Oaks, CA: Sage. pp. 516–29.

Richardson, L. and Lockridge, E. (1991) 'The sea monster: an "ethnographic drama"', *Symbolic Interaction*, 13: 77–83.

Riddell, S.I. (1992) *Gender and the Politics of the Curriculum*. London: Routledge.

Riesman, D. (1964) Foreword to E.S. Bowen: *Return to Laughter: an Anthropological Novel*. New York: Doubleday. pp. ix–xviii.

Riessman, C. (1993) *Narrative Analysis*. Newbury Park, CA: Sage.

Roberts, H. (ed.) (1981) *Doing Feminist Research*. London: Routledge and Kegan Paul.

Ronai, C.R. (1996) 'My mother is mentally retarded', in C. Ellis and A.P. Bochner (eds), *Composing Ethnography: Alternative Forms of Qualitative Writing*. Walnut Creek, CA: Altamira Press. pp. 109–31.

Said, E. (1978) *Orientalism*. London: Routledge and Kegan Paul.

Salisbury, J. (1994) 'Becoming qualified: an ethnography of a post-experience teacher training course'. PhD dissertation, University of Wales, Cardiff.

Sanjek, R. (ed.) (1990) *Fieldnotes: The Makings of Anthropology*. Ithaca, NY and London: Cornell University Press.

Savage, M. and Witz, A. (eds) (1992) *Gender and Bureaucracy*. Oxford: Blackwell.

Scheper-Hughes, N. (1992) *Death without Weeping: The Violence of Everyday Life in Brazil*. California, CA: University of California Press.

Schilling, C. (1993) *The Body and Social Theory*. London: Sage.

Schrijvers, J. (1983) 'Manipulated motherhood: the marginalization of peasant women in the North-Central province of Sri Lanka', *Development and Change*, 14 (2): 185–211.

Schrijvers, J. (1993) 'Motherhood experienced and conceptualized: changing images in Sri Lanka and the Netherlands', in D. Bell, P. Caplan and W.J. Karim (eds), *Gendered Fields: Women, Men and Ethnography*. London and New York: Routledge. pp. 143–58.

Schutz, A. (1964) 'The stranger: an essay in social psychology', in A. Schutz (ed.), *Collected Papers: Vol. II*. The Hague: Martinus Nijhoff. pp. 91–105.

Scott, S. and Morgan, D. (1993) *Body Matters*. London: Falmer.

Shaffir, W.B. (1991) 'Managing a convincing self presentation: some personal reflections on entering the field', in W.B. Shaffir and R.A. Stebbins (eds), *Experiencing Fieldwork: An Inside View of Qualitative Research*. Newbury Park, CA: Sage. pp. 72–82.

Shaffir, W.B. and Stebbins, R.A. (eds) (1991) *Experiencing Fieldwork: An Inside View of Qualitative Research*. Newbury Park, CA: Sage.

Shaw, C.R. (1966) *The Jackroller: A Delinquent Boy's Own Story*. Chicago: University of Chicago Press.

Shaw, I. (1996) 'Unbroken voices: children, young people and qualitative methods', in I. Butler and I. Shaw (eds), *A Case of Neglect? Children's Experiences and the Sociology of Childhood*. Aldershot: Avebury. pp. 19–36.

Silverman, D. (1993) *Interpreting Qualitative Data: Methods for Analysing Talk, Text and Interaction*. London: Sage.

Silverman, D. (ed.) (1997) *Qualitative Research: Theory, Method and Practice*. London: Sage.

Skeggs, B. (1994) 'Situating the production of feminist ethnography', in M. Maynard and J. Purvis (eds), *Researching Women's Lives from a Feminist Perspective*. London: Taylor & Francis. pp. 72–92.

Smith, D.E. (1987) *The Everyday World as Problematic: A Feminist Sociology*. Boston: Northeastern University Press.

Sparkes, A. (1995) 'Writing people: reflections on the dual crises of representation and legitimation in qualitative inquiry', *Quest*, 47 (2): 158–95.

Sparkes, A. (1996) 'The fatal flaw: a narrative of the fragile body-self', *Qualitative Inquiry*, 2 (4): 463–94.

Stack, C.B. (1972) *All Our Kin: Strategies for Survival in a Black Community*. New York: Harper and Row.

Stack, C.B. (1996) 'Writing ethnography: feminist critical practice', in D.L. Wolf (ed.), *Feminist Dilemmas in Fieldwork*. Boulder, CO: Westview. pp. 96–106.

Stanley, L. (1990) 'Feminist praxis and the academic mode of production: an editorial introduction', in L. Stanley (ed.), *Feminist Praxis: Research, Theory and Epistemology in Feminist Sociology*. London: Routledge. pp. 3–19.

Stanley, L. (1992) *The Auto/biographical I: Theory and Practice of Feminist Auto/biography*. Manchester: Manchester University Press.

Stanley, L. (1993) 'On auto/biography in sociology', *Sociology*, 27 (1): 41–52.

Stanley, L. and Wise, S. (1990) 'Method, methodology and epistemology in feminist research processes', in L. Stanley (ed.), *Feminist Praxis: Research, Theory and Epistemology in Feminist Sociology*. London: Routledge. pp. 20–62.

Stanley, L. and Wise, S. (1993) *Breaking Out Again: Feminist Ontology and Epistemology*. London: Routledge.

Stebbins, R.A. (1991) 'Do we ever leave the field? Notes on secondary fieldwork involvements', in W.B. Shaffir and R.A. Stebbins (eds), *Experiencing Fieldwork: An Inside View of Qualitative Research*. Newbury Park, CA: Sage. pp. 248–58.

Strathern, M. (1987) 'An awkward relationship: the case of feminism and anthropology', *Signs*, 12 (2): 276–91.

Strathern, M. (1991) *Partial Connections*. Savage, MD: Rowman & Littlefield.

Strauss, A.L. (1987) *Qualitative Analysis for Social Scientists*. Cambridge: Cambridge University Press.

Strauss, A.L. and Corbin, J. (1990) *Basics of Qualitative Research: Grounded Theory, Procedures and Techniques*. Newbury Park, CA: Sage.

Styles, J. (1979) 'Outsider/insider: researching gay baths', *Urban Life*, 8 (2): 135–52.

Tesch, R. (1990) *Qualitative Research: Analysis Types and Software Tools*. London: Falmer.

Tillman-Healy, L.M. (1996) 'A secret life in a culture of thinness: reflections on body, food and bulimia', in C. Ellis and A.P. Bochner (eds), *Composing Ethnography: Alternative Forms of Qualitative Writing*. Walnut Creek, CA: Altamira Press. pp. 76–108.

Tsing, A.L. (1993) *In the Realm of the Diamond Queen: Marginality in an Out-of-the-Way Place*, Princeton, NJ: Princeton University Press.

Tsurumi, P.E. (1984) 'Female textile workers and the failure of early trade unionism in Japan', *History Workshop*, 18: 3–27.

Turner, B. (1984) *The Body and Society*. Oxford: Blackwell.

Turner, E. (1994) 'A visible spirit form in Zambia', in D.E. Young and J.G. Goulet (eds), *Being Changed by Cross Cultural Encounters: the Anthropology of Extraordinary Experience*. New York: Broadway Press. pp. 71–95.

Van Maanen, J. (1988) *Tales of the Field*. Chicago: University of Chicago Press.

Van Maanen, J. (1991) 'Playing back the tape: early days in the field', in W.B. Shaffir and R.A. Stebbins (eds), *Experiencing Fieldwork: An Inside View of Qualitative Research*. Newbury Park, CA: Sage. pp. 31–42.

Vera-Sanso, P. (1993) 'Perception, east and west: a Madras encounter,' in D. Bell, P. Caplan and W.T. Karim (eds), *Gendered Fields: Women, Men and Ethnography*. London and New York: Routledge. pp. 159–67.

Wacquant, L.J.D. (1995) 'Pugs at work: bodily capital and bodily labour among professional boxers', *Body and Society*, 1 (1): 64–94.

Wade, P. (1993) 'Sexuality and masculinity in fieldwork among Colombian Blacks', in D. Bell, P. Caplan and W.J. Karim (eds), *Gendered Fields: Women, Men and Ethnography*. London: Routledge. pp. 199–214.

Walford, G. (ed.) (1987) *Doing Sociology of Education*. London: Falmer.

Walter, L. (1995) 'Feminist anthropology?' *Gender and Society*, 9 (3): 272–88.

Warren, C.A.B. (1988) *Gender Issues in Field Research*. Newbury Park, CA: Sage.

Warren, C.A.B. and Rasmussen, P.K. (1977) 'Sex and gender in field research', *Urban Life*, 6 (3): 349–69.

Weaver, A. and Atkinson, P. (1994) *Microcomputing and Qualitative Data Analysis*. Aldershot: Avebury.

Weaver, A. and Atkinson, P. (1996) 'From coding to hypertext', in R.G. Burgess (ed.), *Using Computers in Qualitative Research*. Greenwich, CT: JAI Press. pp. 141–68.

Weidman, H.H. (1986) 'On ambivalence in the field', in P. Golde (ed.), *Women in the Field: Anthropological Experiences*, 2nd edn. Berkeley, CA: University of California Press. pp. 239–63.

Weitzman, E.A. and Miles, M.B. (1995) *Computer Programs for Qualitative Data Analysis*. Thousand Oaks, CA: Sage.

Wengle, J. (1988) *Ethnographers in the Field: The Psychology of Research*. Tuscaloosa, AL: University of Alabama Press.

Whyte, W.F. (1981) *Street Corner Society: The Social Structure of an Italian Slum*, 3rd edn. Chicago: University of Chicago Press

Willis, P. (1977) *Learning to Labour*. Aldershot: Gower.

Witz, A., Halford, S. and Savage, M. (1996) 'Organized bodies: gender, sexuality and embodiment in contemporary organizations', in A. Adkins and V. Merchant (eds), *Sexualizing the Social: Power and the Organization of Sexuality*. Basingstoke: Macmillan. pp. 173–90.

Wolcott, H.F. (1990) *Writing up Qualitative Research*. Newbury Park, CA: Sage.

Wolf, D.L. (ed.) (1996) *Feminist Dilemmas in Fieldwork*. Boulder, CO: Westview.

Wolf, D.R. (1991) *The Rebels: A Brotherhood of Outlaw Bikers*. Toronto: University of Toronto Press.

Wolf, M. (1990) 'Chinanotes: engendering anthropology', in R. Sanjek (ed.), *Fieldnotes: the Makings of Anthropology*. Ithaca, NY and London: Cornell University Press. pp. 343–55.

Wolf, M. (1992) *A Thrice Told Tale: Feminism, Postmodernism and Ethnographic Responsibility*. Stanford, CA: Stanford University Press.

Wolf, M. (1996) 'Afterword: musings from an old Gray Wolf', in D.L. Wolf (ed.), *Feminist Dilemmas in Fieldwork*. Boulder, CO: Westview. pp. 215–22.

Wolff, K.H. (1964) 'Surrender and community study', in A. Vidich, J. Bensman and M. Stein (eds), *Reflections on Community Studies*. New York: Wiley. pp. 233–64.

Young, D.E. and Goulet, J.G. (eds) (1994) *Being Changed by Cross Cultural Encounters: the Anthropology of Extraordinary Experience*. New York: Broadway Press.

Index